Films, Literature and Culture

Films, Literature and Culture

Deepa Mehta's Elements Trilogy

Edited by
Jasbir Jain

Institute for Research in Interdisciplinary Studies, Jaipur

RAWAT PUBLICATIONS

Jaipur • New Delhi • Bangalore • Guwahati • Kolkata

ISBN 978-81-316-0009-2

Reprinted 2017

Published by
Prem Rawat for **Rawat Publications**
Satyam Apts., Sector 3, Jawahar Nagar, Jaipur 302 004 (India)
Phone: 0141 265 1748 / 7006 Fax: 0141 265 1748
E-mail: info@rawatbooks.com
Website: www.rawatbooks.com

New Delhi Office
4858/24, Ansari Road, Daryaganj, New Delhi 110 002
Phone: 011-23263290

Also at *Bangalore, Guwahati* and *Kolkata*

Printed and bound in India

to all my research scholars

Contents

Preface

Two factors have led to the making of this volume. First, our ongoing concern at IRIS to engage with the linkages between literature and film studies – a concern which took active shape more than a decade ago and since then, through collective viewings, discussions, workshops, interactions with directors and filmmakers, we have moved towards a better understanding of the medium. The second factor, and the more immediate one, is the three-day seminar IRIS organised in February 2007: *The Diasporic Eye: Theory and Cultural Interpretation*. This seminar focused on Deepa Mehta's elements trilogy – her three main India films. The idea was to explore the larger issues of location, culture and interpretation and move into a dialogue between individual constructs and national constructs.

When an individual migrates, there is never a beginning from scratch. The past travels with him in the form of memories, myths, histories and connections. The diaspora has been seen to adopt mainly three different kinds of stances – critiquing Indian culture in negative terms; exoticising it; and freezing it through stereotypes. There is, however, a fourth possibility that of a living relationship with it. These approaches, when articulated in literature and art serve as a double mirror: the outside sees us through them; we see ourselves in it in some kind of reflection. Suddenly, they encroach upon our right to articulate our own positions and act like interpreters and 'dwar-palikas' (a word Sujit Mukherjee used with reference to Gayatri Spivak and her prefaces to Mahasweta Devi's stories). It becomes our responsibility to evaluate the nature of this representation.

Further to this, there is also the contestation between the individual's right to express and the placement of this expression, whether film or novel, in a larger construct like nation. Art is, more than all else, an independent though not a closed entity. It needs to be evaluated on its own terms and placed within aesthetic judgments. The papers in the present volume engage with several of these issues in search for meaning and relevance and sharpened critical awareness. A note also on the spellings: 'Benaras' has been spelt as 'Banaras' only in Santosh Gupta's paper as the film's advertisements and DVD carry the latter spelling. Everywhere else we have adhered to Benaras.

Several of the essays included in this volume were first presented at the seminar on *The Diasporic Eye* in February 2007. A few other contributions were requested from scholars with similar interests. I take this opportunity of expressing my thanks to all the contributors who have written for this volume and have brought their special expertise to bear on the issues which are our common concern.

1

Introduction

Films, Literature and Culture

Jasbir Jain

Film is perhaps the youngest of the three components present in the title – films, literature and culture – yet its multiform birth has deep roots in the other two. Bharat's *Natya Shastra* centrestaged performance and through it focused on the evocation of emotional responses. Aristotle in *Poetics* established the interconnection between different art forms. Others, down the ages, have stressed this every now and then through their medium – words, colour, stone, clay – and critics like Henry James have validated these spillovers from one art to another in more ways than one. Modern art movements move freely from painting to sculpture, to films and music, and architecture and literature. Yet, each art form chooses for itself different mediums and different ways of producing meaning. Literature depends mainly on words but makes use of sound, rhythm, form and such-like methods; films work out their own medium specifics with the camera eye using language, music, perspective, space, composition, sequence and the human body. When ways of creating meaning differ, then ways of interpreting and evaluating the art form also need to move beyond a uniform application of any approach.

One thing common to most art forms is narrative – this constitutes the impulse and the meaning. And another commonality is its semiotics which sends out clues for interpretation. These two – narrative and semiotics – are also common to disciplines like anthropology and psychology. Clifford Greetz, the renowned anthropologist, has observed that, "A good interpretation of anything – a poem, a person, a history, a ritual, an institution, a society – takes us into the heart of that which it is the interpretation"(18). And the 'heart of it' is culture. Culture exists and envelops us in many invisible ways; art is not the least of these. Freud turned to Greek myths and plays for his interpretative strategies tracing the meaning of archetypal patterns and Sudhir Kakar, in his study of Indian sexuality, has heavily depended on films indicating how deeply these narratives are embedded in our psyches and reflected in our behaviour both conscious and unconscious.

The fact that both the rasa theory and catharsis stress the significance of emotions, goes a long way in identifying the sources of an initial response which often is: 'I like it', 'I don't like it'. But if it were to end there, it would be incomplete. The experience of pleasure is not merely momentary or a choice between being seduced or alienated from the object of our viewing/reading. The Freudian theory of the 'pleasure principle' (in his 1920 essay of that title), takes us beyond this first stage of response to the tension that is at the heart of this experience. The course taken by mental events is "invariably set in motion by an unpleasurable tension, and that it takes a direction such that its final outcome coincides with a lowering of that tension" (Freud 292). This tension, intrinsic to the experience is simultaneously intrinsic to the text for the pleasure generating impulse is opposed by "certain forces or circumstances". This tension, can be understood in aesthetic terms as a parallel to reversal/subversion/irony/discovery and thus becomes an equivalent of plot in emotional terms. Freud's analysis is, of course, far more complex and relates to sexuality but the point it makes about oppositional forces present within the pleasure instinct, is relevant to my discussion.

A transference of this oppositional force to the enjoyment of art is one way of distancing it and subjecting it to a closer examination. This opposition also exists between culture and art. Described as a semiotic system, in itself culture is an abstraction, "Though ideational, it does not exist in someone's head; though unphysical, it is not an occult entity" (Greetz 10-11). In between the two extremes of the reificatory (when it becomes a super imposition and leads us to relate to it as a given, almost a Godhood, not open to criticism) and the reductionist (when it is negated and dismissed as stagnant and discardable) approach, there is a third possibility of looking at it as a living, evolving entity, an organic body capable of growth and of interacting with it at that level.

Working within these parameters, there is a requirement to look at the differences between the two mediums in their ways of expression and our ways of evaluation. Film and literature are both the products of culture and the producers of culture. How do we look at these mirrors that reflect us and at the same time shape us?

Imitation: Representation and Reality

The film, these days with the growing popularity of home theatre, just walks into our living space. The novel remains confined either to the page or our imagination. The relationship between reader and novel is somewhat different from the one between viewer and film. In the first the relationship is one-to-one and works through language, imagination, history and culture; in the second the reception is subjected to the dynamics of group watching, and when this is not the case, the visual image even as it evokes response, in some way stalls the imaginative empathising. The contradictory expressions and statements engage the senses and the emotional response rather than imagination. The film through its visual image and fluidity is a closer proximation of reality. The average viewer tends to constantly bring in the question of its historical veracity. Comments often are – this is simply not possible, this can't happen, historical facts don't support it, laws to the contrary have long existed and often end up in speculative responses to the ending carrying it into the future. Or we treat it as a closed artifact, quite cut off from our life, representative of a make-belief world. A serious piece of art is neither of the two – it is neither a slice of life, nor a casual happening to be dismissed without a second thought. There is need to distinguish between art and reality on the one hand and realism and reality on the other.

Aristotle's view that imitation is natural to men, needs to be expanded upon. It is a special kind of representation. Jonathan Barnes in his essay "Rhetoric and Poetics", has elaborated upon it in these terms:

> Imitation, then is a special kind of representation: it is a matter of representing a so-and-so rather than of representing the so-and-so. It is sometimes true that you represent a so-and-so without there being any so-and-so which you represent. Gibbon represented a degenerate Empire – and there was a degenerate Empire which he represented Manet represented a lunch, but there was no lunch which he represented. To imitate, let us say, is to represent not in the Gibbon fashion, but in the Manet manner. (275)

Representation can take place of an idea, which is populated and expressed through imagination. Representation also automatically, by the fact of selection, acquires a frame and frames are not all-inclusive. Art, in its own right, requires focus – not diffusion. Even if diffusion or disorder is to be artistically represented, it needs framing, which is alike the demand of semiotics and form. Multiplication of frames, repetition, symbolic thrust can help expand meaning, but no piece of art is made up of only parallels or superfluities. In a way if there is an incident or a shot or a subnarrative that doesn't add meaning to the whole, it subtracts from the quality of art. Representation, as it stands like a doorway between writer/director and reader/viewer, makes a demand on the imagination of both.

Realism is a late entry into performing arts, and has been facilitated in some measure by technology. It allows a re-creation of life-like details, which may or may not be real – that is actual. The *real* or reality in philosophical terms, takes one beyond sense perception to the essential quality of the object. In fact it pushes us to look for meaning beyond representation. The visible lies only at a surface level. Reality also includes that which may not be visible or comprehensible. It may go on to include the phenomenological real and the ontological real engaging both the senses and the mind. Realism is a far more restricted term aiming at approximating life, going back to the contemporary times of the narrative and reproducing details which can, for the moment, create a closed world. Roman Jakobson has defined it as a striving for maximum verisimilitude. Jakobson in his essay, "On Realism and Art" (1921), addresses the two different directions the word can lead us to – the intent of the writer and the perception of the reader. The first needs to be validated through evidence, the second is subjective. He further takes it into a discussion of the meaning of verisimilitude and the strategies of projecting three dimensional reality onto a flat surface as in painting, which are ordinarily guided by conventions of art, signs that are immediately recognisable. When the artist rebels or resists these conventional codes, then not only is a new meaning created but realism is also subverted. Several literary devices like condensation or collages, symbolisation, metaphors have been adopted by filmmakers in order to subvert realism and to move beyond it. And in between the crevices, there exists the subtle art of suggestion. A good film, like a poem, suggests; it does not explain and it does not make an overt statement.

The essays in this volume engage with Deepa Mehta's elements trilogy at different levels and different ways exploring the politics, nature of representation, location of the director, relationship of the director with the narratives chosen, sensuality and sexuality, crossing of barriers, space, cinematic techniques, reflection of history, echoes of folk narratives, and extending the films' contemporariness. Each one of them reads the film differently, as a structure, a painting, social history, political critiquing, subversion of dominant ideas, as dialectical image and personal reflection. On the outset there are three locations of the contributors – Uma Parameswaran – a co-Indo-Canadianist – looks at them simultaneously from two different positions. Mehta's frames cannot but remind her of her own. Jennifer Heath, an American, on the other hand, comes to the films as a cultural outsider, willing to unearth cultural nuances. All the other contributors are located in India. Within this last group, one can discern a wide range of sublocations – generational, nationalistic, philosophical, spatial, professional – with the result that there are arguments and counter-arguments, cross-dialogues and disagreements, which weave an exciting network of meaning and provide examples of different ways of reading the trilogy.

Fire (1996), *Earth* (1998) and *Water* (2005) – heat, porousness and fluidity together create a continuum of extinction and continuity working in different ways. The elements surround us, sustain us and constitute the world around us of relationships, institutions, nations, birth and death. They all represent both the destructibility and the vitality of human life. By placing her human characters against these forces, Deepa Mehta has foregrounded the human ability to search for alternatives.

Of the eighteen essays in this volume, Uma Parameswaran has brought into her discussion Deepa Mehta's whole oeuvre and has problematised both her location and the cultural frames. She has additionally placed her among other Indo-Canadian filmmakers. Parameswaran has other essays on Mehta which are referred to and drawn upon for her observations.

Jennifer Heath provides us with an outsider's view of Asian cultures, a way of reading these films in a series and also, through her personal endeavour, a way of reading them stressing the point that visual art is meant to be watched over and over again. Subsequent viewings help unfold its layers and levels of meaning. Heath brings in a freshness of perspective in her approach to the films.

Avinash Jodha is his essay "Packaging India", has taken up a strong stand against the framing of culture guided by marketability. He has analysed the films scene by scene and has substantiated his point of view both supporting and critiquing Mehta's various attempts at de-exoticising India. Jodha's dependence is on the auteur theory – the director as author – which happens to be true at least in the case of *Fire* and *Water*. As a counter-discourse, we have Jasbir Jain's essay which approaches the three films as a personal journey of growth and discovery, a journey which negotiates the conflict between belonging and not belonging and works out a balance. Jain concentrates on the methods of producing meaning and their suggestibility in larger contexts.

Simran Chadha in "Marginalised by Domesticity" works with all the three films and beginning with surfaces and political constructs she moves on to frames both textual and spatial before working out the dialogic relationship between patriarchy and postcoloniality, religion and politics. Using the trope of female sensuality, Madhuri Chatterjee explores women's bodies and the meaning of their centre-staging in Mehta's trilogy as she works with *Fire, Earth* and *Water*.

We also have two essays on *Fire*. Bandana Chakrabarty's and Jayita Sengupta's. While Sengupta works with two films and focuses on the woman question, Chakrabarty's concern is more specifically with sexuality. Sengupta's concentration is on images which she employs for delving both into the conscious and the unconscious and exploring the nature of dreams. In *Fire* there are several dreamscapes – Radha's, Sita's, and Mundu's – and these create a dialogic relationship crossing from individual to society and working across class and gender. The central location of women in Mehta's films, as they confront the categories of patriarchy, religion and nation and as they are marginalised – socially, sexually, spatially is a concern that surfaces over and over again.

Uma Mahadevan Dasgupta's essay serves for the reader as a good introduction to the politics involved in the making of *Water* and the subtler ideologies that hover in the background. The many revisions, rewritings, threats and oppositions are an actual demonstration of strength on both sides: traditional struggles for power that refuse to concede ground and individual struggles for freedom that persist despite great odds. Vijaya Singh's focus on exteriority leads her to work out the parallels between mother-daughter relationships and Mehta's own relationship with her cultural origins. Singh, making use of Said's definition of exteriority applies it to diasporic space and the extension of boundaries through a recreation of the denied space.

Space is a category, which Shamini Shanker-Jain also takes up. She works with spatial metaphors and looks at the structures, the threshold, the pillars, the community courtyard, shared and private spaces with an architect's eye and proceeds to look at the transformation human beings can bring about through their relationships, need for protection and objects of love focusing on the film *Water*. The oppositional categories stretch from one end to another taking over each other's space. The metaphor of the threshold is worked through its many layers moving from Chuyia's entry into the ashram to the national struggle.

Tutun Mukherjee works through fine graphic details, echoes of folk-lore that capture the rhythms of life, and the colours and nuances of *Water*. Mukherjee has looked upon it as an evocative piece of art both as a painting and a social text bringing to dwell on it the historical background of 19th century Bengal. As she works out the construction of dialectical images, Mukherjee also projects the multiplicity of the water metaphor and the multi-images of women in coloniality.

Somdatta Mandal by framing her argument within Mehta's various interviews, takes us behind the camera to the director's mind and threads the narrative through her intentions, aspirations and achievements. Mandal's paper "Representing Partition" focuses on *Earth* and examines the unreliability of Lenny as a narrator. She also works on the problematics of adapting a novel into a film. The cross-relationships are worked out between director and text and author and film in order the sharpen the shifts of each.

It is amazing how one can go on chiselling the ways of looking at a film. Sudha Shastri works with the camera eye but within this she problematises the gaze theory and looks at frames within frames as young Lenny or Dil Niwaz are both watchers-on as well as subjects of the gaze in *Earth*. The dimensions of both exteriority and gaze feature once again in Sudha Rai's essay who applies them to *Water* and explores the text through the multiplicity of the gaze theory working with exteriority, silence, sociological details, spectacle and stylisation. Rai also takes up the subtexts and their subversive power.

Earth resurfaces as the subject of Neelam Raisinghani's essay, who looks at the politico-religious nature of communal conflict and its impact on human life. She takes the film outside the frame to relate to history and social reality as they press on individual lives. Two other essays – Rama Rani Lall's and Santosh Gupta's also move out of the frames to cross class barriers, temporal limits in order to examine tradition. Lall also raises the question of viewership and points out how the ready response of rural women at once dismisses the argument about the law for widow remarriage having been in existence much before 1938. Mehta's compression of time is true to the time lag between the making of a law and the courage to implement it or ask for its implementation.

Santosh Gupta's is the only essay which extends the boundaries of discussion horizontally. She brings in *Banaras* and centrestages the city and its history. In the process three things come in for problematisation – religious tradition, history of social movements and romantic relationships. A fourth element which Gupta takes up is the relationship of the director to the location, which raises another interesting query: how important is this relationship in determining the focus of the narrative? The two films, having chosen different foci, expose different aspects of the city to the viewer.

At the end, one is bound to ask the question, what is it that draws forth these multiple responses: is it the films themselves in their artistic merit? Their closeness to our lives? The rebelliousness within them and confrontation with patriarchal values? Or the reminder that we, as individuals, make history? Perhaps all of them, partly or in full measure. As mirrors that reflect us, and compel consideration of the issues. And they raise questions of representation and reality, location and accountability, irony and subversion and more significantly of aesthetics.

References

Barnes, Jonathan. "Rhetoric and Poetics", *The Cambridge Companion to Aristotle.* Ed. Jonathan Barnes, Cambridge: CUP, 1995.

Freud, Sigmund. "Beyond the Pleasure Principle", *On Metapsychology, Sigmund Freud.* Vol 11. New Delhi: Shreeji Books International, 2003.

Greetz, Clifford. *The Interpretation of Cultures.* London: Fontana Press, Harper Collins Publishers, 1993.

Jakobson, Roman. "On Realism and Art" (F.P in *Readings in Russian Poetics,* 1921). Translated by Karol Magassy. *A Forum for Literary Arts and Culture.* No.9 online edition http://www:centerforbookculture.org/ context/ nog/Jakobson.html.

Kakar, Sudhir. *Intimate Relations: Exploring Indian Sexuality.* New Delhi: Penguin, (1989), 1990.

2

Problematising Diasporic Motivation

Deepa Mehta's Films

Uma Parameswaran

In the Indian Diasporic literary scene, we are having a replication of the debate we had in the 1960s between those who wrote in English and those who wrote in India's other languages, one accusing the other of pandering to the western reader with clichés and stereotypes of pseudo-Indianness, and the other accusing the first of jealousy and fundamentalism. I recognise and am dismayed at the overt and covert antagonisms that toxicise the communication between Indians in India, and NRIs or non-resident Indians. An example of my point can be found in Vikram Chandra's article, "The Cult of Authenticity: India's cultural commissars worship Indianness instead of Art," in *Boston Review* of February 2000. This is an article in which I find all kinds of antagonisms that perhaps the author did not intend; I find its vindictiveness not just in bad taste but symptomatic of a new power structure that could be as neo-imperialist as the Coca Cola-McDonald's empires. Unlike some other diasporas where members visit the original homeland very rarely, there is more traffic among the Indian diaspora, which exacerbates the violence of such exchanges.

Deepa Mehta's work contains many of the traits that Vikram Chandra rightly or wrongly hears his Indian critics protesting against, and that he goes to such lengths to defend. His main contention is that Indian critics insist on the quality of Indianness, a quality that he thinks they define in a very narrow way. On the other side, Indian critics' contention is that diaspora writers exoticise because of nostalgia or diminish India because they write to attract the western reader and the western reader is seduced by exotica and by sensationalising of poverty and violence.

I would like to explore how Deepa Mehta's movies problematise Diaspora Theory. She is a very successful Canadian producer-director. She is very definitely a Canadian, for though she was born in Amritsar in 1949 (some biographies list it as 1950), Canada has been her home since 1973, when she came to Canada with her husband, Paul Saltzman.

She has 15 videos and films or film episodes to her credit, including two episodes in the Indiana Jones series.

At 99: A Portrait of Louise Tandy Murch, 1974 (director)
Danger Bay series, 1984–1989 (director; TV)
Travelling Light, 1986 (director; producer; TV) A documentary about her brother, Dilip, a photojournalist.
Martha, Ruth and Edie, 1987 (co-director with Daniele J. Suissa, Norma Bailey; producer) a film based on works by Alice Munro, Cynthia Flood and Betty Lambert
In Limbo from Inside Stories, 1988 (actor; TV)
The Twin from Inside Stories, 1989–1991 (director; TV)
Sam and Me, 1991 (director; producer)
The Young Indiana Jones Chronicles series, 1992 (director; TV, one episode)
Camilla, 1993 (director)
Fire, 1996 (director; writer; producer)
The Young Indiana Jones: Travels with Father, 1996 (co-director with Michael Schultz; TV)
Earth, 1998 (director; co-writer with Bapsi Sidhwa; producer)
Bollywood/Hollywood, 2002 (director; writer)
The Republic of Love, 2003 (director; co-writer with Esta

Spalding)
Water, 2005 (director; writer)

The films relevant to us are: *Sam and Me* (1991); *Fire* (1996), *Earth* (1998), *Bollywood-Hollywood* (2002) and *Water* (2005). *The Republic of Love* (2003) is an adaptation of Carol Shields' novel set in Winnipeg.

I see *Fire* as an artistic failure, a fissured success. Briefly, I think it fails for several reasons. To give just two of the points that I have discussed in my earlier essays[1]:

1. The cultural allusions she uses for her satire – such as the Taj Mahal, the story of Rama, the observance of Karva Chauth – are heavy-handed and seem to be used more for shock value than for artistic wholeness. I have discussed elsewhere how this esoteric symbolism eludes the cultural outsider and often offends the insider, so that one needs must question Mehta's motivation.
2. It shows in a positive light all forms of sexual love except hetero-sexual marital love. This gives a misogynist message, though that is not the intent Mehta has in mind.

Her *Sam and Me* and *Earth*, on the other hand, are far more artistically complete though each is not without flaws. Analysing why and wherein each succeeds or fails might give us an insight into formulating paradigms of Diaspora Theory, especially with reference to transnational identity, and the ongoing debate between first generation immigrants and their compeers who live in the homeland.

1947–Earth is set in Lahore, which was in India before Partition, and the language is mainly Hindi, though some of the characters include English in a bilingual fashion. The choice of setting and of language problematise, to an extent, the choices faced by the Diaspora in the search for voice.

Mehta repeats certain patterns in all three movies (*Sam and Me, Fire* and *Earth*) but with different degrees of success. In all three, this pairing is a narrative strategy to explore the dynamics of class, race, religious and cultural differences. One of the central relationships in each movie is between a disabled person and his/her caregiver. In all three, the disabled person is higher in economic status but lower in dependency status than the caregiver. In *Sam* and in *Fire*, they are old, colourful personalities, cantankerous and spirited. But in *1947–Earth,* Lenny is a girl stricken with polio, and she spends much of her time with her ayah, Shanta. In all three cases, Mehta excels in realism, and all of us can recognise someone we know in these characters.

Let us consider what makes Deepa Mehta tick, what motivates her to do what she does. In a 1998 interview with Vinita Ramchandani, it is said:

> Being raised in India yet living in Canada, Mehta felt confused about her identity for a long time: "I've never felt Canadian. I used to be upset about being called a 'visible minority,' that's what they called coloured people there. I used to come to India and was called an NRI [Non Resident Indian] here. The problem was not about belonging anywhere; it was a dislike for labels…Now I feel very happy being who I am, Deepa Mehta."[2]

This feeling of not belonging has been articulated by a great many Canadian immigrants. *Sam and Me* is successful precisely because Mehta, consciously or serendipitously, sees that her personal predicament is common to all immigrants. However, though it seems to be the bread and butter menu item for so many writers and scholars, I would say Canada is a place of many solitudes and every immigrant might feel so at the beginning but should grow beyond this feeling that the world is out to get him and only him. Though the statement implies that she has arrived at that point in her own life, the fact that her magnum opus, the trilogy, is set in India and is about Indian issues, makes us wonder about her positioning – consider how many diasporic writers have returned, as it were, to their native setting, and why? In my study of Kamala Markandaya(2000), I said that the cold reception of her *The Nowhere Man,* which speaks of British racism, might have made her return to Indian settings. Moyez Vassanji's *No Man's Land,* that showed up Canadian racism, likewise was his only foray into Canadian issues. Canada, in Rohinton Mistry's works, is only seen in his short stories. Diasporic literature in Britain seems to have grown past that phase of cold-shouldering fiction that criticises racism. It seems that Canada has not yet come to that phase, and Canadian writers opt for the safe space of their native country.

Sam and Me is set in Toronto, and is in English throughout. It is the story of the interaction between an old Jewish man and his young

Indo-Canadian caregiver. Except for the gratuitous and pornographic opening scene where the young man's uncle has sex with a white woman, I thought the movie was a rare treat of life as lived in Canada. As an aside, I should tell you that when the film premiered on CBC television with a lot of pre-publicity, a great many Indo-Canadians, nanis and dadis and all, sat in front of the family television to watch it. The first scene, where Om Puri has an orgy with a white woman, needless to say shocked them no end, and many switched off at that point.

Sam and Me is a human drama that affirms life in many ways. It shows the possibility of communication between generations and between cultures. It is an exemplar of the very Canadian quality of the ability to laugh at oneself; it pokes fun at both Jewish and East Indian emotional extravagance, and at the same time forcefully drives home their poignant histories of diasporic experience.

Sam and Me deals with diasporic life in Canada at two levels through a personal relationship on one hand and various snippets of insightful satire on the other.

Both, the old man and the young, are members of a Diaspora; one is Jewish and tries to escape the new homeland because he wants to die in the old, whereas the other tries to be successful in the new homeland and to bring his mother from the old. Separated though they are by age and economic status, the two men are bound by their alienation in an alien land.

Both are pawns in the hands of others; though the relatives are well-intentioned, they control them and use them to advance their own ends. Even if it is an end as filial or paternal as taking care of their charges, their motivation is that in addition to familial love, they are easing the pressure of their own guilt about their part in placing them in an alien, unsupporting environment. Also both, the Jewish son and the Indian uncle, exploit others in order to establish themselves in the new homeland.

The satire levelled at the Indian characters is far stronger, but in that Mehta exhibits one of the characteristics of the Indian diaspora – not to tread on any toes outside their own ethnocentric community's. But this has another dimension, as I have mentioned elsewhere, namely, the identity consciousness of the Diaspora that the old homeland or their fellow-NRIs are fair game because they are "our own."

What is emerging now is that the old homeland does not quite see it that way. As I say in my central metaphor in my cycle of poems titled *Trishanku*, when King Trishanku enlisted the help of a sage to get propelled to heaven in his mortal state, heaven rejected him saying it would admit a person only after he is dead; shunted downwards, Trishanku was denied re-entry onto earth, because earth said it would not take in anyone once they leave this planet. In my metaphor, I do not mean to say that heaven is better than earth (who would want unending happiness without that pendulum-tension that gives rise to artistic creativity?) but rather that they are two different spaces, and now NRIs are discovering that earth does not care to welcome them like a proverbial prodigal son afer all.

While on the topic of humour, it makes sense to discuss *Bollywood/Hollywood* next. It is a delightful, hilarious comedy, superficial and yet zeroing in on the hollowness of one aspect of diasporic life. It spoofs Indo-Canadians all the way, and if one of the Canadian characteristics is to laugh at oneself, it perhaps comes from the immigrant sensibility of resorting to self-disparaging humour in order to defuse one's anger at oneself or at others. Rana Bose does this remarkably well in plays such as *Baba Jacques Dass* and *On the Double*. This film is also a spoof on the Bollywood stereotype, with a great many songs and dances that are there for no reason, and exaggerated *hai-hais* from overfed uncles and aunts and mothers, and a general atmosphere of chaos where everyone seems to know and get what they want, rather than feel lost. Rahul is the son of very rich parents, who live in Toronto. And note that yes, there are a great many very rich Indians who live in ostentatious houses in Toronto and Vancouver, and have garish, ostentatious parties. Of course, the film exaggerates but that is the nature of satire. Rahul's mother wants him to get duly engaged before his sister's wedding, and absolutely forbids him to marry the white girl he was dating at the time. In typical Bollywood fashion, she conveniently dies in a freak accident soon afer his sister's marriage is fixed. In order to keep up appearances, Rahul hires a consort from a nightclub with the name of Sue (acted by Lisa Ray), whose black hair and appearance fit the bill. Sue says she is hispanic, and during the course of training her to be an

Indo-Canadian fiancee, Rahul falls in love with her. Again, with typical Bollywood connivance, it turns out she is an Indo-Canadian herself, incidentally showing that the diaspora is to be found in every profession, including the proverbial oldest profession.

There have been many negative comments on the film, including racist ones such as a comment by Nix on an online review site, <beyondhollywood.com>. This reviewer says:

> As is the case with all Ethnic movies, the leading man is not so enthralled with his ethnicity's insanely closeted customs and traditions, but by movie's end will learn to embrace them fully. Which leads me to this observation: If the West offers up so much corrupting influences that it causes these Indian families so much emotional distress (as *American Desi, Bend it Like Beckham,* and now *Bollywood* seems to attest to), why *are they here in the first place?* I guess hypocrisy doesn't stop at the ethnicity border.[3]

No one would say this of any white comedy. (I have quoted this at length to give an example of the racism an NRI often experiences in everyday life, varying versions of, "Go back to your own country.")

Indeed, *Bollywood/Hollywood* has often been compared to that hugely popular comedy, *My Big Fat Greek Wedding* (2002). One must note that both films were released in the same year and so it is not a case of one copying the other. I loved *Bollywood* because it is pure entertainment, and though exaggerated, pinpoints many traits of the Indian diaspora, such as overprotectiveness and over-control on the part of parents, the garishness of the rich diaspora and the workaday world of the poor ghetto – Sue's Panjabi father is a blue-collar worker – and all the hypocrisy and high living that is part of the diasporic scene. A comparison between the two films might show that Mehta scores over Vardalos in many ways, though perhaps an insider would notice that her satire of Indian-diasporic culture is far more hard hitting than Vardalos of hers. Clearly Vardalos' version of her culture is affectionate whereas Mehta means to hit hard. Just as she slams heterosexual love in *Fire,* she slams diasporic culture in this movie. There is hardly any character, main or minor, who is likable, leave alone admirable. But again, note that the Mehta's satire (notwithstanding the review quoted above) is almost totally against Indo-Canadians and not against Canadian society as a whole.

This film was made at a time when Mehta was bruised and battered with all that had gone on in her attempt to film *Water*. Barred from filming it in Varanasi, attacked and demonised by fundamentalists, Mehta came home to lick her wounds and recoup. In this period she made yet another film – *The Republic of Love,* which is based on Carol Shields's novel and so not having little of Mehta's own voice. Of the latter, she says she was enthused by the simple love story.

"I promised myself that I would not do *Water* again until I stopped being angry," Mehta says. "I could feel it: I would look at the script and I would get that horrible feeling in the pit of my stomach, of being attacked – like someone knocking you in the solar plexus and taking the breath out of you. When I could think of *Water* and not miss a breath, I knew the feeling of anger had gone." [4]

The two films, *Bollywood* and *The Republic of Love,* seem to have revitalised Mehta enough to enter the fray again. *Water* was filmed in Sri Lanka and premiered in April 2005.

Let us take another statement of Mehta to see what motivated her to start the trilogy. In a 1997 interview with Paul Kirkland, she says,

> "It was important to set it [the films] in India because the story is happening there. It is a microcosm of India, the challenging of traditions. I seriously wanted to break the stereotypes of India, the 'exotic' India of the Raj and the princes and the mysticism. Exotic India doesn't really exist."[5]

The problem as I see it is that the opposite is nearer the truth – that the average person in Canada has a very negative perception of India and no one exoticises it – Mehta seems to have the Britain of the 1950s in mind – when nostalgia for the lost empire continued to exoticise India. Today, even in areas of religious quests, we do not hear of exotic sadhus and snakes or of exoticised philosophical musings of mystics, but of down-to-earth topics such as the physiological bases of why yoga or a certain type of diet are good for a healthy body, and which therefore is good for nurturing a healthy soul. All the books that have made it to the headlines now, whether it is Rohinton Mistry's *A Fine Balance* or Anosh Irani's *The Song of Kahunsha* paint a grim picture of India. So, it seems to me that Mehta has got off on the wrong foot about her mission, and this accounts for many of the shortcomings in her films, the main one being trying too hard to make a point, to flay an issue to death, even issues that are already dead. Mehta's comments about her motivation and the whole issue of protest of the filming itself come in the way of our critical appreciation of the film as art.

If one could ignore for the moment these distractions, *Water* is beautiful in many ways. It speaks volumes through such cinematographic techniques as light-and-shade effects. Most old houses, as we know, used to be fairly dark inside, but Mehta uses this aspect of realism to symbolise the darkness of widows' lives. The outside scenes of the bright river are in deep contrast to life within the Widows' Home. Mehta conveniently eschews statistical probabilities by making Chuyia the only child among a large group of old women, and Kalyani the only young woman.

Chuyia is an eight year old widow who is admitted into this home, and is befriended by two other widows. One is Shakuntala, who is literate and keenly aware of the injustices of their plight and intent on protecting Chuyia from the prolonged torment. The other is Kalyani, beautiful and illiterate, who shares the little girl's love of freedom, and is being enslaved into selling her body to help run the Home. This is set against Gandhi's freedom struggle, which is a calling for Narayan, the rich young man who comes home after writing his Law exam. So here we have a leader, a cause, and followers who seek to realise the dream of a new India.

It's no coincidence that Deepa Mehta's heroine is named Kalyani, the heroine of Bimal Roy's *Bandini*. The parallels are worth noting. First is the remarkable resemblance between the two actresses, Nutan and Lisa Ray. Then there is the story. Nutan's character, you may recall, for one cannot easily forget Bimal Roy's classic. Her lover, Bikash, had left to serve freedom's cause, but got married to someone else. Kalyani ended up working for Bikash's shrewish wife, and crazed by her father's death, she poisoned the woman, and is in prison when the film opens. She is befriended by the idealistic jail doctor who wishes to marry her. When she runs into Bikash again and finds out about his patriotism, she chooses to go with him rather than with the doctor.

The film owes much to that other Master, Satyajit Ray. The muted scenes between Shakuntala and the swami, and the stark gaunt tableaux of the group of widows show the muteness of their life, in much the same way that Satyajit Ray used to focus the camera on stills of people rather than on still life.

In the context of developing a Diasporic theory, it might be worth looking at the fact that each generation of the diaspora seems latched on to the India of their childhood, or perhaps the India of their parents' lives. In Jhumpa Lahiri's *Namesake,* for instance, her delineation of her mother's generation generates more positive response than her delineation of the present generation, which reinforces if anything the stereotype of ABCD (American-born confused-desi) culture. One could, for instance, study the parallel between the film version of *Namesake* and *Water* and follow this thought further, or look at the cinematographic techniques that Mehta has borrowed from the old masters.

The two films, *Bandini* and *Water*, share a Gandhian backdrop; a Gandhian hero; and an imprisoned woman. Kalyani in *Water* is even more imprisoned than her namesake in the earlier film. Both are about the plight of women, trampled by the unforgiving and merciless feet of a misogynist society. In those earlier movies, as we know, a woman who has slept with a man never gets to sleep with anyone who really loves her or ever get married. Mehta keeps to the old script. Kalyani, ready to marry Narayan, discovers that his father has been one of the men who have used her service, and so does not get to marry Narayan. While Bimal Roy's Kalyani goes to her figurative death by choosing a dying man, Mehta's Kalyani goes to her literal death by walking into the river. In short, Mehta has no doubt shown the hopelessness of widows' lives but does not really break with tradition.

The points made so far are familiar diasporic territory – to revisit the past with an aim to relate it to the present. The problem with this approach is that though the past is usually depicted well, the present is a fractured appendage and seldom succeeds. Mehta's final note on the screen reveals this fracture in no uncertain terms. *Water* is set in Varanasi in 1938. Varanasi is what Mehta had in mind, though the actual location ended up in Sri Lanka. The date is clearly shown on the screen at the beginning of the movie, along with quotations from

Manu, and the end of the movie has a paragraph on the screen that says: "There are over 34 million widows in India according to the 2001 census. Many continue to live in conditions of social, economic and cultural deprivation as prescribed 2000 years ago by the Sacred Texts of Manu." This circular movement, a standard structure for literature and drama, is very misleading in this context. One tends to conclude from the word "many" that this is the condition of life for a majority of widows then and now. The blame for this misperception is, one might say, the reader/viewer's and not the writer/director's. But that is one of the problems with much diasporic texts – Where are the lines drawn? Who draws them? The argument splits the readership into polarised constituencies, as I have discussed in an earlier essay on Mehta (Parameswaran, 2007).

The script is quite stilted, everyone speaking with a stiffness the issues Mehta so clearly wishes to bring forward – Gandhi's moral revolution; the debauchery of zamindars; the fatuous justification that Narayan's father forwards when he says brahmins can sleep with anyone they choose and that the women they choose should consider themselves privileged; the hopelessness of widows' plight and the cruelty of society towards widows. Even simple messages – that widows are given only one meal a day and that they have to fast for the good of others – are belted out rather than acted out. There is a loaded conversation between a swami – he is a good swami, philosophical and wise (note that Mehta does not debunk holy men) – but that too is very streamlined into making points rather than blending with emotions. Shakuntala says she still feels worldly desires, but there is nothing in her face or actions to let on that there is passion within. She does become passionate, however, when she realises what has been done to Chuyia, and her race to the railway station to give the little girl into Gandhi's care is moving. It is somewhat contrived that Narayan should be the one to take the child in his arms as the train speeds away. Seems to me that he should have thought of her much before this; it does not say much of him that he totally ignores Chuyia's existence the moment Kalyani dies – true his heart is broken and all that, but this was the child that brought Kalyani into his life, the child that acted as intermediary with his letters, the child who made his life worth living. However, even in the generally stilted dialogue, there is one line that stands out – when Kalyani says that the lotus might stand in dirty water but is always pure, Mehta is referring to Kalyani's own purity despite being a prostitute.

One of the points Mehta clearly wishes to make is how widows were forced into prostitution, but I have misgivings about the way it is presented. Kalyani is the only one who seems to be in the profession in that whole house of forty or fifty women. Even more unconvincing is that little Chuyia is sent off to the same hangman's noose; for one thing she is, we are told, about eight years old; for another, whereas we are told that Kalyani is allowed to keep her hair and forced to keep her beauty so she can please the clients, Chuyia is sent off without any explanation with her plain single cloth and shaven head. I would have been more convinced if one, there had been at least one more prostitute or one more child in the home, and two, if Chuyia had been falsely lured by being given clothes and allowed to grow her hair and primed as it were for her role as an earning member for the Home, and then brutally sent to the sacrificial altar of prostitution. We know that virgins fetch a high price in the profession, and that could have been played up. Several persons with whom I discussed the film thought that Chuyia was sent to Narayan's father's house, but I do not think so. I think Mehta has effectively conveyed the prevalence of this abuse by having a staircase that seems identical to the one Kalyani climbs, a back staircase such as every manor-home would have had in those days. Narayan calls his father a liberal thinker who could be persuaded to agree to him marrying a widow, and it does not seem in character that he would take an eight year old child.

I would have liked to see Chuyia lose her chubbiness – to show rather than merely tell that they get only one meal a day. Also, Lisa Ray is a far cry indeed from Nutan. I had some questions about the realism of some scenes – a wedding taking place almost next to burning pyres, for example.

The interviews, commentary and comments that are included in the DVD, as I said, detract rather than add. Mehta, for instance, says she has never considered herself a feminist, and this seems an unnecessary caveat. The lead actors apparently are not fluent in Hindi, and this might account for the ineffectiveness of the dialogue and the fact that Mehta makes dialogue minimal. Narayan (John Abraham) talks of how he had to practise walking in a dhoti, and Lisa Ray of how she had to get used to the sari. These additional comments rather detract from our appreciation of the film, just as the protest over the filming overshadows any discussion of the content and techniques of the film.

The question that haunts those who live in India is perhaps the same with which I began – how many good representations of widows' lives written and directed by resident Indians have been silently ignored, and why does a non-resident Indian's film get so much media and world promotion? It is not a question of whether Deepa Mehta deserves the attention she has got so much as why is it that others of comparable achievement do not get the attention they deserve?

Notes

1. Uma Parameswaran. *Writing the Diaspora: Essays on Culture and Identity.* Jaipur: Rawat Publications. 2007. (This volume is a collection of essays published over the span of three decades, and includes three essays on Deepa Mehta.)
2. Vinita Ramchandani. "Passionate Plots." (6 Dec.1998): no page number. <www.the-week.com/98dec06/>
3. Nix. "Review of *Bollywood/Hollywood.*" Internet site: <beyond hollywood.com>. Posted May 9, 2003.
4. Paul Kirkland. "Deepa's values are down to Earth." *Toronto Sun* 25 Sept. 1999.
5. Paul Kirkland. "Deepa Mehta takes on the customs of India in the first of three works." *Toronto Sun* 24 Sept. 1997.

3

Ruler of Love's Republic

Deepa Mehta Seen from the US Southwest

Jennifer Heath

My first encounter with South Asian cinema took place in Lahore's Shalimar Gardens when I was fourteen. My father was a United States diplomat in Afghanistan and our family had gone on holiday to Visit History. Not for us vacations at the beach or ski resorts.

My mother kept a firm hand on my little brother, pointing out carvings and crumbling walls, while my father recited ghazals. I stumbled along behind, dreaming as always, and soon found myself wandering alone across a vast flat expanse and through a corridor of what appeared to be opposing armies of butterflies. My head was down, my mind elsewhere – "blue skying," as my mother called my habit of mentally disappearing. Someone shouted. The butterflies charged. I looked up just in time to see that the bright colour and noisy flutter were in fact hundreds of stampeding men, naked to the waist, strapped to massive multi-hued wings and heedless of the girl trapped between them. I gasped. I ran. My parents stood on a parapet next to a bank of movie cameras, my father waving frantically, my mother doubled over with laughter.

Forgive me. I open this essay with a personal reminiscence, because I was asked to write about the Indian-Canadian filmmaker, Deepa Mehta, from an outsider's – a Westerner's – point of view. I have no choice, of course. I *am* an outsider. But I want to come clean at the start that I am not a total Euroamerican neophyte.[1]

Like many in the United States (including, I suspect, Indians), I had never really heard of Deepa Mehta until 1996, when *Fire* appeared accompanied by ugly headlines from India: Molotov cocktails hurled at movie screens; theatres burned. Then *Earth,* in 1999, arrived without nasty fanfare, and then, in 2005, again with nasty publicity, came *Water*. I cannot remember when I have been more taken by narrative film. As with certain novels we adore, re-read, and never loan, I am attached to Deepa Mehta's exquisitely told, archetypal "Elements Trilogy."

(Incidentally, I'm gravely disappointed to hear – through the grapevine, as I have no definitive source – that this series is to remain a trilogy. But there are, after all, *four* elements. I am hereby pleading for a fourth movie. Although air may seem a little wispy, and Mehta may not wish to become envapoured, I can list numerous subjects that might be tackled under that rubric – not least the nuclear arms race between India and Pakistan, for example, a real-life sequel to Partition, *Earth*'s devastating theme.)

When I was invited to write this piece, I realised the best approach was to conduct a private Deepa Mehta Film Festival at home in Colorado. I am a devoted movie watcher, but not a "fan," that is, I pay almost no attention to celebrities, actors, directors, or any sort of Movieland minutiae. I have been a visual arts critic and curator, but am hardly a film scholar and know little about history and even less about theory. So I felt I could not begin to understand Mehta's signature films without first experiencing some of her other, less important work.

A search on Google revealed a fairly substantial oeuvre all new to me. I hoped these "Canadian" films, as let's call them, might offer insights to Mehta's aesthetic and philosophical sensibilities. My first realisation was that Deepa Mehta is not necessarily reliable.

I had to make choices, lest my personal festival drag on, so I eschewed Mehta's 1974 debut Canadian film, *At 99: A Portrait of Louise Tandy*, and the documentary series, *Spread Your Wings,* which she made with her (now ex-) husband, Paul Saltzman. Disappointingly, for it might be a pre-echo of *Water*, I could not locate her first film (or even its title), a documentary about a child bride based on the experiences of a family servant, made before Mehta left India for Canada in 1973.[2] It might also reflect that poignant segment in *Earth,* when a six-year-old girl is married to an old dwarf in a marvelously strange wedding ceremony where Hinduism and Christianity intersect. The sleepy child barely notices what's happening, but focuses on her wedding present, a hand-me-down dolly.

I was frustrated not to find *Travelling Light*, Mehta's 1985 tribute to her photojournalist brother Dilip. Nor could I get hold of *Sam and Me*, her first feature film in 1991, apparently about a friendship between an Indian boy and an old Jewish man. Mehta lists *Sam and Me* along with the trilogy as concerned with "where one's own voice stop[s] and the baggage of tradition begin[s] ... the conflict between the individual and the voice of tradition."[3] This is one of her most vital themes, recurring in almost everything she does at various levels of hub and intensity.

There is also a small host of Mehta productions that struck me as likely to have been labours less of inspiration than for pay. We all have to meet our bills. Therefore, for my private – and extremely limited – film festival, I skipped such fare as *The Young Indiana Jones Chronicles*, which Mehta directed for George Lucas in 1994, or *Danger Bay*, a 1984 television production.

It helps me appreciate *Bollywood/Hollywood* a bit more knowing that Mehta made it in 2003 as a sort of respite-and-recovery project, to gather back her profound courage and cheer herself up during the period she was forced to shut down production of *Water.*[4] But I found *Bollywood/Hollywood* boring, l-i-t-e to the point of nothingness, a meringue that has been whipped so long it passes its peak and dissolves. (Might *it* be the fourth element, air?)

Bollywood/Hollywood grapples comedically with the usual – or best known in the West – Indian themes: arranged marriage vs. marriage for love, overbearing mothers (the Indian matriarch in the West is gradually capturing a place among her Italian, Jewish, and Irish sisters), food, the tension between immigrant generations, and so on,[5] all wrapped in a formulaic farce of deceptions and mismatches. It was met with mixed reviews.[6] About.com referred to it as a "collision of conventions ... decidedly unsurprising" and "yield[ing] precious little traction. ... self-reflexive ... a rote American romantic comedy";[7] BBC called it "predictable ... the music average, the choreography rather unimpressive," while conceding that "Mehta still manages to put a fresh and funny spin on the proceedings."[8]

In a review that's nearly as clichéd as the film, Rotten Tomatoes called *Bollywood/Hollywood* "a fun-loving-romp of a movie...about following your heart."[9] Seattle, Washington's Post-Intelligencer – panting with it's-a-small-world-after-all eagerness – declared that *Bollywood/Hollywood* "reveals nothing if not that the complicated machinations of East Indian musicals aren't all that different from our own brand of cinema fantasy" and sums up by calling it "a feisty, featherweight comedy that makes the case that even the most flamboyant cinematic conventions are as universal as they are exotic, especially when they conspire to produce that glow of happily ever after."[10]

Surely, this laboured fluff is a map of Mehta's fragmented mind after plans had been destroyed for *Water*, its set torn apart and tossed into the Ganges by enraged mobs fuelled by fundamentalist Hindu groups, which issued death threats and burned Mehta in effigy. A good comedy always has substance, but *Bollywood/Hollywood* seems lost, neither here nor there – trapped at a crossroads between nostalgia and gentle satire. At least it yielded the lovely Lisa Ray, who I believe took over for Nandita Das in the original cast of *Water*, after filming was stalled, the actors dispersed, and everything had to be rebuilt in Sri Lanka from its original location in Varanasi.

How can we help but be sympathetic with Mehta, not to say outraged on her behalf and on behalf of free speech and expression everywhere? Yet it's not unreasonable to expect *Bollywood/Hollywood* to be less self-indulgent, considering the filmmaker's acute perception and talent. Regardless of uncertainties, Mehta is *privileged* to straddle two cultures,[11] and owes it to that privilege to do a smarter job. Mehta's goal to "break" stereotypes about India,[12] which she realises magnificently in the Elements Trilogy, is a missed opportunity in *Bollywood/Hollywood*, considering the rapacity of cultural appropriation today and that Bollywood is as trendy now as, say, Krishnamurti and all things Indian were for Westerners in the 1920s and '30s.[13] Bollywood is currently enjoying peak popularity in the West, with fashionable Manhattan and London film showings, Bollywood parties, Bollywood aerobics and dance classes, and even an elaborate musical theatre production, *Bombay Dreams,*[14] featuring music by A.R. Rahman (the prolific and brilliant composer who also writes for Mehta's films), all "simplified ... and target[ed for] the average American."[15]

Camilla, second on my festival calendar, suffers from a surfeit of loose ends. It was made in 1994, with screenplay by Paul Quarrington, based on a short story by Ali Jennings. It certainly has amiable moments, a road picture in which a young and an old woman find each other and through one another find themselves. (Had I been able to see *Sam and Me,* I might have uncovered a connecting thread and perhaps clues about why Mehta chose to direct *Camilla.*)

Each woman is a musician breaking away from what is or was once expected of her. Frida – Bridget Fonda – has a husband (Elias Koteas) who, incomprehensibly for a Euro-Canadian in this day and age, tells her with a straight face, "your place is with me ... that's how it works." A statement that would have seemed far more appropriate in *Fire.* Camilla – Jessica Tandy – is more believably infantilised by her middle-aged son (Maury Chaykin), for whom she relinquished true love when he was little.

The few reviews I found appreciated – as did I – its good performances, but slammed the film as "disjointed and unfocused [with] some sweet and humorous moments";[16] "romantic slush ... lacks a little something in the credibility department";[17] "ordinary ... [not] worth a backward glance ... dull, vapid."[18] Despite the happy ending, where second chances are seized, the film comes alive only when Camilla revisits her old, still burning love affair (with Tandy's real-life husband Hume Cronyn). The film is invaluable as the last one ever made by Tandy, who died in September 1994.

For all its indifferent direction, *Camilla* is nevertheless very Mehta indeed. To larger or smaller degrees throughout her films, she inevitably questions women's functions and place (and that of men, who are equally confined by custom). East or West, Mehta inexorably examines how we, female or male, might burst the chains of convention. She recurrently explores issues of integrity and wrenching conflicts within love, hate, fear, free will, and letting go.

So what's wrong? Why is *Camilla* so flimsy and muddy? As the closing credits rolled, it occurred to me that the problem is that there's no India here to provide Mehta with ballast. The exception, a merest token, is an immigrant Canadian cop – Officer Kapur – played by Ranjit Chowdhry, who was excellent as Mundu, the jealous, double-crossing servant in *Fire*, but in *Camilla* is blankly benevolent with little to do. Mehta has said repeatedly in interviews that despite her own (and others') confusion and chronic attempts to brand her or box her into one or another social space, she refuses to choose between cultures. Across the years, she has evolved into a product of both East and West and the result is that she has become a third entity: herself.[19] This Bothness of Being, this – privileged – dual territory where Mehta resides, is key to her vision. It is what makes her able to see broadly and therefore able to challenge hidebound Indian traditions, as well as to penetrate Western classifications of what she calls "the 'exotic' India, of the Raj and the princes and the mysticism."[20] Indeed, India is a spiritual heartland for many Westerners who know little about the country or its cultures and languages beyond the ashrams they visit.[21] But *Camilla* was made between *Sam and Me* and *Fire*, before Mehta may have fully recognised who she is, become comfortable transiting cultural boundaries, or had the authority and resources to do so.

Republic of Love, made in 2003, after *Water*, charmed me. Its greatest flaw is that like *Bollywood/Hollywood*, it lacks visual depth – as if it were made for television, on the cheap – but it is a heart-warming film, full of grace and breath. Mehta wrote the screenplay (with Esta Spalding) from a novel by Carol Shields. Since established filmmakers usually choose their projects, I can only assume that the book somehow appealed to Mehta's creative and emotional needs. I have not read the novel, but wager that the Indian references in the film are Mehta's, not Shields'! It is as if Mehta has finally embraced her "bothness," and – as was sadly not evident in *Bollywood/Hollywood* – has learned how to handle and exploit it successfully *as art* on both sides of the cultural divide.

The Elements Trilogy is where Mehta *became* as an artist, story-teller, and director, seriously embodying her "bothness." In those films, she utilises everything she's got, travelling between time, space, cultures, and continents, able to manoeuvre around the cul de sacs and blind corners constructed of ancestry, heritage, religion, and customs, and to examine Indian history and culture with a cool, relatively objective eye. She is among those leading the way to address social justice. Like my knowledge of film generally, my acquaintance with serious Indian cinema, beyond the magnificent Satyajit Ray and a few others,[22] is embarrassingly inadequate. Nonetheless, I am under the impression that the use of film as a forum for social change, rather than for simple storytelling, has been a particularly Western – more European than American – practice, and rare even at that. Entertainment – money – is the name of the game everywhere, yielding trite love tales, trivialised literature, or rehashed religious allegory. But I suspect that there is – my explorations of Indian visual artists tells me that there *must* be[23] – an underground, experimental film movement in India as yet virtually unknown to the West, except among a few cognoscenti.

Mehta's inclusion of *Bollywood/Hollywood* in the background on a television screen during an early scene in *Republic of Love* is cute: one imagines she could be sticking it in the faces of all those who disliked it. Rather than the usual background elevator tunes (and whatever was trying to happen musically in *Camilla*), Mehta overlays this Euro-tale with Talvin Singh's compelling compositions. Indeed, when Fay – played by Emilia Fox – and Tom – Bruce Greenwood – fall in love at first sight, Singh's music explodes like a collision of planets.

Fay is aptly named: "fay" derives from Middle English for faith and fairy, and from Old English for "fit or join closely."[24] She is fancifully and naively idealistic about love, a folklore museum curator who researches and collects artifacts of mermaids, otherworldly symbols of enchantment. Fox's performance, though somewhat more deliberately grounded, was reminiscent of Ray's in *Water*. Ray plays a widow/prostitute, Kalyani, in dreamy, weightless, childlike gestures, and like a sea fairy of ancient – universal – lore, having had only brief happiness in the human world, returns in despair to the waves from whence she came. Fox's Fay, on the other hand, must come to grips with reality, develop her land legs, as it were, despite *and* because of her disillusionment.

Mehta further invokes India in *Republic*'s set and colours. Fay lives in an apartment decorated with Indian cloths and knick-knacks (O exotica!). Throughout the film, as romance blossoms, the hues (especially grassy greens and orangey corals) heat up from modest Euro-bland to steamy, ostentatious, saturating, and rewarding. When the affair sours and hearts are shattered, the colours disappear almost entirely, exchanged for concrete, steel, and glass, whose mirroring textures are sharp and hostile. When the lovers reunite, vigour also returns. Partly with this use of colour and the force of Singh's music, Mehta reminds us in *Republic of Love* – as she does in the Elements Trilogy – that all human endeavours are laced with absurdity, whimsy, and self-destruction, and that these fade in and out of every life, simultaneously ambiguous and overwhelming.

When, with a wedding and a kiss, *Republic of Love* closed, I realised that Deepa Mehta's films, East or West, are all love stories.

I had finally reached the Elements Trilogy in my private film festival. Although I'd seen *Fire, Earth,* and *Water* when they originally appeared in theatres, each remained fresh to me on second, and even third, viewing.

I started at the beginning, with *Fire*, the story of a middle class Indian "joint family," a concept utterly alien to most Americans, who allow children to incur debts at will, separate from the rest of the family's requirements (even underage youth may carry credit cards in the United States, though parents can be forced to pay their bills). Individualism has its price, but there must be compromise between our responsibilities to the community (tradition) and to ourselves as independent creative beings (individuals).

No matter whether westerners "get it" about Indian family customs. *Fire* is so skillfully written by Mehta, so complete in its characterisations and clear in its trajectory, that she has obfuscated our cultural limitations, leaving us with no doubt about the repression, contempt, sorrow, and barrenness lived by this clan, and the two women – daughters-in-law, Radha (Shabana Azmi) and Sita (Nandita Das) – ensnared in a household where each person is consumed by narcissism. Mehta has drawn such a full picture that it would make no difference if the story took place on another planet. We feel the loneliness, desire, need, and cruelty at their core, and we root for the flowering of fulfillment, by whatever means, however illicit.

It "isn't only the tangible pleasures of a lesbian relationship that created such heated reactions," Gary Morris writes of the violence that met *Fire* in India, "...This beautifully shot, well-acted film is a powerful, sometimes hypnotic critique of the rigid norms of a patriarchal, post-colonial society that keeps both sexes down. All of Mehta's characters are trapped in their own lives, but two of them find a way to escape by discovering who they really are."[25]

Sex is only a portion of what is at issue here – this is a film less about lesbianism than about human emancipation – for the erotic is only one side of love, notwithstanding those riots in India, as well as bigotry in the West about homosexual relationships.[26] Fire is a sensual, rich, gorgeous film, hardly explicit and seemingly shot at dusk, the light is so dim, aptly oppressive. It is profoundly refreshing not to endure long, unreal sex scenes, but to enjoy lyric subtleties, where one bare breast tells all.

Republic of Love supplied me with an epiphany, giving me to understand that Mehta's very most basic, very most bottom line, very most driving concern is love. Love's multiple truths stretch far beyond sentimental or romantic definitions. Exemplifying this, Mehta introduces a little girl into each Elements film, as embodiment of innocence, empty vessel, personifications of hope and love.

In *Fire,* the child is Radha, shown in flashbacks with her loving parents, her mother encouraging her with a parable about mountain people who have never seen the sea. The wide imagination is evoked: "you just have to see without looking." The grown-up Radha is visionary and Christ-like, forbearing wife of Ashok (Kulbhushan Kharbanda, magnificent in all three films). Eventually, she is sacrificed on the altar of tradition, manifested as a speechless, tyrannical mother-in-law, Biji (Kushal Rekhi), who lights the punitive kitchen fire. "[T]he tragicomic presence of Biji [is a] potent symbol of an impotent Old India – wizened, mute, helpless, carefully dressed and powdered each day, and carried around the room with a ridiculous little bell in her hand, which she can ring to indicate distress or need."[27]

Radha is the first to peel back the layers that conceal love, to grasp tenderness, compassion, and friendship and what it means to live authentically. Her younger, more modern, rebellious sister-in-law and eventual lover, Sita, initially responds viscerally to her own frustrated yearnings. She represents the future, insecure and full of chaotic promise. "This tradition business is overrated," she announces. After their first love making, a scene so touching it brings tears, Sita, frightened and unsure, whimpers, "Radha, did we do anything wrong?" The older woman considers calmly, inscrutably, and finally concludes, "No." Love, Mehta tells us, is never wrong, and neither is the freedom to want love. Love is the least we deserve. Radha's countenance and maturity are exquisite; she does indeed see the ocean even when isolated in the mountains.

The lovers try to escape, to somehow make their own way, but Radha is delayed by her integrity and sense of duty. She is, after all, the bridge between those aspects that are in fact good and might succeed if tradition and individuality could be balanced. Her husband does not care what she has done – he is caged by his self-absorption, a righteous antithesis to love, willing for the sake of his own satisfaction to ignore what's happened. By her refusal, Radha is doomed.

Sita, bewildered yet determined, waits for Radha and their new life to begin. Radha appears, battered, burned, probably dying, and purifying rain – love – washes the screen.

Because I came of age in Afghanistan and because my mother was Irish, *Earth* is, for me, the most gripping of the Elements Trilogy.

It takes place in 1947 in Lahore at the moment of India's independence from Britain and during the throes of Partition, the awful time of "cracking India" (a later title for Bapsi Sidhwa's semi-autobiographical novel, originally published as *Ice-Candy-Man*, and on which the film is based). The geopolitical repercussions of the events that split Pakistan and India resonate today, with such atrocities as Pakistan-sheltered Al-Qaida and the Taliban, who torment Afghanistan, the conflict over Kashmir, or the India-Pakistan nuclear arms race. When I was growing up, my family called Partition "Revenge of the Raj," our commentary on how the British, not wanting to be booted out of India therefore left a legacy of hatred and divisiveness. It is pus from an open sore still seeping, occasionally storming, always dangerous, affecting the whole world.

Once again, Mehta has chosen a tale that centres around a little girl, a somewhat spoiled, very bright, and highly privileged Parsi child named Lenny (Maia Sethna), who is lame, perhaps symbolic of the vulnerability and neutrality of the Parsi (Lenny's mother: "The neutral position isn't comfortable." Lenny's father: "Think Swiss. If they can do it, so can the Parsi."). The brutal events of Partition are seen through Lenny's eyes, a device that, Stephen Holden of the *New York Times* wrote, "cannot do them full justice."[28] Perhaps not, but it provides an intimacy that may be hugely effective in alerting people to those terrifying times and their consequences.[29]. It is quite likely that *Earth* was many Americans' first introduction to that history which so impacts us now.

Earth, too, is a love story. Love within families. Love among friends. Love of two men for one beautiful woman, Shanta (Das), Lenny's *ayah.* Love between nurse and child. Love of place and home.

In *Earth,* the land is the object of desire. My mother, who was born before Ireland gained its bloody independence from Britain in 1923, liked to say, "If you open an Irishman's heart, you will find the word LAND writ large upon it."[30] In Ireland, from the Anglo-Norman invasion in 1155 CE, right through to the late 20th century, people were forced to leave their homes, the beloved dirt, rocks, sea, flora, fauna, and generations of tribe and family that defined them as Irish regardless of their differences. So it is in *Earth*, with the Muslim, Sikh, and Hindu friends surrounding Shanta, diverse with differences yet all defining themselves as belonging to India. Today, just as there is India and Pakistan, there are two Irelands. This trick of the British – its policy of population exchange – was carried out, as well, in Palestine and Cyprus.

In *Earth*, the idea of land is constant, illuminated in nearly every shot by yellow, ochre and gold. As violence and hatred grow, feelings of indignation and dread become palpable, present in every face and demeanour. Early on, the anger and trepidation are expressed most vehemently through the character of Mr. Singh (Gulshan Grover), coming to blows with an Englishman, who, arrogant bigot though he maybe, is also suffering a personal partition: he is British, yet the only home he knows is India, where he was born and reared, and which, with independence, is now rejecting him (and his place in the white ruling class).

Universally, in mythology, women represent the Earth. The *ayah* is nurse, nurturer, and steward of that which is powerless: the children and the land. Enmities and upheavals slowly amplify, but for awhile, as one of her friends notes, "only the group around [Shanta] remains the same ... like moths to a flame." She is place, dwelling, hearth. (By the same token, they – Muslim, Hindu, Sikh – are also guardians for the defenseless child, each in their way watching out for her.) Shanta stands for the land and pays the cost in vengeance and butchery. Caring one night for sleepless Lenny, she finds a doll, which the child, having witnessed the slaughter of a man by rioters, has ripped apart. Their world has fractured and split, and Shanta struggles, sobbing uncontrollably, to mend it.

"Love makes angels of the wicked," says someone in *Republic of Love*. Love is also shadowed by fear and loathing, such that sometimes the heavens turn and the angels themselves become wicked. So it is in *Earth*, as friends persecute and slaughter one another, until they ravage the land herself, in the person of Shanta, carried off screaming and helpless to an unknown fate, unwittingly betrayed by a child.

Water, about widows shunned, discarded, and exploited by family and society, is the flip side of *Fire*. Both films tackle directly the question of women's actual humanity, defined almost entirely by their husbands. When husbands are gone, or when, as in *Fire*, wives violate some rule of absolute devotion, the women are expendable.

Water was met with much praise in the West, not only because it triumphed over devastating adversity, but because it is quite possibly the most visually stunning and perhaps the most easily accessible of the Elements Trilogy.

Naturally, a child leads the way. When a rebellious eight-year-old widow named Chuyia (Sarala) appears at a widows' house on the edge of the Ganges, lives change. Meanwhile, outside the walls of the women's cloister, the independence movement is growing under Gandhi's leadership in the late 1930s. Chuyia, feisty, fun loving, and convinced that her parents will soon return for her, disobeys house decorum, disrupting the complacency of its inhabitants. Chuyia is befriended by Kalyani, another young widow living upstairs, out of sight, a prostitute pimped by an avaricious old widow and an eunuch. Kalyani and a progressive, well-to-do nationalist named Narayan (John Abraham) fall in love, despite taboos. It is little Chuyia who enables this affair. Like Shanta in *Earth* and Sita in *Fire*, Kalyani is barely out of childhood herself, teetering on the cusp between old India and new.

Swept up by Chuyia's insubordinate energy, as well as the possibilities she sees for Kalyani's escape and happiness, a thoughtful, middle-aged widow named Shakuntala (Seema Biswas), who seems to run the house, is forced to question her own faith. Her maternal instincts are aroused – motherly love that will do anything to save her children – and as tragedy befalls first Kalyani, then Chuyia, Shakuntala takes action.

Water is the most redemptive of the Elements Trilogy and moves beyond the issue of India's outcast widows. Shakuntala becomes Chuyia's saviour, even as Gandhi is becoming India's. As the freedom train leaves the city carrying Gandhi and the brokenhearted Narayan away from the site of his sorrows, Shakuntala rushes to hand him the abused, traumatised little girl, giving Chuyia a chance at deliverance, a chance at life, one person saved, the first step toward liberation.

In the 5th century BCE, the Greek Empedocles came upon the notion that all things are composed of four primal elements: fire, earth, water, and air. Two active and opposing forces, love and hate – affinity and antipathy – act upon these elements combining and separating them into infinitely varied forms and possibilities. Reality is cyclical. At the beginning of a cycle, Empedocles taught, the elements are bound together by the principle of love. When hate penetrates the cycle, the elements separate. The world evolves from chaos into form and back to chaos again in an eternal cycle.

It is love that reunites everything, and love that unifies Deepa Mehta's great master works.

Notes

1. My butterfly adventure happened in the late 1960s. Pakistan's film industry, modelled after Bollywood, was and still is based in Lahore and thus called Lollywood. In Afghanistan, during a brief period of liberalisation in the late 1960s and '70s (before the Soviet invasion of 1979), we watched not only Lollywood movies, but Bollywood, as well, in the public cinemas, which no longer exist. Today, religious conservatism reigns supreme, but in the capital city of Kabul, many own DVD players and thousands of Bollywood films are sold daily. Lollywood, meanwhile, has languished and, according to a young scholar in Lahore, Haider Sayyid, in a personal email correspondence on May 17, 2007, "Lollywood's output these days is meager. Pathetic. Only about thirty or forty films a year. But in the '70s and '80s, there were ten or more studios putting out a hundred or more films a year. Some say it has fallen because

of competition from Bollywood and TV, but I would also suspect the growing conservatism here affects it."

2. Kathleen Caughwell. "Movies Grounded to 'Earth' Political Upheaval in 1947 India is the subject of the second film in director Deepa Mehta's trilogy." *Los Angeles Times*. 9 September 1999.
3. Wyndham Wise. "Bollywood North: An Interview with Deepa Mehta." *Take One*. September-November 2002. p. 36
4. "It took me about three months to decide what I wanted to do next ... something that was life-affirming, that was fun, that was foot-tapping, that made me glad to be alive..." "Interviews and Conversations: Deepa Mehta." *Talk Cinema*. 21 September 2003. www.talkcinema.com.
5. The best film, in my opinion, to grapple with cross-cultural issues of Indian immigration remains Gurinder Chadha's *Bend it Like Beckham* released in 2003.
6. By now, movie reviews can be found online (and there is an endless supply of amateur reviews, sometimes more interesting and insightful than the pros). The archives of reputable newspapers and periodicals are also often now found on library archives available on the Internet, but do not necessarily reveal page and section numbers.
7. Jürgen Fauth. "Bollywood Hollywood: Different Wood, Same Tree." About.com: World Independent Film, No date. http:// worldfilm.about.com/cs/bollywood/fr/bollyhollywood.htm.
8. Maya Bellap. "Gloucestershire Films: Bollywood/Hollywood (2003)." BBC.CO.UK. Updated 8 February 2003. http://www.bbc.co.uk/gloucestershire/films/reviews/a_f/bollywood_hollywood.shtml.
9. Author unknown. "Info & Tidbits on Bollywood/Hollywood (2003)." *Rotten Tomatoes*. No date. http://www.rottentomatoes.com/m/bollywoodhollywood/about.php.
10. Sean Axmaker. "Featherweight comedy makes valid points about the universality of cinema," *Seattle Post-Intelligencer*. 5 September 2003.
11. Having myself been born and grown up outside the United States, I empathise entirely with the homesickness, purgatory, and mistreatment of the immigrant, but I also see this plurality as an honour and advantage, especially in a world of increasing globalisation.
12. Paul Kirkland. "Deepa's values are down to Earth." *Toronto Sun*, 25 September 1999.
13. Jiddu Krishnamurti, 1895-1986, was a protégé of theosophist Annie Besant, 1847-1933, a leader of the Hindu nationalist movement, president of the Theosophical Society in London and founder of the

Central Hindu College at Varanasi. Besant declared Krishnamurti to be the new Messiah. Krishnamurti rejected the role of guru, yet his Western admirers were legion, including C.G. Jung and Joseph Campbell.

14. I mention *Bombay Dreams* merely to make a point about how all-things South Asian have been experiencing a new heyday. In fact, *Bombay Dreams* opened at New York's Broadway Theatre in 2004, a year after *Bollywood/Hollywood.*

15. Neilesh Bose. "Bombay Dreams." *Theatre Journal*, Vol. 56, No. 4, December 2004. p. 703.

16. *DesertNews.com.* No date. http://desertnews.com/movies/view/1,1257,268,00.html.

17. Channel 4 Film. No date. http://www.channel4.com/film/reviews/film.jsp?id=101743

18. James Berardinelli. "Camilla, a film review." *Reel Reviews.* 1995. http://www.reelviews.net/movies/c/camilla.html.

19. These kinds of statements by Mehta are found in numerous places, for example: Lacey Liam. "East meets west in Deepa Mehta's film." *Globe and Mail* [Toronto] 20 September 1997, and Ramchandani, Vinita. "Passionate Plots." *The Week*. 6 December 1998. www.the-week-com/98dec06/enter.htm.

20 Paul Kirkland. 'Deepa's values are down to Earth." *Toronto Sun*. 25 September 1999.

21. I am chagrinned to report that several Americans I asked who are involved in Westernised variations of Indian spiritual practices knew little or nothing about Mehta's Elements Trilogy nor about Bollywood films. This was hardly a scientific poll, but it surprised me, until I realised that cultural India, of course, is not the point for these earnest followers of Americanised Hindu deities and scriptures, anymore than American Buddhists bear much resemblance to those in, say, Tibet. In another short, informal survey, I found that indeed many acquaintances and colleagues had seen the Trilogy and treasured them. One woman – half Jewish, half Norwegian, reared in Minnesota – told me that when her father died in early 2007, she retreated with DVDs of *Fire, Earth,* and *Water,* discovering in them some consolation and insight to her own grief. I asked her to elucidate, but these things cannot necessarily or easily be described in words.

22. As another cross-cultural filmmaker, Mira Nair has produced some hits (*The Namesake, Monsoon Wedding, Salaam Bombay)* and misses (*Kama Sutra: A Love Story)* and may be the best known of Indian movie directors in the United States. Far more interesting, however, are the lesser known

new breed of artists, such as Onir, who in 2005 produced a low-budget drama, *My Brother Nikhil*, the story of a gay man's struggle with HIV/AIDS.

23. In the process of curating a travelling art exhibition about the culture and politics of veiling, as a visual complement to my anthology, *The Veil: Women Writers on Its History, Lore, and Politics* (University of California Press, 2008) – and in particular reference to a chapter by Jasbir Jain titled, "*Purdah*, Patriarchy and the Tropical Sun: Womanhood in India" – I sought out Indian artists and discovered a vivid and dynamic community of contemporary painters, photographers, sculptors, video and performance artists.

24. *Webster's Seventh New Collegiate Dictionary*, Springfield, Mass.: G. & C. Merriam Company, 1965. p. 305.

25. Gary Morris. Bright Lights Film Journal. "Burning Love: Deepa Mehta's Fire," http://www.brightlightsfilm.com/30/fire.html.

26. There were no protests against *Fire* that I'm aware of in the United States and Europe, but this does not mean it was not despised or boycotted or that the West is free of prejudice against homosexuality. According to the United States Department of Justice/Federal Bureau of Investigation, "Hate Crime Statistics, 2004," one in six hate crimes are committed against sexual orientation.

27. Gary Morris.

28. Stephen Holden. "India Torn Apart, as a Child Sees It," *New York Times*, 10 September 1999. Aside from his misgivings about showing history through a child's eyes, Holden's review is highly praiseful of *Earth*.

29. I was teaching civics and journalism class at Naropa University when *Earth* came out. I made seeing it a requirement and found that most of my students responded deeply to it. It is a marvellous teaching tool, particularly in a country where world history is no longer taught in public schools ... if it ever was.

30. This was not original to my mother, but I do not know the source. Doubtless it was and continues to be a truism tripping off many Irish lips.

4

Packaging India

The Fabric of Deepa Mehta's Cinematic Art

Avinash Jodha

> *This is not a just image, it is* just *an image.*[1]
>
> Jean-Luc Godard

> *There are no good and bad movies, only good and bad directors.*[2]
>
> François Truffaut

The auteur theory of film criticism, a major influence in the French New Wave cinema of the 1960s, envisions the director as the author of the film. Alexandre Astruc's notion of *caméra-stylo* or "camera-pen" had some prominent champions in the directors and film critics like Truffaut, Godard, Chabrol and Rohmer.[3] Film criticism since, has been through a spate of theories, primarily from the field of literary criticism – New Criticism, Semiotics, Structuralism, Psychoanalytic theory and the theories of Culture Studies. Nevertheless, the *auteurist* positioning of the director as the primary creative force still holds its ground as both good and bad directors leave discernible patterns of their individual milieu, technique and vision in their films. The *auteurist* filmmakers are still a major source of inspiration for the directors world over, particularly those who strive to make films that bear their distinct signatures.

Deepa Mehta has been acknowledged as one of the representative directors of South Asian diaspora. She has carved out a niche for herself in the media as one of the flag bearers of the freedom of expression. While a number of other diasporic directors have dealt with the troubles, traumas, tears and laughter of the Indian community abroad, Deepa Mehta has taken her take on India in a big way. There are few directors both in the west and the east who have proclaimed universalistic representations of nations in their films in spite of the fact that there have been some amazing period films that have depicted significant historical moments and some other films that have concentrated on small regions within the nation states. Satyajit Ray's cinema is an outstanding example of regional cinema that exceeds the barriers of the specificities of time and space and touches universal human concerns. Ray, somehow, abstained from claiming his cinema to be the conscious representation of India.

Deepa Mehta stands apart in this context as she is quite specific about her agenda as a filmmaker particularly in the context of her trilogy on India. In one of her interviews – she is a prolific interview giver – she says:

> There are several conceptions that prevail in the west about India. There is firstly the spiritual India—a place where you go and find nirvana. Secondly, there is the conception that India is entirely poverty stricken, with a permanent kind of begging bowl attitude...
>
> It is uncomfortable and difficult for some filmmakers to produce works that destroy these perceptions. India brings specifically fixed images in many western minds, and the minute you start de-exoticising that, you have you deal with Indians as real people, and there is a pressure not to do that.[4]

In yet another interview, in Toronto, Mehta pointed out:

> It's amazing how ignorant people are about India over here. The audience here is fed on a diet of Satyajit Ray on the one hand and the Raj on the other.[5]

Deepa Mehta's restlessness with the existing stereotypes of India in cinema apparently provided her the fuel to come up with her elements trilogy – *Fire, Earth* and *Water*. The trilogy is her manifest attempt to blast all the prevailing myths and shatter all the stereotypes about India in the west and to correct the dietary malnourishment caused by the movies of Satyajit Ray by providing a more wholesome diet of India to the western palates. However, in both her pronouncements west remains at the centre.

Public proclamations of ideological or artistic intent and concerns have sufficient media-appeal but any such manoeuvre, in more ways than one, relegates the work of art to the backseat and severely jeopardises the artistic credibility of the artist. If a work of art, a film or otherwise, necessitates explicatory interventions by the artist the work as an artistic entity stands in bleak waters. Choice of a mammoth subject or a controversial issue stands no ground if it is not supplemented with the requisite artistic treatment. In fact cinematic art, subjects notwithstanding, can be the only tenable benchmark to gauge the comparative worth of directors.

A crucial difference between good and bad directors is the way they negotiate their ideological affiliations with their cinematic art – do they impose meanings or are they more subtle, are their images literal or multilateral, how much do they presume and assume the responses of the viewers and are governed by them, what are the artistic risks they are ready to take, how much of their art is clumsily visible or deftly hidden? All these questions acquire a greater significance in the context of the films made by the diasporas as there are inescapable political and socio-cultural implications. Mehta's unequivocal assumption of the responsibility to de-exoticise India and to 'wipe out two thousand years of imposed training'[6], even if in a limited measure, deserves all the applause as any such enterprise should but what still remains a crucial subject of enquiry is whether the fabric of her cinematic art is tenacious enough to carry the burden of her ideological intent?

Her first film *Fire* is her take on the real middle class of real India and the reality of the cumbersome burden of tradition. There are some visible structures in the film – the structure of Hindu tradition projected primarily through repeated references to the *Ramayana*, the mythological and historical nomenclature, rituals of homecoming and fast keeping; the structure of the middle class family with its patriarchal, economic and power equations; the structure of the house the family inhabits; the structure of the city, and the spaces private and public.

A striking aspect of Deepa Mehta's treatment of space within the film is that out of some 90 scenes in the movie 71 scenes take place within the house. As for the external spaces – there is the sequence at the Taj Mahal, six extremely short shots of the streets, two of the roads, one shot of a vegetable market and one of a park the family visits. With these there is the opening shot of a mustard field that recurs thrice in the film at climactic moments. Beside these spaces two scenes take place at Julie's parlour, four at the Swami's ashram, one scene of *Ram Lila* (folk enactment of *Ramayana*) and one outside an open eatery. The outside world and its influences are severely minimised and Mehta's camera keeps its focus on the three levels of the house – the ground floor houses Jatin's video parlour and Ashok's take away, the first floor where the family lives and the roof which is visited only by the female members of the house for a breath of fresh air, or to have a peep at the moon, or for girl games.

The idea is too painstakingly visible; Mehta wants to convey the truncated world in which the family lives. The outside excursions are primarily for the males in the house but they too are fixed for Ashok – the Swami's ashram, for Jatin – Julie's beauty saloon, for Mundu – the early morning street to fetch milk. If the women want to go out they have limited choices like the vegetable market or the Nizamudin shrine, which is a special liberty that they take on *Karva Chauth*. Mehta squeezes the spatial possibilities for her character to a strangling extent. Madhu Kishwar, in her review of *Fire*, raises some pertinent questions about Mehta's understanding of Indian culture and Hindu family life:

> An unrealistic element in her depiction is that the *Fire* family seems to live in complete isolation. This *Fire* family strangely enough never gets a visitor, even at the ritually important moment when the young couple returns from their honeymoon. The post-marriage period is usually filled with guests and neighbours in Indian families....The total isolation of this family is not only unrealistic but also claustrophobic.[7]

The claustrophobic treatment of space gets worse as the viewer moves into the house – there is a drawing-cum-dining space in one part of which lies Biji's bed beside a big window and beneath the overseeing presence of a framed photograph that in all probability is of her deceased husband. Within this common space there is a dining table, a sofa, a TV with a flower vase situated below a poster on the wall that reads 'Home Sweet Home'. There are two other posters that depict painted scenes from *Ramayana* and *Krishna Lila* (episodes from Hindu God Krishna's life). This common space has doors that lead to a small kitchen and the two bedrooms one for each of the couples. The rooms are fairly similar, a double bed, a dressing table and a big window from which the lights are so bright that nothing outside can be seen, but there are slight differences between the two rooms. Deepa Mehta makes sure that the rooms have a bearing of their masters' characters. There is a poster of Vivekananda on Ashok's wall and the posters of Bruce Lee and Jackie Chan in Jatin's room.

The beds in the brothers' rooms are even more interestingly placed while Jatin and Sita sleep on the bed that is double and is together; in Ashok and Radha's case the double bed has been separated into two and the most amusing part of this bed-business is that the only people in the house who seem to have a mosquito threat are Radha and Ashok. There are mosquito nets on their beds while Biji, Jatin and Sita sleep challenging the Delhi mosquitoes. Mehta leaves nothing to the imagination of her audience; the mosquito nets become a device to further establish the stagnant marital relationship between Radha and Ashok. Mehta's every single prop is designed to continually reemphasise already established ideas. She hammers her intended meaning to an extreme that any other interpretive possibilities are virtually ruled out.

Mehta, as a director, has an obsessive love for the creation of contrasts and polarities and she carries them to strenuous limits. One very significant aspect of *Fire* is the organisation of the scenes and the interweaving of three major threads of the narrative – *Ramayana* tradition, middle class life and revolt. The scene sequences give a clue to Mehta's method: the first reference to *Ramayana* is when Radha asks Mundu to take Biji upstairs and show her the *Ramayana* video. As Mundu does so, Radha and Sita linger into a conversation about Radha not having children and when Sita says, "Ashok Bhaiya is a saint" and Radha responds, "Yes he is…" immediately the next scene presents Mundu masturbating in front of the TV with his back to Biji. The word 'saint' is followed by Mundu's masturbation. When Sita comes up the scene is back to *Ramayana* on TV showing the sequence of the trial by fire and Mundu expounding on the emotional appeal of the scene for Biji, who unable to articulate her anger is helplessly crying. Next there is a close up shot of the poster of Ramanand Sagar's *Ramayana* at Jatin's shop, followed by Jatin's renting of a porn-movie to a slimy looking character with a cheap Hindi cinema number '*Tu cheez badi hai mast mast*' playing in the background.

In another sequence Jatin is engaged in a prolonged kiss with Julie and it is followed by an early morning shot with the sound of temple bells and the prayer 'Om Jai Jagdish Hare' in the background and a milkman chanting 'Sita Ram Radhe Shyam'. Next there is the *Ram Lila* sequence; the character who plays Hanuman is shown smoking a *bidi* (country made smoking sticks), again it's the trial by fire scene with Ashok watching the Swami more than the *Ram Lila* and killing a fly in the process. The scene finishes with the Swami saying "Poor Ram" and immediately afterwards the rooftop of the house – where Radha licks blood from Sita's leg in a loudly suggestive manner. Things do not stop here; Mehta keeps playing the editing trick over and over again. One scene offers Jatin licking the toes of Julie followed by a shot of Ashok pressing the feet of the Swami. And immediately after the beautiful *Quawalli* at Nizammuddin, the 'Allah Hoo, Allah Hoo' melts into the groans of Mundu masturbating yet again.

Mehta also manages humour in this otherwise serious film. And again she relies on editing skills for the purpose. In the scene that presents the family having food together Ashok mentions in a solemn manner that the Swamiji needs an operation because "Swamiji's testicles are too large for his loincloth"; while Sita gives a suppressed chuckle Ashok points out that it's a serious matter. In another scene sequence, there is a long shot of Swamiji with Ashok and words that are heard are "You fucking bastard, it's all your fault!" At first it produces the impression that Ashok has said this to the Swami and for a moment it appears that things are going to take a major turn but as the camera moves closer it turns out to be Jatin who is abusing Mundu for exposing him. And then the major scene, in which Mehta must have expected a rollicking laughter, comes after Mundu is caught in his fairly routine masturbations in front of the TV. The family watches *Ramayana* together, in all probability as prescribed by Swamiji in view of Mundu and Jatin's sins. Mundu suddenly inspired gets up and tries to touch the feet of Biji and even as he asks for forgiveness he says, "What could I do my batteries were overflowing I had to discharge them!" While Jatin abuses him, Ashok unperturbed breaks into a spiritual speech "mistakes in the soul journey are inevitable."

The context of Mehta's ire is unmistakable. For her, Ashok is as lost a pervert as Mundu or even worse because while Mundu, despite his callous masturbations, has a redeeming feature in the fact that he is simply giving vent to his repressed sexual urge, Ashok professes to be superior. Even Radha identifies her own sexual urge for Sita with that of Mundu. However both the Swami and Ashok are beyond redemption implying a similar fate for the sex abstaining spiritual leaders right from Vivekananda to Mahatma Gandhi to the modern day Swamis. Thus *Fire* presents the real picture of the middle classes of India torn between *Ramayana* and sex, between Swamis and Hong Kong bound Julies; passive males and passionate women doomed into dead marriages by tradition without even the option of a divorce, or possibilities of socialising or entertainment beyond soap opera *Ramayana*. The women are so pushed by tradition on one hand and insensitive males on the other that the only choice left for them is to explore the enlightened possibilities of lesbianism. This is Deepa Mehta's answer to the stranglehold of patriarchal tradition, a revolt that is bound to destabilise the constraining Indian traditional set up if not topple it altogether.

After establishing the reality of contemporary urban India Mehta turns to one of the most traumatic moments of the twentieth century, the partition of India. Based on Bapsi Sidhwa's novel *Ice-Candy-Man*,[8] *1947–Earth* was made on a grander scale. A look at the subject, star cast and cinematography reveals the film to be amazing cross between popular Hindi cinema presentation and parallel cinema intentions. The treatment of spaces and the scene sequences bear the stamp of Deepa Mehta's characteristic style. Out of some sixty-five scenes, forty-two scenes take place within the four walls of the Sethna house; another truncated world with its heavy curtains, high walls, garden, servants' quarters, and its own banyan tree. A house, where each of the major communities is represented through the servants – a miniature replica of the good old tolerant India in a colonial setting.

The scenes at the Sethna house represent peace and harmony and they are interspersed with fifteen scenes of the streets and the roads – a majority of these scenes present the violence of partition. Deepa Mehta's bloodstained canvas of partition is very carefully constructed to include all the established images of partition – two shots of mobs storming the streets, one shot of mob tearing a man apart, one shot of police perpetrating violence, one shot of train full of murdered people, one shot of people departing with their belongings, one shot of child marriage, one shot of the humiliation of the new convert and the last shot of the mob carrying away its prize, a Hindu woman. Mehta does not miss out a single opportunity to graphically present the acts of violence heard, said, reported from the days of partition.

Artistic renditions of sensitive historical events perform a very crucial function in moulding the imagination of a nation. They enable the collective conscience of the nation to come to terms with its own past, to learn its weaknesses but more importantly they people have the ability to unearth the buried threads of belonging, threads that can be held on to and consolidated by future generations. Also art can shame a nation like no history or documentary evidence can. It has the potential to convert time-space specific mishaps into permanent tumours, marks of disgrace that have to be carried along by each generation and allowed to get worse without any possibilities of redemption. The emphasis of an artist changes everything. Mehta's approach to the subject of partition is clearly indicated by her choice of material from Sidhwa's novel. While she has carefully picked all the major instances of violence and atrocities, she has completely skipped over a significant part of the novel that deals with the frantic search for Ayah by Lenny and more importantly by her mother and aunt.

The last scene sequence in the movie is carefully contrived to leave the viewers appalled and bewildered: the shot of disheveled Ayah being carried away by the triumphant mob is followed by the shot of grown up Lenny, who had been reminiscing the story so far, and she says, "After that I didn't see Ayah again, some people said she married the Ice-candy-man, some say that she was reunited with her family in Amritsar but I could never forgive myself for betraying her." It is followed by the last frame that offers the statistical figures of the number of people killed and dislocated by partition. The movie winds up on a strong note of paralysing helplessness that brings the curtains down on any possibilities of resistance or fighting back. Ayah and so do the other victims have to be relegated to the recesses of the guilts of personal betrayals.

Mehta exposes the historical and contemporary vulnerability of the Indian peoples but forgets to establish their ability to resist and fight back. The gory narrative of partition is not posited with a challenging narrative of resistance but on the contrary with a rather tame looking exploration of marital possibilities by a young babysitter that has been called 'an epic romance set against the bloodstained canvas of partition' (the punch line of the film). It is very important to examine Mehta's negotiation of the artistic balance between the two threads of the narrative i.e. the narrative of partition and the narrative of Ayah's romance. The triangular romance, in its own right, is less than ordinary. Ayah simply appears to consider the choices available to her.

The romance in the film has its inspiration in popular Hindi cinema; each of the lovers Dil Nawaz and Hassan, has a fair allocation of scenes and songs with the Ayah. Shanta in the beginning is quite generous with both the lovers so there is a fondling-cuddling-kite-flying song with Dil Nawaz, and next there is a blushing-smiling-cycle-ride song with Hassan. In 'Banno Rani' song Dil Nawaz takes the lead only to be stumped later by Hassan-Shanta physical union song *'Yeh Jo Zindagi hai'*. One song meanwhile is dedicated to the prevailing fear. Ayah's eventual choice of Hassan comes as no surprise at all and Mehta further simplifies matters for Ayah as she makes Hassan propose that he would marry Ayah, go along with her to Amritsar and will become a Hindu, that there are no such proposals in the novel is immaterial. Mehta's pepping up of Ayah's romance has a commercial appeal as it allowed her space for a few patent Hindi cinema songs but beyond that the narrative of romance from the very beginning stands no chance against the sweeping tide of partition.

Mehta's formulaic presentation of Ayah's romance is matched by her stock characterisation in the film. She fails to capture the complexity of Sidhwa's characterisation. The characters that have been called a close group of friends by Mehta have been carefully constructed, to bear the characteristic traits of their corresponding religions. Each one of them fits into established stereotypes – all the Sikhs in the movie are impulsive and are the first to grab collars, Hindus are shrewd and submissive, Parsis are bum lickers and chameleons or at best neutral. Only the Muslims offer some diversity in the form of pious Imam Din, sensitive Dil Nawaz and secular Hassan. Hassan with his earring and dazzling white pajama kurta can pass off as a Hindu or anyone. He kisses like a Hollywood actor and squats like a rustic Indian.

There is a marked difference of emphasis in the corresponding approaches of Sidhwa and Mehta. A significant part of Sidhwa's novel concentrates on the aftermath of the partition, the efforts to recuperate and to restore life to its normal order. More than any official efforts it were the efforts of the people like Lenny's mother, her aunt and Godmother (a character who doesn't find a place in the movie) that played a vital role in the rehabilitation of the dispossessed. Mehta's Lenny dismisses Ayah as a sore memory, sealing her fate and of many others like her but Sidhwa's Lenny cannot forget her Ayah so easily. She roams around in the streets of Lahore accompanied by Himmat Ali and Sharbat Khan in the hope of getting a glimpse of her Ayah.[9] Lenny's mother and her aunt who appear as ineffectual, ordinary Parsi women in the movie take great risks in the novel. They smuggle rationed petrol to help their Hindu and Sikh friends to run away and also to arrange convoys to send kidnapped women to their families across the border.[10]

They finally trace Ayah and despite all the threats and pleadings from the Ice-candy-man and the sluggishness of bureaucratic circles manage to send her back to her family in Amritsar.[11] The valiant efforts of such people, their extended arms to help their fellow beings and their contribution in restoring sanity do not find a place in Mehta's movie simply because she is unable to think beyond the dramatic appeal of the last scene of Ayah being brutally carried away. Her choice of the moment of closure in the film could as well have been the point of embarking into the story if at all she had sought to posit a narrative of resistance with the narrative of destruction and had wished to strike a balance between human tragedy and human resilience.

Earth was professedly made by Mehta to bring the truth of partition to the fore and to end the long silence of the western filmmakers on this Indian holocaust.[12] The reason of silence, according to Mehta's theory, was that it might have put the British in a bad light but Mehta's *Earth* obviates this fear because the movie produces a strong impression that the rifts in Indian society and its self-destructive tendencies would have broken it apart even without the British hand. The responsibility of the British in the partition of India in *Earth* appears as phony as Mr. Sethna's claim that "before the British there was no syphilis in India"; and Mr. Rogers' response that the "Indians would not be able to blame everything on the British for long" is a resounding vindication of the British who couldn't help facilitating the division of India.

Water, the last movie of the trilogy, presents the third dimension of Deepa Mehta's cinematic art – her romance with colours. After the forebodingly prescriptive caption from Manu, the viewer is confronted with a surfeit of natural beauty; a long shot of a pond full of lotus, intensely green grass and trees, a bullock cart, a man carrying two buckets of water on a bamboo, almost a painting. Deepa Mehta has also taken a lot of care in her use of light and sound. Two major sources of on screen light in the film are the countless earthen lamps and the light from the perennially ablaze pyres on the *ghats*. The fourth element wind proves itself amazingly cooperative by remaining mute. As the film proceeds further this interplay of colours goes on and on, providing a contrast to the white garbs and the blank faces of the widows. Deepa Mehta creates another polarity, another contrast – awesome natural beauty pitted against appalling human misery and she has her reasons for doing so, in yet another interview she comments:

> *Fire* was a very warm palette, *Earth* was a very red palette and *Water* had to be bluey green. My cinematographer and myself took the palette from the elements itself. Their world is so harsh that outside it we wanted it to be as beautiful as it can be. Something that is not accessible to them yet they are living it to show the irony of their lives.[13]

Deepa Mehta makes this statement without any irony. Setting of a film in a particular environment, locale, socio-cultural context plays an instrumental part in the existence and the experience of the film as an organic entity. Godard, in response to his approach towards nature in his movies, comments, "It's like the body. And words and action in movies are the spirit or the mind. And these days the body is almost completely forgotten."[14]

Landscapes and locales have a definite, though evolving, relationship with the people and patterns of life that inhabit them. Great directors like Godard and Ray have persistently attempted to explore the interplay of infinite subtleties that exist between external and internal spaces. Nature in their movies is never an appendage to the storyline or a mute backdrop against which the human drama can be enacted. At the same time these directors avoid indulgence in nature for its own sake or for its scenic appeal. Satyajit Ray offers a significant clue:

> The cinema is superbly equipped to trace the growth of a person or a situation. And to do that – to depict a social situation with the utmost truth and to explore human relationships to the utmost limit – one must eschew all the short cuts that have been artificially imposed over the years by non-artistic considerations. I should also like to banish from my films every last trace of the theatrical and even the pictorial or prettified – two of the most common cinematic impurities.[15]

Water's cinematography reveals a predilection for *the pictorial or the prettified* that reduces nature, in spite of the abundance of landscape shots, to a redundant external detail devoid of depth and subtlety. Nature's resplendence in *Water* performs two simplistic artistic functions: first it offers a perennial contrast, as acknowledged by Mehta, to the misery of the widows' life and second it accentuates the romance between Narayan and Kalyani. The former has its roots in the exoticist notion of 'social destitution in the heart of nature's abundance' and the latter is strongly steeped in the formulaic presentation of popular Hindi cinema romance. Nature in either case is reduced to a subservient role, as an object of human awe or a soothing backdrop to human drama.

Narayan and Kalyani's romance, much like the depiction of romance in *Earth*, has all the ingredients of Hindi cinema – 'love at first sight', breathtaking landscapes, captivating music, smuggled letters, social restrictions, meetings in dusk but in spite of every prop the intensity of love is somehow missing. Mehta attempts to stiltify the relationship by her insistence on Narayan's carrying a copy of the Sanskrit classic *Meghdootam* (Kalidasa's tribute to the spirit of love).Mehta's emphasis on the aesthetic appeal takes *Water* away from the ground of reality. The film glides over a thousand other corrupt practices that have spawned over the *ghats* of Ganga in the name of religion. The holy river itself has borne the smudge of the excesses of its devotees and yet the only blot on the face of Ganga in *Water* is the widows' ashram. Outside the ashram the world remains perfectly poised and the river itself manages to remain beautiful calmly reflecting the lights from the pyres in its tranquil waters. Mehta's failure to contextualise the Hindu widows' plight within the larger frame of ritualistic malpractices shifts the entire burden on Hindu religion and more so, on the scriptures that in her movies appear to sanction and even advocate victimisation of women.

Mehta's trilogy bears no traces of growth in her art of characterisation. The majority of characters in *Water*, except Shakuntala and to some extent Chuyia, are personified ideas devoid of the complexity of human character. The fathers of Narayan and Rabindra represent the ugly decadent face of upper caste and upper class Hindus. Rabindra is the representative of the new generation of English educated Brown Sahibs who relish English wine and take pride in quoting English poets alongside their inheritance of upper class privileges. Narayan is a progressive Gandhian who loves to quote from Kalidas' *Meghdootam* and simultaneously correct Rabindra's slurs in quoting English poets. Madhumati is the regular tyrant matriarch, who has mastered the equations of patriarchal traditional Hindu society to her own advantage. Kalyani is Hindi cinema's basic 'damsel in distress' and Gulabi the eunuch is the characteristic procurer, the go-between the Seths and widow homes. Mehta reiterates the stereotypes and establishes a clear line of distinction between the good and the bad characters; there are visible heroes and villains, victims and victimizers and well identified targets.

The fissures in Mehta's cinematic art correspond to her ideological and artistic limitations. Her art is choreographed by her allegiance to specific polemical concerns or ideas and their marketability. These compromises severely undermine her cinema's potential to depict human situations and relationships in a convincing manner. In her trilogy the 'idea' takes precedence over art – *Fire* seeks to validate the revolutionary potential of western lesbianism in the context of decadent Hindu society; *Earth* appropriates the history of partition in its gruesome aspects and offers no signs of hope; and *Water* takes a stride into the colonial past of India to reemphasise the inherent depravity and corruption of this ancient civilisation that still remains beleaguered to these practices. Mehta's trilogy offers no sense of continuity or traces of growth in her understanding of India or signs of depth in her belonging to India. The only thread that binds the fabric of her *Fire*, *Earth* and *Water* together is the thread of ideological and artistic inadequacy. It would be preposterous even to faintly attempt a comparison of her trilogy with Satyajit Ray's classic Apu trilogy. Mehta's advocacy of a 'cause' and her reformist zeal is a smokescreen that has strong commercial and media appeal but beyond it her inheritance of India is an inheritance of loss and depravity.

Notes

1. See MacCabe, *Godard: Images, Sounds, Politics* (1980).
2. See François Truffaut's 1954 essay *Une certaine tendance du cinéma français* ("a certain tendency in the French cinema"), quoted here from Auteur theory – Wikipedia, the free encyclopedia2.htm
3. See Auteur theory – Wikipedia, the free encyclopedia2.htm. Online. Internet.
4. See Richard Philips. "An Interview with Deepa Mehta". wsws.org. Online. Internet. 6 August 1999.
5. See "An interview with Deepa Mehta", *The Asian Age*, Toronto. Feb 9, 1997. Quoted here from Madhu Kishwar, "Naive Outpourings of a Self-Hating Indian: A Review of Deepa Mehta's 'Fire'." naïve outpourings.htm. Online. Internet
6. Richard Philips, Int. Deepa Mehta Speaks with WSWS. wsws.org. Online. Internet. 15 May 2006.
7. See Madhu Kishwar "Naive Outpourings of a Self-Hating Indian: A Review of Deepa Mehta's 'Fire'." naïve outpourings.htm. Online. Internet.

8. Bapsi Sidhwa, *Ice-Candy-Man* (1988, New Delhi: Penguin Books India, 1989)
9. *Ibid.*, 209.
10. *Ibid.*, 242.
11. *Ibid.*, 274-277.
12. See Richard Philips. "An Interview with Deepa Mehta". wsws.org. Online. Internet. 6 August 1999.
13. See Preeti Thandi. "Tumultuous Water: An interview with Deepa Mehta". mybindi.com. Online. Internet.
14. Hal Hartley, Int. Jean-Luc Godard "In Images We Trust". *Filmmaker.* Vol. 3, No. 1 (Fall 1994): 14, 16-18, 55-56.
15. See Bert Cardullo, Int. Satyajit Ray "Revisiting Satyajit Ray". *Bright Lights Film Journal*. Online. Internet.

5

The Diasporic Eye and the Evolving I

Deepa Metha's Elements Trilogy

Jasbir Jain

Deepa Mehta's elements trilogy is firmly located in India and India's history and the present: Delhi, Lahore and a substitute Varanasi with a substitute name. Except for the British officer in *1947–Earth*, foreign characters are absent. While *Earth* focuses on the 40s, *Water* on the 30s, *Fire* looks at contemporary India of the 80s and the 90s, of the postfeminist and post Babri Masjid period. Therefore, in terms of filmmaking, Mehta journeys from the present to the past, step by step, looking for roots, causes and explanations. For all practical purposes, the films are women-centred but the female body and its sexuality is delinked from procreation. Not a single child is born in any of the three films even if child characters are centrestage and occupy important roles. Except for *Earth,* the other two films have been conceptualised and written by Deepa Mehta, announcing a much more intimate relationship with the themes, than in the case of selection from stories written by others.

Intimately woven with India and its cultural values, these films have received a wide-ranging response. There has been a very strong appreciation on one hand and vociferous criticism on the other where Mehta has been accused of scandalising the national sentiment. Mehta is not the only one to be subjected to negative criticism. Others before her, like Satyajit Ray, have also been subjected to similar onslaughts. Ray's Apu trilogy, even as it won raving reviews for its aesthetic dimensions, came in for criticism for its framing of India's poverty.[1] Such a reception raises two related questions: the relationship between art and nationalistic ideology and the location/purpose of the filmmaker.

Addressing the first, one would like to pretend that a film is a self-enclosed entity, complete in itself, that art has value in terms of acting, cinematography, imaging and all else that goes into it. But this is not so. A film is a communication (not propaganda), it is dialogic (not imperial or one-sided in its tone) and it reaches various audiences across cultures, classes and gender. Thus somewhere along the line, some kind of ideology gets linked up with the thematic thrust. *Lagaan* (2001) made by Aamir Khan is one such example where nationalistic fervour and a patriotic defence underlie the making of a film. Others of this kind are the whole lot of Manoj Kumar films and Aamir Khan's *Mangal Pandey* (2005), leading one to conclude that a film does in some way or the other indulge in cultural framing with varying degrees of concern for realistic portrayal and emotional fidelity.

It is simply not possible to employ the same yardstick to every film but there is often a glamourisation of heightened emotions in films like *Lagaan* while an isolation of the themes of loneliness, abandonment and struggle in films like *Salaam Bombay*. Mira Nair's *Salaam Bombay*[2] won for itself both appreciation and brickbats. Why? Those who see us negatively pose a threat to our self-complacency. They hold up a mirror into which we are afraid to look. And the diaspora is always suspect. (No matter how badly the stay-at-home writer/director savages us in low grade movies). Thus location becomes important. Cultural images do not necessarily convey the same meaning to other culture readers/viewers. I recall that once when I referred to the implications of the *Ramayana* episodes in *Fire*, a foreign friend of mine suddenly woke up to their significance. There is always a great deal in any piece of art that is culturally rooted but cannot be explained; a part of which may often be part of an oral tradition. In a film even the body language, which is often culturally constructed, carries meaning and may evoke quite a different response in the 'other' culture viewer. The point I wish to make here is that a great deal that goes un-elucidated in the Mehta films as far as the foreign viewer is concerned, would lead us to conclude that Mehta is not specifically targeting the non-culture viewership.

Mehta's many interviews, the criticism on the grounds that she is located abroad (read Uma Parameswaran's essay in this volume which adopts this view)[3], the controversy at home – all stress the importance of location – (a) for the filmmaker (b) for the native critic located abroad (and consequently part of the frozen culture and distant from the fluidity of the home culture) and (c) for the native critic more at home with the politics of culture. My location is in the third category and for the moment I am going to bypass Mehta's own statements and responses and attempt to capture my own responses to her films wherein I would like to place them in a continuity signifying an evolving relationship of the director with her 'self' and her inherited cultural tradition.

The Films

When *Fire* was first screened in India, I saw both the Hindi and the English versions. My first response was that it was a foreign film more at home in English. The setting, except for the outdoor scenes like the visit to Taj Mahal and the memory sequence of the girl sitting in the field with her parents and the occasional visit to the shopping area, could be easily lifted into any foreign setting. The cinematography and the semi-dark scenes reinforced this feeling. The scenes were slick, they moved quickly into each other, were often cut short at the point of merging into another, the double-function fast food joint and video parlour almost solely managed by women (not a common sight in 1996 in middle class India), were all a little distant, and their apartment could easily be an immigrant home abroad. Strangely enough though the home is crowded, the film is thinly populated. No relatives encroach on their space, there are no nodding neighbourhood acquaintances, no community feeling, festivity or celebration, no parental associations. The only two outward extensions are Julie, her parents and the Swami. The Ram Lila performance and the wedding procession are additional sites/sights.

Almost all of these could be transported anywhere else except for the charpoy on the terrace. Even swamis are easily transported. *Fire* is dominantly a film of confined spaces both emotionally and physically. The outdoor scenes hardly enter the imagination and at times, like the morning *doodhwala* (milkman) totally eliminated by the late 70s by Mother Diary, are unrealistic details. Biji's bed is in a passage cum lounge, where the family TV also occupies a place. The women move in and out of their rooms down to the kitchen and back again. Privacy and freedom both are missing and power is shared by the old woman – bed-ridden and paralysed – and her elder son Ashok, emotionally and intellectually under the sway of the Swami. She with her bell, controls movement, music, laughter, dress and behaviour code and he controls the money and the hierarchically structured roles.

The two ends of the film are governed by memorials and shrines – the Taj Mahal, signifying the immortality of love, and Hazrat Nizammudin's shrine signifying the immortality of the spirit. Nizammudin, a Sufi saint, represents here the freedom from religious ritual.[4] The Sufi discourse is in direct contrast to the Swami-Ashok discourse largely based on the *Ramayana* which celebrates *maryada-purshottam* Rama and a code of conduct tuned to public reception. It also addresses, even though obliquely, the Babri Masjid context by commenting on the irrational hold of orthodoxy. *Ramayana* forms a powerful subtext in the film with the recurring references to it – through Swamiji's discourse, Ram Lila performance (with its cross dressing), clippings from the TV serial and the symbolisation attached to *agnipriksha* – trial by fire.

Uma Parameswaran has at one point objected to the names and suggested that Ashok's wife should have been named Sita (apparently because of his obsession with the *Ramayana* narrative) and that allusions should have been more in a one to one relationship.[5] But by deviating from such expectations, Mehta has simultaneously achieved three things – she has selected a subtext which has constructed the notion of womanhood in India, but has then go on to disturb it by breaking away from its main narrative in order to serve the ideological function of the film's narrative.[6]

The spaces and the cinematography together insist that the film is about the nature of freedom and the movement is from illusion to self-discovery. Radha and Sita are not the only ones looking for freedom, even the two sons are fretting against the control of orthodoxy in half-measures unable to come to terms with their uneasiness with the roles they are made to fill. Mundu adheres to the stereotype of a servant who exploits in return for being exploited and emerges as a conniving potential blackmailer.

There are several scenes that through recurrence draw attention to themselves and to the fact of their centrality to the meaning of the film: the references to *Ramayana*, the field sequence, the reference to procreation and the possible birth of a baby (thrice in the first fifteen minutes), scenes in front of a dressing-table and kissing scenes. Each repetition supplements or reinterprets or contrasts with the earlier occurrence. The field sequence defines Radha's character and attitude. It is a constant reminder to her of wide open spaces, of the sea beyond the limits of land, of the need to 'see' without looking. This field sequence is both a memory and a dream and shapes her whole being as well as her later relationship with Sita.

There are several scenes in front of the dressing table. Sita, soon after her return from her honeymoon, cross dresses and indulges

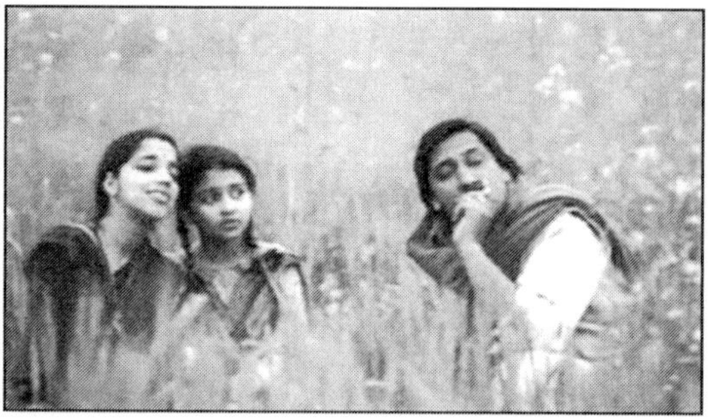

The third occasion of this dreamscape

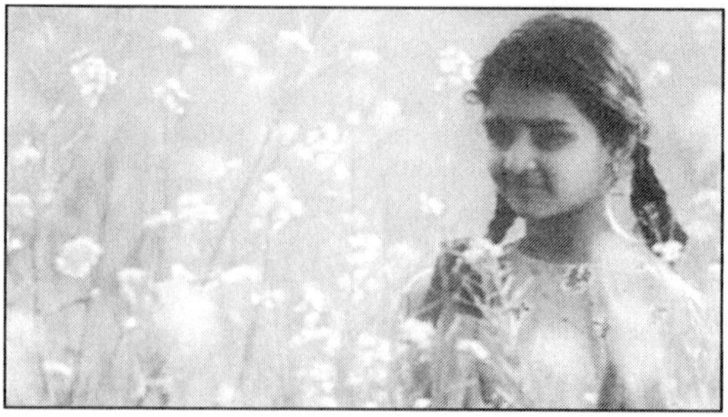

The fifth and final occurence of Radha's dreamscape

herself by looking at the mirror. Later Jatin and Sita, as they discuss their compulsions, are reflected in the mirror. The mirror as a narcissistic reflection features a great deal in Sita's room.[7] In Radha's room it is not so centrestage, though there is one scene when Radha sits in front of it and is lost in contemplation. The mirror, in her case, is substituted by the memory of the childhood scene in the field. This too occurs at least five times and if one notes carefully, its recurrence is marked by difference. In the first the mother is centrestage, subsequently it dims, then later it is magnified and finally the child emerges more confident and assured and is also more clearly visible with the parents hardly to be seen – this is the last time when this dreamscape is repeated. One needs to take note of these connections to the meaning of the central narrative and the tentative connections being made between the inner psyche and the outer world. The reflections in the mirror indicate both the desire to be loved and the reality of not being loved as well as Sita's consciousness of her body.

There are at least four kissing scenes in the films – the two girls, Jatin and Sita, Jatin and Julie and Ashok and Radha. Each kiss denotes a different emotion. The women's kiss is full of exploratory desire, tenderness and love, Jatin's is a disinterested one of ownership and is in direct contrast to the earlier kissing scene with Julie, where the kiss is full of passion and is a lover's kiss. Ashok's kiss starts as one of punishment but changes into one of release from his own repressed sexuality. It is simultaneously a release from his adherence to the Swami's advice and a yielding to his own nature. Ashok, acted by Kulbhushan Kharbanda, is a complex character. His portrayal here carries a resemblance to the role of Tiloka in *Ek Chadar Maili Si*[8] except that Tiloka spends his sexuality and Ashok does not. Both of them treat their women with contempt. The main influences on him are the Swami with his constant talk of good and evil, Swami Vivekananda whose portrait adorns his bedroom and Gandhi whose need for the other as a testing ground for his own moral strength is emulated by him. In the background lurk the differences in the lives of these two men. Swami Vivekananda, even as he placed religion at the centre of national life, advocated activism and upheld masculinity as an ideal[9] while Gandhi's ideological belief was in non-violence and his vow of celibacy was taken as a measure of self-restraint. In his case it was "the imperatives of desire straining against the higher purpose of unfettered service to community".[10]

Ashok has none of these strengths. His abstinence is directly related to Radha's barrenness, and his stand is closer to Manu's edict in which the two – sex and procreation – are linked together.

There is another oppositional discourse in the film. Radha's name directly links up with Krishna and the openness of the Radha-Krishna relationship, the mainstay of which were flirtation and festivity, dance and music – in short, an openness of spirit. The two – the moral control of the *Ramayana* and the community sharing of the *Krishna-Lila* where the mischievous boy has an open affair with a married woman older than him, don't go together. These situations hint at basic incompatibilities.

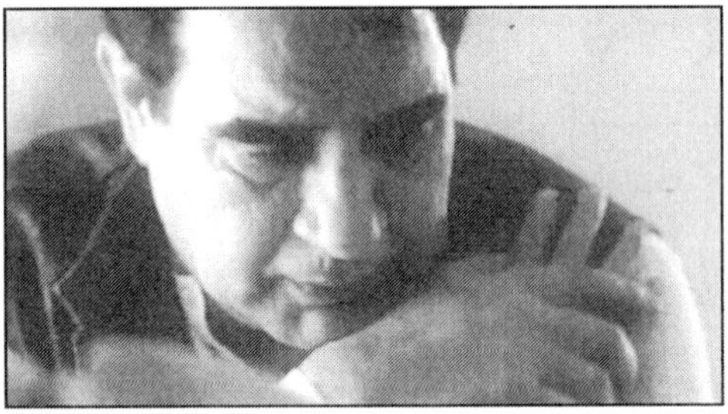

Fear of the female touch (*Fire*)

The Radha-Sita relationship is directly contrasted with Ashok-Radha and Jatin-Sita relationships. The latter two are utilitarian and non-caring. In the Radha-Sita relationship there are no impositions on the will of the other. Even the Jatin-Julie relationship is a lop-sided one but not so the one between the two sisters-in-law. Whether the lesbian desire is rooted in the dissatisfaction with the heterosexual relationships or in biological difference has been mooted by several critics. Ratna Kapur builds up a case for the latter and foregrounds Sita's agency as she takes the initiative of planting a kiss on Radha's lips.[11] Gayatri Gopinath refers to Radha's dreamscape

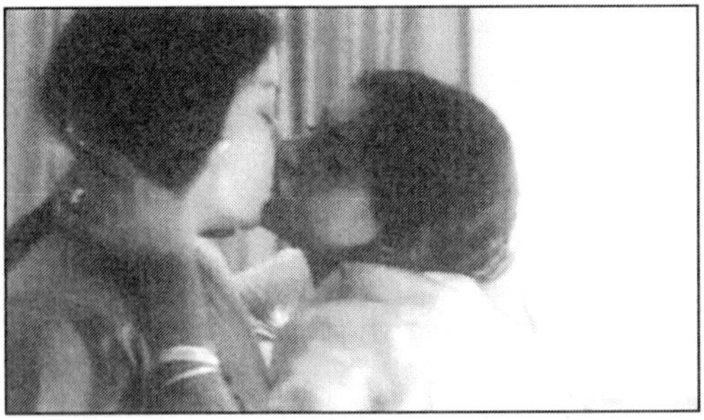

Desire and self-discovery

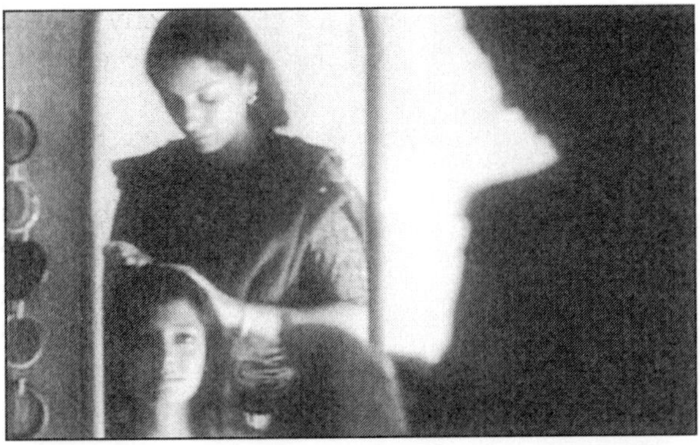

Reflections of love

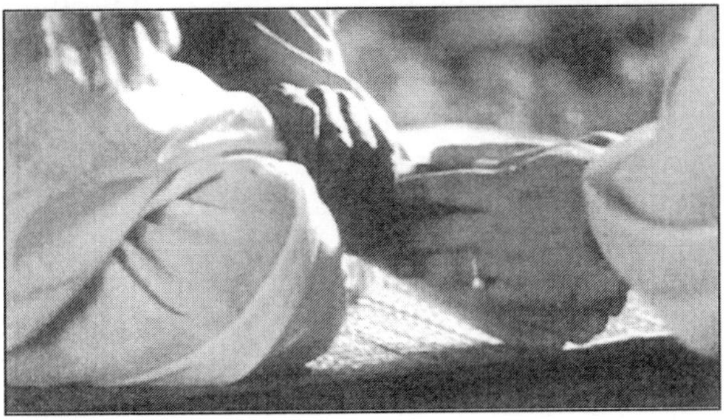

Swami and the devotee

and her mother's exhortation to see things differently, "to 'see' without literally seeing", a fact that points to the "need for a particular strategy of reading sexuality outside dominant configurations of visibility, desire and identity [.....] it suggests an alternative mode of reading and 'seeing' non-normative erotic and gender configuration as they erupt within sites of extreme hetero-normativity" (Gopinath 741). With controls imposed on Sita's cross-dressing, her dance and music, restricted to the close confines of the home and the business-like, yet curious, examination of the violation of her virginity, a scene inserted to make several points, the most important of which being the sexual innocence of Sita as also the cultural value attached to virginity, all focus on Sita's discomfort in her new home.

The disillusionment which began during the honeymoon visit to the Taj Mahal (note Jatin's distance and body language in the Taj Mahal scene), is now complete with the dry matter-of-fact experience

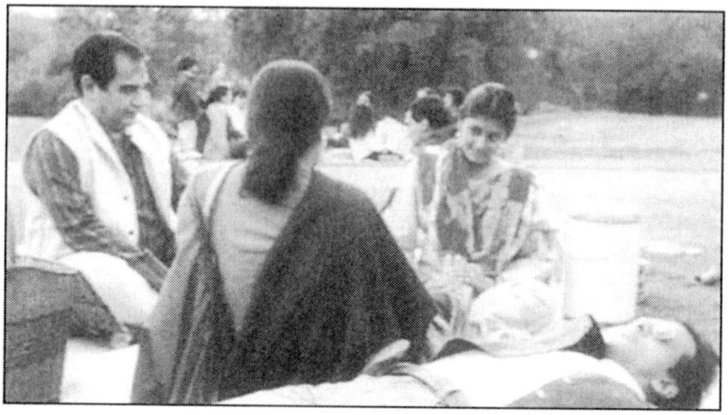

Women as lovers: Sita massaging Radha's feet

of the sexual act. Sita's efforts at establishing a normal relationship are endless but the only response she gets at a human level is from Radha. Despite these emotional setbacks, Sita's respect for her own body and her self-image survive her loveless relationship. Their desire for each other is born out of the need for touch and for sharing. The picnic scene like the hair-oiling scene make this sufficiently clear. Combing the hair of another, applying oil, massaging are all acts that fall within the orbit of filial relationships.[12] Massaging the feet of an elder is accepted. That Sita's doing so in the picnic scene is the act of a lover is not evident to the family, even as it is apparent to the audience. Any interpretative act depends on a number of factors, one of which happens to be the information one has. One may stretch the interpretative act to read these scenes as those of courtship. Chris Straayer has observed that in many ways, female bonding is "the antithesis of love at first sight, as it is built upon specific personal environment" (Straayer 350-351).

Fire is a film of contrasts and the meaning is produced through oppositions and variations on the same theme. *1947–Earth,* on the other hand, is a film of juxtapositions and parallels through which the political anxieties of two different classes are projected. Also it concentrates more on open spaces that allow interaction between different groups and genders. Open spaces contextualise the locale with its monuments and architecture and capture the past. It is a very Indian film in its showcasing of festivities, romance and songs. The kite-flying scene facilitates a romantic closeness while Pappoo's marriage scene is bereft of the upper class wedding celebrations that would cater to the non-cultural viewer. Instead it subverts it by showing the unequal marriage. In the first few minutes of the film there are four songs; there is also a love triangle. *Earth* is based on Bapsi Sidhwa's *Ice-Candy-Man* and is focussed on the evil, the unleashed beast, inside all of us that leads to mindless violence. Dil Nawaz the Ice-candy-man, is the dynamic character in the film. He takes on role-playing as an astrologer, dervish and so on. He is ready with a couplet on the drop of a hat and it is he, who when he faces the violence of the partition, discovers the animal within all of us. *Earth* is thus a film not only about politics and conflicts of religions but also about colonialism, violence and revenge – the total debasement of the human being.

Earth had its own share of controversy and came in for some very bad reviews – as a simplistic representation of partition, as a distortion of the reality and as a typical Bollywood movie. Deepa Mehta's professed aim, however, was to demonstrate the futility of violence and the multi-ethnic grouping was to show how good will and bonhomie are given the go-by.[13] It was the actuality of the event of partition that was the real strength of the movie, the re-living of this in celluloid was bound to affect her (and the Indian viewership) deeply. In terms of aesthetics, the film is an improvement on the novel which has a thin narrative and Lenny as the observer-narrator (in the novel) has far too mature responses. Lenny serves as a link between the two classes as she has free access to both and is gifted with a native curiosity, which allows her to slip under the table or be a voyeur without any compunction whatsoever – experiences that send her into adulthood sooner than desirable.

Earth has a clear-cut division into two halves – the first with its moments of sharing, mild flirtations, kite flying and community get-togethers with politics a growing concern, the second is unrelieved in its grimness, disruption, oppression, broken friendships and violent hatred. Hassan's concern for others – his Sikh friend, the bereaved Dil Nawaz, Shanta, the girl he loves – is pushed back by Dil Nawaz who destroys the two lovers. This rising crescendo is accompanied by intermittent noises in the background – Nehru's 'Tryst with destiny' speech, the beat of Shanta washing the clothes, the sounds of the riots and finally the blasts. These four stages also mark a stage by stage destruction of the abstract idea of trust and express a mixture of hope and anguish (Nehru's speech), rage at the helplessness in face of

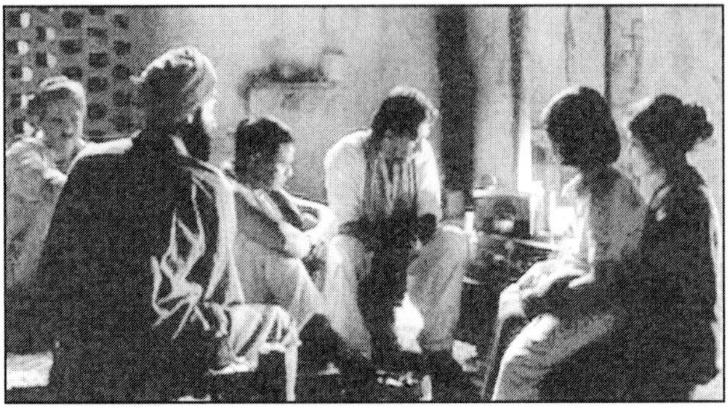

Tryst with destiny

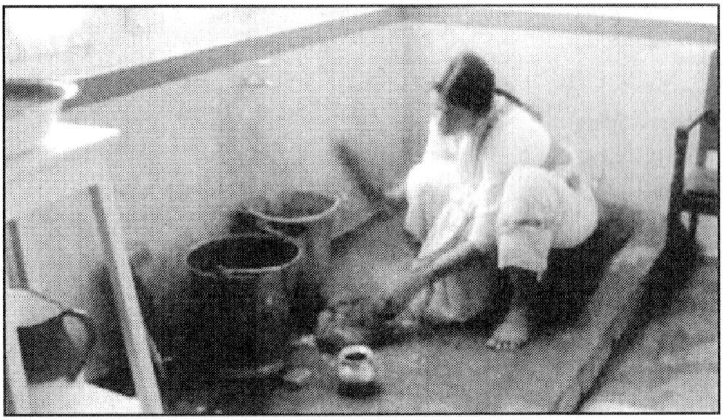

The rage within

the events (washing the clothes), and lawlessness and chaos (the arson and the blasts).

Enveloped in controversy, *Water,* the third film of the trilogy, is markedly different from the other two and is insulated against the outside world except for the four entry points – the entry of new widows, the homecoming of Narayan, the invisible control the rich have over the widows and the references to Gandhi where his hold over the Indian mind is commented upon. The widows' home has its own 'Madam', like that of a brothel and it also has its own share of jealousies, thefts and sycophancies. In fact women – all Brahmin widows – at different stages of their life are represented – beginning with Bua and ending with Chuyia to form this single-sex family. Right from the point of Chuyia's entry the two power-centres are clearly identifiable – the coarse, greedy and self-obsessed Madhumati and the quiet, reserved and self-contained Shakuntala. In contrast to the lazy self-indulgent habits of the older woman, Shakuntala never has an idle moment. She is always engaged in some activity or the other – grinding, stitching, reading and so on. The plot revolves around the power dynamics of these four characters: Madhumati, the power-wielder; Shakuntala – the protector; Kalyani – the exploited and Chuyia – the catalyst. In order to enter into this experience of deprivation, one has to begin with Chuyia through whose eyes, bewilderment, non-acceptance and emotional relationships one enters this world. Chuyia is impulsive, non-judgmental, unaware of the rules and spontaneous in her responses. She bites Madhumati, screams aloud, stomps her feet, chases the pup, gets out of the temple queue of the widows, buys the laddoo resisting her own temptations, and shares her food with the pup. She is not yet tamed or hardened and holds on to her trust in others. Love and hate have a strong meaning for her. When she wrings Mithu's neck, the hatred is directed towards his mistress, a hatred arising out of her love for Kalyani. In *Earth*, we have a similar scene with Lenny pulling apart a rag doll when she is disturbed by the violence around her. In both cases the violence moves in two direction – inwards as the emotions conflict and outward toward society, breaking the frame of representation, The

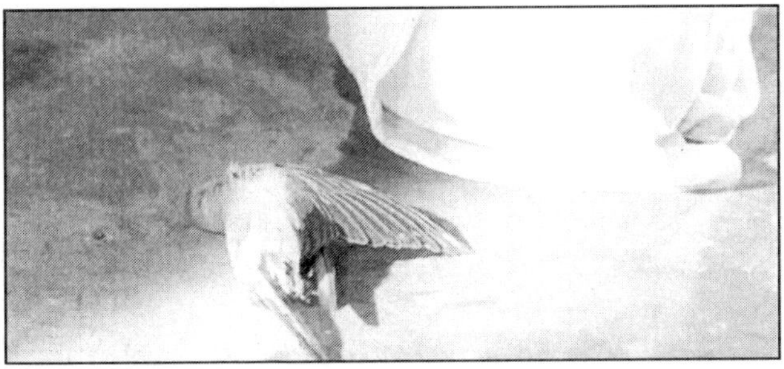

Trapped in helpless rage

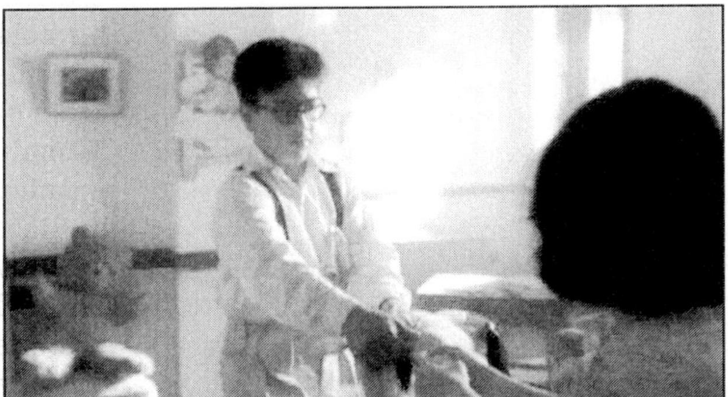

Violence replayed: Kids at work

symbolic actions stand out by itself. Aware of the fact that she cannot go home, Chuyia is still unable to acknowledge this fact in an open statement: the longing still pulls at her.

The god-figure of *Water* is Krishna (not Rama). Kalyani has a small nook devoted to him and he is their confidant. Chuyia is made to act the role of Krishna when she is decked up in all finery and colour (in contrast to her normal widow's wrap). As Krishna, the behavioural norms are relaxed. The grimness of the widows' home is relieved through such celebrations and through the emotional support they can garner for themselves. The friendship between Chuyia and Kalyani sustains them as they play together, talk about poetry or about Krishna or Narayan. In such scenes their emotional selves emerge. The rain-scene is symbolic of this relief and of the vitality of emotions and evokes the associations with 'saawan' in Indian culture and folk songs, where 'saawan' is associated with the arousal of sexual desire.

Water critiques Brahminical values but it also goes beyond this to bring in a host of other issues related to value-structures, colonial stupor and social change. Once again, as in *Earth*, the revenge motif is strong. Mithu's death is avenged through Chuyia's prostitution. Like Dil Nawaz a moment of trust is exchanged for betrayal. The film reflects on the potential for change – the priest by the riverside is not a stereotype. He becomes a channel for social change; Shakuntala, who has overlaid her mind with spiritual faith as means of restraint and numbing of desire allows her innate sympathies to yield to reason – as if she is just waiting for an external support; even Narayan's mother changes as she understands the enormity of the unjust system and Deepa Mehta herself has changed, but of that a little later. In all this Kalyani-Narayan romance acts only as a means of change. The interplay of will and choice is a constant undercurrent in the film – in significant as well as in ordinary things. *Water* has been criticised for its ending. My personal response, however, is different. Had Narayan asked for her – as Uma Parameswaran suggests – it would have been sentimental and vaguely hinted at Chuyia taking the place of Kalyani at a later date. A single man really had no business even to inquire about her. And later, caught between the teeming crowd, only a known face could have helped her. Chuyia is being handed over not to Narayan but is being placed in Gandhi's custody.

The simplicity of the surroundings and the mild, subdued tones, the minimal dialogue reflect the pervasive silence of the women's lives and the use of the music of the 30s, of the bhajans played on the gramophone, strike a nostalgic note for many an Indian viewer and offer a refreshing change. This use of music amounts to intertextuality, as does the use of Nehru's speech in *1947–Earth* and the *Ramayana* subtext in *Fire*. Songs from an earlier age or other films, bhajans (as in *Fire*), repetition of scenes or images from some earlier movie of the director, all are uses of intertextuality. Several aspects of these intertextual references will fail to come through to a non-cultural audience. I say this in substantiation of my point that the director's concern for a western viewership (if it is there), has not affected her concern for aesthetics and the trilogy, despite its artistic flaws, works in a continuity for Deepa Mehta.

The Filmmaker

The trilogy reflects on Deepa Mehta's relationship with India as she explores the socio-cultural problems, patriarchal institutions like marriage and family, religious interventions in politics, the politics of caste and gender, she also focuses on the human need for freedom and the development of an agency. Each of the three films questions the location of power – and concludes that power is shared and shareable. The opposition, at times, comes from this co-sharer located at the other end. The paralysed mother and her passive elder son share it in *Fire*; the British and the aggressive crowds do so in *1947–Earth* and the two women – Shakuntala and Madhumati – hold it from different ends in *Water* as do the enlightened priest and the orthodox Brahmins. Those, from amongst the powerless, who have

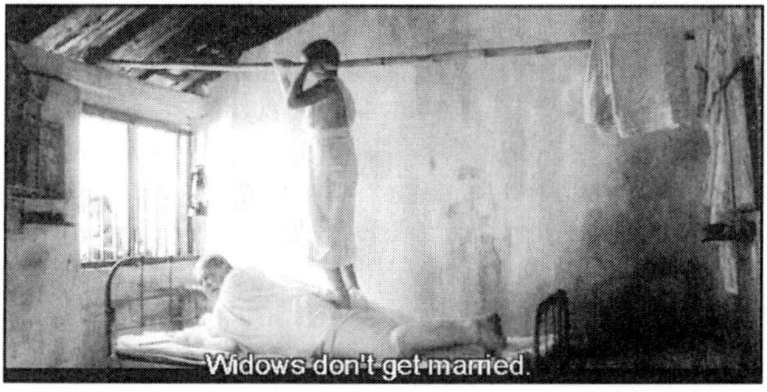

Reversal of control

acquired a share in power have done it through their own agency and in *Water* it is also through resistance. Not so in the other two films where sharers in power adhere to similar principles.

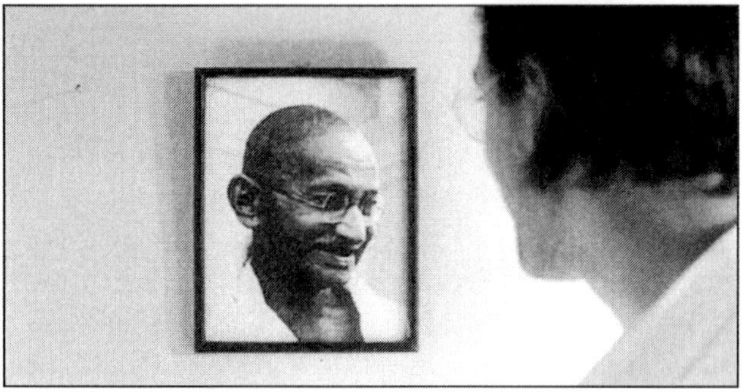

Winds of change

An additional continuity is established, in all the three films, through the Gandhian discourse. *Fire* mimics Gandhian celibacy and asceticism and his relationship to women as a test for his own strength, *1947–Earth* blames him for the division of the country but in *Water* he is seen as the messiah, the saviour who, like a fresh breath of air, can introduce change. There is a polyphony of voices about him. The eunuch and Madhumati repeatedly refer to him and blame him for attempting to do away with untouchability and social discrimination; Narayan's friend, in his affiliation to British culture, considers Gandhi to be of nuisance value; Narayan's mother reproaches him for trying to implement Gandhian ideas and Shakuntala believes him to be the saviour who can be trusted to look after Chuyia.[14]

This relationship with Gandhi also reflects an evolution of Deepa Mehta's relationship with India, Indian culture and Indian history. Significantly her other subtext, which finds a place in all three films is the contest between a humanistic discourse and violence. Radha's search for freedom, to find the sea beyond the land, to see without looking is constantly hedged in by control. She finds the courage to find her way only when a constructive relationship strengthens her. Hassan and Dil Niwaz represent opposite attitudes. Hassan says that "Jit is my brother" and offers even to convert and migrate in order to be accepted by Shanta. He resists violence and is always the peace maker. The most tragic event is perhaps not the ending but Hassan's murder when a co-religionist kills him. The total debasement of Dil Nawaz is completed later by another act of betrayal when he betrays the trust of a child as he inveigles himself into her confidence and is instrumental in the violence against Shanta. The futility of violence in terms of human loss is not merely in the death toll but the destruction of all finer emotions of life.

In *Water* the turning point comes when Shakuntala asks Chuyia 'How do I look?' and Chuyia tells her 'You are old'. If youth is over and life is passing you by, then perhaps it is time to act. Prior to this she applies turmeric on Chuyia's scalp, looks after her in other ways but after this she almost consciously shoulders the responsibility for her and Kalyani and demands the key in order to set Kalyani free. This concern for the human has been an important aspect of Gandhian thought who, despite his asceticism, looked upon the human being as a subject and not an object. The striving towards a higher self is a necessary step towards freedom.

The Diasporic Framing

Deepa Mehta has herself refuted the idea that her target audience is in the west. At a Press Conference on *Water* at the 2006 Taormina Film Festival she spoke to Philip Hoschka and made three points: she did not make her films for the west; the issues were more important to her, if the subject interested her, she went ahead without any fear of the taboos; and that her underlying subtext was a search for peace. Hassan in *Earth* was the 'peace' man as are Gandhi and Narayan in *Water*. She also made another statement that she divides her time almost equally between India and Canada thus placing herself in a sub-division of the diaspora that spends more time in India than a fleeting holiday.

In another interview, with Richard Phillips, she attacked western perceptions of India. The west chose to see India as (a) spiritual (b) poverty-stricken (c) or the country of Maharajas and palaces. Mehta observed, "India brings specifically fixed images in many western minds, and the minute you start de-exoticising that, you have to deal with Indians as real people, and there is a pressure not to do that."[15] A natural fallout of this is that real people grow, they evolve and traditions do not remain frozen. In one of her many interviews, she, with reference to *Water* explained the title as symbolic of a fluid tradition. Traditions "should never become rigid", lest they start to stink like stagnant water.[16]

The diaspora is, in no case, a homogeneous group and its emotional ties and relationship with the home culture will vary according to its attitudinal base, reason for emigration and the generation living abroad. A first generation adult migrant carries a cultural baggage and an emotional involvement that is difficult to neutralise or rationalise. Any attempt to introduce ethnic culture to the west can be viewed with suspicion – whether it is a translated text, cultural myth or a socio-political reality. It is difficult to determine as to the dividing line between genuine concern and showcasing in response to market strategy. And again all diasporic showcasing is not the same. In an earlier article I have appealed to the value of authenticity (as defined by Lionel Trilling).[17] I want to apply a similar test to Deepa Mehta through an examination of the 'endings' of these three films and the notion of 'guilt' as it is introduced and handled.

All the three films have mixed endings. None of them is free of a tragic association. The ending of *Fire* is not only an escape to freedom but the image that lingers is of Radha with her half-burnt clothes, anguished face and an overwhelming consciousness of failure and rejection, very much in need of succour. The loneliness, the rain, all add to the heaviness at the heart of this journey. Despite this it is a victory, one for which the price has been fully paid and is symbolic of a life after failure (and after patriarchy) – not a cause for celebration in itself but a better alternative to what they have experienced.

It is not Shanta's captive body being dragged out in *Earth* that is the ending. The image in itself is a powerful one of rapacious hunger and extreme helplessness and lingers in memory. But the real ending is Lenny's feeling of guilt. A guilt which is not only Lenny's but should be everyone's, including Dil Nawaz, the British, the political leaders and the frenzy-driven masses. The individual is superseded by a felt collectivity of guilt at a very human level which is passed on to the viewer.

Strangely enough this sense of guilt is absent in *Fire* and is underplayed in *Water*. The child Chuyia links her feeding Bua the laddoo and Bua's death but Shakuntala tells her not to worry about the consequences, Bua would have gone to heaven. The taboos are not worth worrying about. Guilt, however, is not felt by the real culprits. Narayan's father dismisses his act irresponsibly, justifying it on the basis of his brahminhood. Instead the guilt is passed on to Narayan who is – in his departure from home – trying to atone for his father's act. In *Water*, the sense of guilt descends on a collectivity and the atonement lies in social action. Shakuntala begins the process by rescuing Chuyia from the fate Madhumati has marked for her. The ending of *Water* is marked by a continuity – the moving train is destined to move towards a more hopeful future. Guilt thus shifts ground in all the three movies, as it shifts from familiar code-based issues to larger socio-political ones. It is this that transforms a 'mere' showcasing to an act of art with the purpose of making the audience uncomfortable, of puncturing a sense of complacency.

Sudesh Mishra has pointed to the persistent dilemma of locating or describing diasporic subjectivity and warns against a 'deterritorialisation' of identity (Sudesh Mishra 17-23). No easy division into 'them' and 'us' is possible. What saves the trilogy from a purely market showcasing is the anger and the love that work in unison with an artistic purpose. Moving from film to film, Mehta's relationship with herself has clearly evolved as it has with the culture of her origins.

Notes

1. Nargis Dutt was one of his critics. She made the comment that he was exporting poverty. Western critics like Bosley Crowther and Francois Truffaut were even more critical and saw no worth for Ray's films about peasants. The Ray trilogy came together between 1955-1959. For more details see en.wikipedia.org/wiki/satyajit_ray
2. *Salaam Bombay* (1988). Mira Nair was both the storywriter and the director of the film.
3. Also see two other essays by Uma Parameswaran "Disjunction of Sensibility: Deepa Mehta's film *Fire*" (1999) and "When Elements Travel: Deepa Mehta's Films and Diasporic Dilemmas" (2000). Both are including in *Writing the Diaspora: Essays on Culture and Identity* (Jaipur: Rawat Publications, 2007). In "Disjunction of Sensibility" Parameswaran targets the hybrid sensibility, criticises the naming of the two women as Radha and Sita and the sermonising iconoclastic references to Rama (269-270) and recommends adherence to simple rules of allusion. In the second essay she is critical of this straddling of two cultures (275).

4. Idries Shah writes about the Sufi way of life, "The Sufi learner is developing through his exercises a new way of seeing things. He is also acting, reacting, differently in a given situation than he otherwise would" (141). Sufism treats tradition as fluid and ritual as dispensable several of the bhakts of the bhakti movement had a similar philosophy. Uma Parameswaran in an Appendix to her essay "Disjunction of Sensibility" refers to C.M. Naim's observation that Hazrat Nizammudin's dargah is Mehta's natural choice because of Nizammudin Auliya's "homoerotic bond with the legendary poet Amir Khusro." Naim goes on to suggest that Mehta should have looked, for a model within the Hindu tradition.

5. Mehta, "Disjunction of Sensibility," 267-268.

6. See Lisa Cartwright, 129.

7. Sita's narcissistic preoccupation could be termed narcissistic scopophilia whereas Mundu's prying into their privacy in *Fire* and Lenny's into Shanta's room when Hassan sends Lenny home and enters Shanta's room, fall into the category of voyeuristic scopophilia and part of the 'looking' trope – the gaze being transferred to a character.

8. A film based on Rajinder Singh Bedi's novel of the same name translated into English by Khushwant Singh as *I Take This Woman*.

9. See Sudhir Kakar's comments on Swami Vivekananda in *The Inner World*, 162-165; "In Vivekananda's view, the development of the modern Indian identity had only one legitimate basis: the traditional Hindu world-image [.....] Vivekananda was passionately convinced that the regeneration of religious vitality required a massive effort in raising cultural consciousness so that the Hindu world-image could come to pervade every form of individual and social endeavour....". And later Kakar adds, "Again and again, as a grown man and a nationalist leader, Vivekananda comes to India's (and his own?) need for manliness..." (174). Vivekananda more than once asserted that it was a man-making religion, a self-assertive manhood that was required.

10. Kakar in *Intimate Relations* writes about Gandhi "the imperatives of desire straining against the higher purpose of unfettered service to community" (97) Kakar also observed that Gandhi's celibacy was the 'mainspring of his political activities. It is from this repudiation, the ashes of sexual desire, that the weapon of non-violence [...] was phoenix-like born" (96).

11. Ratna Kapur, 193-194.

12. We have an equally powerful scene of a woman combing another woman's hair in Kalpana Lajmi's *Rudaali*. The act indicates a caring relationship.

13. See "Interview with Richard Phillips (http://wsws.org.oarticles/1999/aug.1999/meh-106shtml) in which she pointed out that partition was a very uncomfortable subject for the British. Mehta described *Earth* as an anti-war film and went on to comment on her use of the group of intimate friends.
14. In Bapsi Sidhwa's fictional version, even Chuyia's mother wants to add Gandhi's portrait to her pantheon of gods (Sidhwa, *Water*: 11)
15. Interview with Richard Phillips; http://www.wsws.org/articles/1999/aug.1999/meh-106shtml.
16. See http://inhome.rediff.com/movies/2005/sep/23deepa.htm.
17. "The Poetics of the Diaspora: Authenticity and Aesthetics," unpublished keynote address delivered at a conference in Ludhiana, 22 March, 2007. Trilling in *Sincerity and Authenticity* (1972) distinguishes between the two terms of his title. Sincerity concerns the relationship with the moral being of the self but authenticity goes on to embrace a whole civilisational discourse.

References

Arora, Poonam. "The Production of Third World Subjects for First World Consumption: *Salaam Bombay* and *Parama*". *Multiple Voices in Feminist Film Criticism*. Eds. Diane Carson, Linda Dittmar, and Janice R. Welsch. Minneapolis: University of Minnesota Press, 1994.

Cartwright, Lisa, and Nina Fonoroff. "Narrative is *Narrative*: So What is New?" *Multiple Voices in Feminist Film Criticism*. Eds. Diane Carson, Linda Dittmar, and Janice R. Welsch. Minneapolis: University of Minnesota Press, 1994.

Fire, Dir. Deepa Mehta, Perf. Shabana Azmi, Kulbhushan Kharbanda, Nandita Das, Javed Jaffery. 1996

Gopinath, Gayatri. "Nostalgia, Desire, Diaspora: South Asian Sexualities in Motion", *Sociology of Diaspora*. Eds. Ajaya Kumar Sahoo and Brij Kumar. 2 Vols. Vol. 1 pp. 729-748. Jaipur: Rawat Publications, 2007.

Kakar, Sudhir. *Intimate Relations: Exploring Indian Sexuality* (1989). New Delhi: Penguin. 1990.

— *The Inner World* (1981). Delhi: OUP 1988.

Kapur, Ratna. "Too Hot to Handle: The Cultural Politics of *Fire*", *Translating Desire: The Politics of Gender and Cultural in India*. Ed. Brinda Bose. New Delhi: Katha, 2002.

Mehta, Deepa, Interview with Arthur J. Pais, Sept. 23, 2005 http://inhome.rediff.com/ movies/2005/sep/23deepa.htm.

— Interview with Richard Phillips http://www.wsws.org/articles/1999/ aug.1999/meh_106.shtml.

— Interview with Subhash K. Jha http://www.glamsham.com/movies/ interviews/deepa_mehta1.asp.

— Press Conference on *Water* at the 2006 Taormina Film Festival. http:// www.filmscouts.com/SCRIPTS/Interview of m/File=3120

Mishra, Sudesh. "Diaspora Criticism," *Introducing Criticism at the 21st Century*. Ed. Julian Wolfreys. Edinburgh: Edinburgh University Press, 2002.

1947–Earth, Dir. Deepa Mehta, Perf. Aamir Khan, Nandita Das, Rahul Khanna, Maia Sethna, Kitu Gidwani, Kulbhushan Kharbanda, Raghuvir Yadav (Based on Bapsi Sidhwa's novel *Ice-Candy-Man*) 1998.

Parameswaran, Uma. "Disjunction of Sensibility", *Writing the Diaspora: Essays on Culture and Identity*. Jaipur: Rawat Publications, 2006.

— "When Elements Travel: Deepa Mehta's Films and Diasporic Dilemmas", *Writing the Diaspora: Essays on Culture and Identity*. Jaipur: Rawat Publications, 2006.

Shah, Idries. *The Sufis*. New York: Anchor Books, A Division of Random House, (1964), 1971.

Sidhwa, Bapsi. *Ice-Candy-Man* (1988) New Delhi: Penguin, 1989.

Straayer, Chris. "Sexual Representation in Film and Video", *Multiple Voices in Feminist Film Criticism*. Eds. Diane Carson, Linda Dittmar, and Janice R. Welsch. Minneapolis: University of Minnesota Press, 1994.

Trilling, Lionel. *Sincerity and Authenticity*. Cambridge, Massachusetts: Harvard University Press, 1972.

Water, Dir. Deepa Mehta, Perf. Seema Biswas, Lisa Ray, John Abraham, Sarala, Manorama, Waheeda Rehman. 2006.

6

Women's Bodies, Women's Voices

Exploring Women's Sensuality in Deepa Mehta's Trilogy

Madhuri Chatterjee

Gender and sexuality are crucial constituents of the pleasure of cinema, even if evaluation and enjoyment may differ from person to person. Deepa Mehta explores the paradigm of female sexuality and its representations within the larger patriarchal superstructure. In the process, she brings to the fore the simmering Hindu right wing tensions about representations of female sexuality that were being covertly nursed through the last two decades in India. Post Foucault, we know that sexuality when represented or perhaps translated into culture is much more than a simple manifestation of a physical desire, it is politics.

Deepa Mehta's first film *Fire* (1996) makes an effort to depict the freedom and possibility in the articulation of female sexual need, which is often condemned. Also in the process, the film draws some distinction between natural lines of affiliation and sexual attachment. While the second film of the trilogy *1947–Earth* (1998) is against the background of Hindu-Muslim politics and insurgency where women's bodies were muffled and castigated, *Water* (2005) – the last film of the trilogy – construes the gendered subaltern resistance to both patriarchy and matriarchy and the director delicately draws the nexus of incongruity between perceptions of nationalism and female sexuality in the film. To subtly rephrase it in Jasodhara Bagchi's note "The Indian womanhood is [here] transfixed on an essentialist historical juncture to define Indianness" (102-103).

Cinema is definitely a mode of cultural production and therefore its understanding depends on the imperatives of genre, sexual economics and diversity. This feminine sensibility is enhanced by cinematic representations and narration, opening new semiotic plenitude. However the many ambiguities can be debated if the parameters are understood and acknowledged thus – "Femaleness is constructed and the terms of such construction need to be sought in the dominant modes of ideology (patriarchy, colonialism, capitalism). In this it is the investment of need and politics of control that representation both signifies and serves that is at stake" (Sundar Rajan 129).

Clearly all three Deepa Mehta´s India films are focused on these issues. In an interview she expresses her views, "*Fire* deals with politics of sexuality, *Earth* with politics of sectarian war and *Water* with the politics of religion" *(Hilary Magazine).* They are part of a process of globalisation and expose different narratives of female sexuality that strive to redefine identity through these differences. She explores the social acceptability/unacceptability of relatively new understanding of family, desire, sexuality and pleasure and the location of these (series) – in the changing notions of identity. There is also an examination of the social agencies that render women vulnerable to charges like (i) moral corruption (ii) weakening of/inimical to community connections and identity (iii) challenging masculine dominance(Gabriel 55). The narrative constitutes an interpretive commentary on culture, society and politics. Often the films play out in celluloid terms the tension between culture and sexuality.

Fire, a beautifully crafted sensual film, portrays an allegory where the country seems to be struggling between tradition and modernity and questions women's roles, It's the suppression of desire and the flame of sensuality that propels the story. The film begins against the background of Taj, where the newly married couple Sita (Nandita Das) and Jatin (Javed Jaffrey), try to understand each other. On returning home, Jatin leaves his wife and promptly joins his mistress. The young wife soon learns to bond with her sister-in-law, Radha (Shabana Azmi), who is also left to fend for herself while her husband's evenings are spent with the Swami who preaches abstinence and warns that desire is the root of all evil. Both the marriages are a farce.

"Sexuality" as pointed out by Kakar, is the creation of a two-person universe, where the affirmations of the female body and the recognition of her feminine soul take place simultaneously (Kakar144). What the society wants is juxtaposed with what an individual wants. The moral issue takes a hold over their lives and the individual's desires are pushed back and suppressed. Both the sisters-in-law observe a conventional behavioural code before their mother-in-law. Jatin is insensitive to Sita's desire for love or romantic ideas of a married relationship yet he tries to take Sita brutally to fulfil his duty to the family. For Sita this becomes a very trying experience, leaving her emotionally estranged from her husband.

The Sita-Radha relationship shatters the male constructed roles for women. The film, in its own way, questions the social norms which deny the individuality of women and discriminate against them on grounds of morality. Their resistance evolves in the form of female bonding. The emotional and psychological selves are discovered through the physical.

Deepa Mehta's film explores the socialisation process and questions subordination or compliance to the norms defined by patriarchy. The women are placed centrestage. Apart from the condition of victimhood and rebelliousness, the films also focus on transgressive behaviour, which violates the norms of traditional morality and constitutes a deviation from the socially approved moral norms of sexual relationships. In *Fire,* Radha and Sita trespass into zones not acknowledged as legitimate, and define a new relationship through individual questionings and go on to deconstruct the patriarchal situation.

Touch is important to the women, as their repressed desire pushes them to explore and discover the sense of their body seriously. Ironically, the men abstain from this touch especially where their wives are concerned. The gesture of oiling someone else's hair or massaging the elder sister-in-law's feet become intimate sexual acts in the process. In one climatic scene Radha's clothes catch fire and she is enveloped in flames while her husband Ashok leaves the home with his mother in his arms. The act becomes a kind of *agnipariksha* (trial by fire) for her. She finds her way to Hazrat Nizamuddin's shrine where Sita awaits her. The narrative moves away from constricting frameworks to render the acquisition of agency possible for both Sita and Radha. As Jasbir Jain puts it "an act of transgression breaks the control of others over the body and compels society to reformulate its boundaries in whatever limited measures" (136). Radha and Sita transgress the male discourse which entraps them. They do not sweep aside the existing order, rather they assert their own discourse on the masculine one, by breaking it up, subverting it and in a sense, re-writing it. The film is open-ended – there is no finality of closure but a remarkable journey into the feminine psyche and space. It presents no resolution but definitely interrogates human relationships.

1947–Earth is based on Bapsi Sidhwa's novel *Cracking India (Ice-Candy-Man)* and presents a neutral and objective account of the traumatic event of the partition through the eyes of Lenny, the child protagonist and narrator of the story. In problematising gender and religion, the theme becomes a significant testament of a gynocentric view of reality in which feminine psyche and experiences are presented with unique freshness. The gynocentric perspective determines the narrative strategy and affirms the fact that women's voices and issues are central to every society because they define all human relationships and social constructs. The body also becomes an integral part of it, for as Susan Bordo has observed. "The body is not only a text of culture. It is.... a practical, direct locus of social control; it is a metaphor of culture" (13). Showalter expands it: "A theory of culture incorporates ideas about women's body, language and psyche but interprets them in relation to the social contexts in which they occur. The ways in which women conceptualise their bodies and their sexual and reproductive functions are intricately linked to their cultural environment. The female psyche can be studied as the product of construction of cultural forces" (16). In a visual medium, it is not only important how women look at their bodies but how men look at them, how they dress and behave, the manner in which they are used by the director, by the narrative and by the women themselves. Sexuality or the violation of it through seduction or rape, its procreativity or barrenness, its location within space all acquire meaning which can either reinforce conventional perspective or produce a counter discourse.

The central consciousness or the narrative eye is Lenny (Maia Sethna) a young lame Parsi girl. Lenny's lameness does not becomes a source of self-pity or a constrictive force on her psyche. She remains assertive and holds her own when it comes to the crunch. And who is the formative influence on Lenny? Her ayah Shanta (played by Nandita Das), a flame of sensuousness and female vitality around whom the male lovers constantly hover. She acts like the queen bee who controls the actions and emotions of her male admirers: the cook, the house gardener, the butcher, the compactly muscled masseur and the Ice-candy-man. The ayah's constituted role as a spectacle, as the subject of the look, is evident in the way her body is arranged with respect to the camera, the movement of the body and how the gaze is selectively invited to parts of body considered sexual. Her costumes/blouses are also dazzling and multi coloured. Ironically the woman needs to be careful how she dresses, behaves, generates life and in short what she does with her body.

The first half of the film revolves around the interplay between these characters – Lenny, Shanta, Hassan (played by Rahul Khanna) and Dil Nawaz (Aamir Khan). Shanta takes Lenny around whenever she goes and this is how she knows and makes friends with Dil Nawaz and Hassan, who are both in love with Shanta and though she flirts with both, she loves Hassan which leads to their downfall. The partition disturbs their group but the measure of ayah's power is seen when she objects to the political discussion among her multi-religious admirers, as she fears discord. The Ice-candy-man defers to her wish and says "It is just a discussion among friends, such talk helps clear the air but for your sake, we won't bring it up again" (157).

The massacre sets into motions events that turn Lenny's world upside down. The once charming Ice-candy-man turns into a near madman, with vengeance and murder on his mind. The Muslim masseur, the only voice of reason amongst ayah's admirers, implores the group to "stand by each other". Lenny's family is spared the slaughter because of the neutral stand of the Paris.. But when the Muslim mob arrives at their gate, they want all the Hindu servants including the ayah. The destruction of innocence by desire and greed wearing the garb of religion and nationalism becomes the price of this sectarian war. Diasporic writing often recalls a moment of trauma in the homeland what Derrida referred to as an "impossible mourning" and what Juliet Mitchell clarifies creates a breach that even if the incident is expected, the experience cannot be foretold.... In trauma we are untimely ripped" (Mitchell 121) The characters also start dealing with their personal demons. Eventually some die, some convert, some live and some come through unharmed but not unscathed.

The directorial gaze even while framing the female body for exhibition and erotic impact can code it differently. Particularly when there is an act of transgression. It raises questions related to self, being and personhood. She becomes the 'other.' Also the women in matters of articulation, reproduction and management or even something as fundamental as the control of one's own body, are seriously, fundamentally and much too often deliberately disadvantaged – sometimes to the extent that it is longer remains merely a hegemony – masculine or otherwise but is a blatant intimidation, repression and subjugation (Mulvey 837). In *1947–Earth*, the female voice is heard and yet retained substantially within a narrative controlled by masculine and patriarchally sanctioned desire, whether individual or collective. The film raises questions regarding the boundaries imposed on the female body, which acquire significance in the larger social discourse. There is a strong sense of territory in *1947–Earth,* The ayah holds her own ground in the beginning but she is later wrenched away from it. The film closes in on the image of invasion and of occupied territory. Shanta is tossed between two faiths, two identities and two places/spheres, a symbol of dispossession and displacement.

Water is set in 1938. Following the Hindu tradition, after the husband's death, the widows are forced into an ashram where they do penance for their sins. The film is seen through the eyes of Chuyia (Sarala) an eight-year-old girl who is woken by her father's words: "Do you remember getting married?" "No" she sleepily replies. "Your husband died. You're widow now", "For how long?" She asks. Bereaved of a relationship she is not old enough to value she is placed in a widow's house, where her head is shaved and she is forced into a life of deprivation and control.

The action mainly takes place in the ashram where Chuyia is deposited to spend the rest of life in renunciation. There are fourteen women who live in the small, dilapidated two-storey house built around a central courtyard. The ashram is financed through prostitution and charity, Madhumati (Manorama), is the virtual commander of this home, maintaining a contact with the outside world through the pimp Gulabi (Raghuvir Yadav), an eunuch who keeps Madhumati supplied with Ganja and gossip. Gulabi helps Madhumati to prostitute Kalyani (Lisa Ray) – the second youngest of the widows – by taking her across the river waters to the customers. She is valued for her beauty and is the only widow whose hair is not shorn. She is further segregated within this segregated space, living and eating above the main quarters. Kalyani is the lotus flower living in dirty water, a metaphor offered in the film. The ashram provides no "ashraya" for anyone and the water (Holy Ganges) and ashram are all tainted with impurities "we have a collective amnesia about our own problem. *Water* is about three women trying to break that cycle and trying to find dignity and trying to get rid of the yoke of oppression, and if it inspires people to do something in their own culture, that's what's important" (Mehta to CBC). Deepa Mehta's film dwells on the rituals that the inmates of the ashram have to perform, in the name of tradition and how the punishment of excommunication is forced on women – even a girl child like Chuyia – for no fault of theirs. It is a self-effacing regime of fasting, purification and denial of bodily desires additionally loaded with the stigma of being inauspicious. *Water* explores gender in the context of issues like widowhood and prostitution.

The socio-moral code of religion excludes women not only from power structures and social constructs but also from her own body, the idea of a self and her sexuality. Once again it is the female body which is deprived and constrained. The concept of purity critiqued in *Water* imposes a lot of control over desires and senses, and imposes a social control through forms of behaviour and relationships. Kalyani's body however is not marginalised through deprivation but centralised through prostitution. Amidst the adversities of their approved lives, the film also focuses on the individuality of the characters and is a critique of the silencing of women's voices, a denial (their bodies) and thwarting of their desires. Shakuntala (Seema Biswas) is the most enigmatic widow. She is good looking, and a sharp, dark person. When she exudes anger, even Madhumati leaves her alone. Disturbed by what she around here she seeks counsel of Sadananda (Kulbhushan Kharbanda) a gentle-looking priest in his late forties or early fifties who recites scriptures. He gives her the necessary intellectual input to separate true faith from the hypocrisy and superstition that makes the life of the widows' a misery. In the climatic scene, it is again her effort that saves Chuyia's life as she carries her to the train in which Narayan is travelling. In the first part of the film, the focus is on Sarala, in the second part on Ray, and in the third on Biswas. The socio-political elements are gradually woven in without destroying the intimacy of the space. Explaining this social segregation of the widows, Narayan says "one less mouth to feed, four less saris, and a free corner in the house, disguised as religion it is about money." Chuyia believes that her stay is a temporary one and her mother will take her away and she repeatedly asks. "when will we go home?" At a later point she acknowledge the fact that this will not happen but she is unable to gave up all hope.

Once again, it is through Chuyia as an agent, that Kalyani meets Narayan (John Abraham), a Gandhian, who attracted by her, is bold enough to defy tradition and offer marriage to Kalyani. Thrilled at the prospect of a feast, the child lets out the secret to Madhumati, which creates all the chaos, who then menacingly enters Kalyani's room, throws her to the floor, shears her long black hair, and locks her up until she "comes to her senses." The act of shaving Kalyani's hair brutally is shown in a string of close ups and conveys the loss of her youth and beauty, emphasising the act as one of blatant violation of her body. When Shakuntala, over the protests of other widows, unlocks the door to Kalyani's room, her quiet act of rebellion leaves everyone speechless.

A liberated Kalyani walks out of the house but to no avail. Once again she is ferried across the water, (water which is supposed to wash away all sins) but the portico of Narayan's house, leads to her to her tragic end. Finally Kalyani drowns herself. *Water* clearly exploits the symbols: hair (beauty and individuality), water (in its destructive and life enhancing aspect), colour (white) (unfulfillment), and windows/door – open, they signify the hopeful self, closed they symbolise the trapped, tormented self.

Water balances hope with despair. Shakuntala's dominant nurturing instincts come alive and she finds the strength to question the traditions that govern the lives of the widows. Shakuntala concentrates in her character what the feminist feel is very important for a woman to realise her individuality – the feeling of self-worth. Also one way to transcend the body, to learn to treat it as a medium and not a "self" is to bring it under the control of will and women in raising their voices are compelled to question all social constructs – be they religious, political or romantic. To realise the self, the nature of desire needs to be questioned As opposed to Kalyani who is a figure of victimisation, Shakuntala is a figure of resistance and resilience.

Deepa Mehta creates new narratives of being and becoming, of renewing and reclaiming. The body operates as a metaphor on many levels – as the site/object of violence, as both participant in and victim of resistance, as a figure of sexual politics, as an icon of nation/culture. Each cluster stands for one major thread of the narrative. It is the women in the films, who provide insights and nuances of the atrocities of culture/history/society, whether perpetrated by figures or events The female body is seen to have a history which is related to its embodiment in different social contexts – marriage, procreation, barrenness, desire, bonding in *Fire*, transgression and violence in *1947–Earth,* and widowhood and victimisation in *Water*. The women's bodies and voices offer multiple representations of the turmoil that marks our reality.

References

Arabi, Peegah. Interview, *Hilary Magazine,* Saturday, June 2, 2007.

Bagchi, Jasodhara. " Introduction" *Indian Women: Myth and Reality*. Ed. J. Bagchi, Hyderabad: Sangam Books, 1995.

Bordo, Susan R. "The Body the Reproduction of Feminity: A Feminist Appropriation of Foucault" *Gender/Body/Knowledge: Feminist Reconstruction of Being and Knowing*. Eds. Alison M. Jaggar and Susan R. Bordo. New Brunswick: Rutgers University Press, 1989.

Fire. Dir. Deepa Mehta, Prod. David Hamilton. Perf. Shabana Azmi, Nandita Das, Kulbhushan Kharbanda, Javed Jaffrey, 1996.

Gabriel, Karen. "Designing Desire: Gender in Mainstream Bombay Cinema," *Translating Desire*. Ed. Brinda Bose. New Delhi: Katha, 2002.

Jain, Jasbir. "Body as Text: Women Transgressors and Hindi Cinema," *Films and Feminism*. Eds. Jasbir Jain and Sudha Rai. Jaipur: Rawat Publications, 2002.

Kakar, Sudhir. *Intimate Relations: Exploring Indian Sexuality*, New Delhi: Penguin, 1989.

Mehta, Deepa, Interview to Diane Kristine, CBC, November 9, 2005 [Broadcast]

Mitchell, Juliet. "Trauma, Recognition, and the Place of Language", *Diacritics*, 28.4.1998

Mulvey, Laura. "Visual Pleasure and Narrative of Cinema," *Film Theory and Criticism*. Eds. Leo Braudy and Marshall Cohen, New York: Oxford University Press, 1999.

1947–Earth. Dir. Deepa Mehta, Prod. David Hamilton, Perf. Aamir Khan, Nandita Das, Rahul Khanna, 1998.

Showalter, Elaine. "Feminist Criticism in the Wilderness", *Writing and Sexual Difference*. Ed. Elizabeth Abel, Sussex: The Harvester Press, 1982.

Sidhwa, Bapsi. *Ice-Candy-Man*. New Delhi: Penguin,1989.

Sunder Rajan, Rajeshwari. *Real and Imagined Women: Gender, Culture and Post Colonialism*. London, New York: Routledge, 1993.

Water. Dir. Deepa Mehta, Prod. David Hamilton, Perf. Lisa Ray, John Abraham, Sarala, Seema Biswas, 2005.

7

Marginalised by Domesticity

The (Un) Desirable Women of Deepa Mehta's Trilogy – *Fire, Earth* and *Water*

Simran Chadha

> Her head was shaved, she was dressed in a white sari, her bangles were broken and the red dot (pottu) on her forehead was removed. Since then the only place she has gone to is the temple. She has not been allowed to attend any weddings, even those that took place in her own house. When asked who prevented her from attending weddings, she laughed and said: "Of course the people and the shastras."
>
> Martha Alter Chen, *Perpetual Mourning*[1]

It may be politic to begin this essay with the polemics of the Indian Right wing regarding women, not only because of the deep dialogic relationship they enjoy with Deepa Mehta's films but because ascetic widowhood remains one of the defining realities of Indian womanhood, both rural and urban. With an eye towards ferreting an ancient Hindu past, the Hindu Right actively labours to fashion an essential Hindu wife as it does the essential Hindu nation – both, according to the pressing needs of its chauvinistic agenda. One witnessed however an unprecedented spurt in the public visibility of the female members of the Sangh and its Samiti's, especially in the violence that followed the Ramjanambhoomi issue. In signposting this shifty ideological stance manifest by the Right in recent times, Tanika Sarkar sees this as the tacit nexus that the Right establishes between women, domesticity and the Hindu nation.[2] While conceding that this new "communalised female subjecthood" certainly unsettled notions of "female victimhood" vis-à-vis "male inflicted violence", Sarkar astutely avers that the Right found itself on shaky ground and women, it was decided, in their own interest, were best "housebound", notwithstanding the "public potential" they had displayed. The Sangh and its Samiti's reined in their women, save of course for a few of its prominent female politicians.

While representations of the Indian woman as subaltern have fired the western imagination since time immemorial or more specifically since the colonial conquest, a new category, that of the Good Indian woman often works to nuance the ill-balanced equation even further. In this, the liberal sprinkling of Indian exotica is coupled with the spiritual strength or *Shakti* – the feminine Hindu principle– as exemplified for instance by the devoted Hindu wife played by the actress Tabu in Mira Nair's *Namesake*. Such representations are what the Right deems worthy of emulation, exemplifying as they do the very teachings of its ideological honcho, M.S Golwalker. This gender hierarchy postulated by Golwalker finds unquestioned and widespread acceptance not only because of its tonal similarity with the *Manusmriti* but also because he insists that it is a truth as natural as the *vatavaran* itself, hence objective and altruistic. The Hindu woman as homemaker must abide by the *Pativratadharma*, a word that resonates with male control of female sexuality. The auspiciousness granted to her by her marital status is deified further through sartorial accessories, such as the *sindhoor*, red bangles, *mangalsutr* and also certain equally elaborate rituals and mythological legends.[3] With heterosexual domesticity tacitly institutionalised as the defining paradigm, the question of choice for women, if at all, looms large? What are the consequences of choosing otherwise and how does the social mechanism work to maintain its status quo? It is with these questions that I approach Mehta's woman-centred trilogy – *Fire, Earth* and *Water*. As a diasporic filmmaker straddling both Bollywood and western traditions of filmmaking, to what extend does Mehta (as the Right insists) raid her third-world 'homeland' for images of the exotic, the spiritual and the subaltern. Images that have found a virulent presence in representations of the space mapped by the colonisers onto the land they named India. Moreover, with the raging debate on Sati touted since the imperial times and continuing to the more recent controversy over the Sati of Roop Kanwar, why does Mehta choose instead to focus on the practice of ascetic widowhood[4]? In raking up a longstanding debate along with issues of child-marriage and widow-remarriage, (in her other two films, *Fire* and *Earth* as well), does the filmmaker trilogy stand the litmus test of female empowerment? As these are the questions I purport to answer during the course of my paper it appears apt to quoting Mehta on her espousal of feminist politics: "I think it's slightly naïve of me to think that films make a difference. But what it can do is to start a dialogue and provoke discussion."[5]

Beginning our discussion with the trope of the auspicious Hindu wife implies taking into account her societal counterpart – the inauspicious and ill-omened Hindu widow. An equally elaborate behavioural and dress code conditions this aspect of womanhood. The control unleashed by the Manichean aesthetics of widow/wife serves to secure not only the worship of the male husband (with rituals such as *Karva Chauth*), but also facilitates the internalisation of a gender hierarchy in the guise of tradition and scriptural truth. The image of the widow as Mehta uses it explains rather limpidly her feminist politics. Firstly, the representation is almost bereft of the romanticism that dodges other popular Bollywood representations of Hindu widows.[6] Moreover, the time frame she chooses for her film is the clime of the Gandhian era – 1938, a time when the modern Indian nation was being imagined into being. The strident nature of the mass freedom movement, the radicalism regarding untouchables and the form of self-critical *swaraj* leavened by Mahatma Gandhi implied a new power-bloc and therefore new forms of knowledge. Mehta relates this determining moment of the past to a contemporary present where despite multiple changes of power the practice of ascetic widowhood continues to flourish. Deploying to advantage, the plastic art of cinema, Mehta establishes the dialogue that time-present shares with time past. The final shot with which the film closes, is that of the widow Shakuntala (played by Seema Biswas) who after having cognised the ambivalence inherent in scriptural (as in literary) writing and interpretation, breaks the limitations of a deep rooted indoctrination and conveys to safety the child widow Chuyia (played by Maia Sethna). In this defining shot, charged with the euphoria of the Gandhian moment, Shakuntala, her back to the audience, throws a backward, over the shoulder, slow and accusing glance at her audience. Cinematically, this draws the audience into the narrative and in doing so breaks the spell or what Coleridge has referred to as that "willing suspension of disbelief", so essential to for the art of representation. Drawing the audience so unabashedly into the narrative structure, serves only one purpose, that of linking the fictive with the empirical or real. Pregnant with meaning, the sequence does signal new beginnings – for Chuyia the child widow, for Shakuntala the now emancipated middle-aged widow, but it leaves wide open for a contemporary audience, the space for questioning and possibly change.

Looking at the recent past of the modern nation or the how the onset of modernity meant to cleanse India of its evil and superstitious past, Mehta shows change cannot be wrought with half hearted, sidelong glances at the woman's question. In advocating re-marriage for child-widows, the politics of the Mahatma at best insisted on austerity for older widows, strengthening though obliquely the practices of ascetic widowhood. Maybe, it is true that history paints the past in larger than life colours.

Along with the Hindu nationalism, the dictates of Brahminical liberal humanism kept intact the symbolism associated with the figure of the widow. Showing how the concept of widowhood is integral to all of society and not as alienated an institution as it appears to be, Martha Alter Chen, in her illuminating study on Hindu widows shows how in being projected through the "institutions of marriage, kinship and caste...the social institutions that regulate the lives of widows also regulate the lives of women" in general.[7] The laws that govern widowhood extend through the social body of laws governing Hindu society and have therefore a very direct impact on the lives of real women, who are conditioned from childhood to fear widowhood and avoid it through piety and devotion.

In being the sacred cow, the widow is conspicuous as the "abject" defining by her shadowy visibility the very idea of domesticity and gender hierarchy. To exemplify my contention, I use Julia Kristeva's concept of the "abject", as posited in *The Powers of Horror*. Explained as the reaction evoked by sewerage, an open wound or even the skin that forms over milk, the abject is literally revulsion. Ironically the symbolic order must have an abject if it needs to define the meaning of desire, from which springs its own self-definition. The object of abjection, as opposed to the object of desire must be expunged from the societal order for it refers to the threatened breakdown in meaning caused by the loss of the distinction between subject and object or between self and other. Using Kristeva's example for such a reaction is the corpse, serving to remind us, rather traumatically of our own materiality. The abject in being "radically excluded" must need be situated at a place outside the symbolic order for in disturbing "identity, system, order" it sets the defining boundaries for the same.[8] Quoting Kristeva: "The corpse, seen without God and outside of science, is the utmost of abjection. It is death infecting life"(Kristeva, *Powers*: 4).

Complicating the issue, the widow as Mehta portrays her, although expunged is nonetheless the very object of desire, and desire as Kristeva deems is very much a part of the symbolic order of things. Mehta's construction thus amplifies meaning beyond the monolithic of western thought. The widow in this context is associated with both – fear and what Kristeva in a different context has referred to as *jouissance*. [9]

With the constructed sanctity of the domestic space held in balance by the polluted widow, the obvious question is why are association of the in/auspicious, tied so firmly to women and the destinies they bring with them to the domestic hearth and whose interests does this serve? The two figures marginalised by domesticity, yet ruling the realms of imagination are the courtesan and the widow.[10] Unlike the courtesan, however, the widow is unfortunately not relegated to archival speculation though the debates regarding Hindu widowhood predate the colonial.[11] In drawing a cartography of desire around the widow means locating the anomie as the very displaced centre around which society organises itself and herein lies the critical insight that Mehta brings to a long-standing debate.[12] Desire, as Mehta texts enunciate, is palpable in the very act of being jettisoned into realms of abjection. The contention of this essay is to show that the witch-hunt for widows and its age-old discourse renders obscure and even blankets the cartels of male desire.

Not entirely on a tangential note, Ashis Nandy draws attention to the efflorescence gained by the "epidemic" of Sati during the late eighteenth and early nineteenth centuries.[13] This as Nandy states was mainly due to the "British colonial intrusion into Indian society", that too despite the legislations passed by the British government banning, in various forms, the practice of women burning themselves on the funeral pyres of their husbands.[14] Yet, as records testify, Sati continued to be revered, vacillating between a "primitive Malthusian means of population control in famine ridden Bengal", to the vouch-safing of societal respectability for the families stigmatised with westernisation:

> in families seduced away from the path of traditional virtue by the new colonial culture, Sati became a means for securing social status and renown for virtue. We have already noted that the rite enjoyed some popularity among the upwardly mobile sections of Bengali society and they found Sati a new means of sanskritization. Important parts of urban Bengal accepted this new means as legitimate: even when the family of the suicide was prosecuted there was no loss of caste, infamy or disgrace; the family in fact gained in social stature and were 'backed with applause and honor'.

Unlike Nandy's "rage against all women" or Chen's kinship patterns, Mehta traces the gnarled roots of misogyny desire and knowledge that claims the sanctity of the *smritis* (the shastras, Vedas and the Puranic stories). While Mehta flirts dangerously with the issue in her earlier two movies, it is with *Water* that the fat is in the proverbial fire. With *Fire*, Deepa explores rebellious vistas of desire, as they exist between women; relationships, as Tanika Sarkar notes, a homophobic Right refuses to even as much as acknowledge. Interviewing a *pracharika*, Asha Sharma, about the controversy regarding *Fire*, Tanika quotes:

> Asha Sharma expressed her revulsion against what she called 'interrelationships among women' – she could not make herself say the word lesbianism. She was emphatic that such '*vrikriti*' – a product of western culture – should be banned, as well as its sympathetic portrayal.

Fire exposes humdrum domesticity as hampering, not only for women but men as well, as for the pornography-inflicted husband in the movie, who does not want to join the family business, as he does not want to marry Sita (Nandita Das) or his Chinese girl friend, for that matter. But women, it is clear, cannot skirt such dangerous liaisons; their aspirations must centre on domesticity. In the absence of male company, the text posits the spouting lesbianism between the sister-in-laws, played by Nandita Das and Shabana Azmi, onto modes of loneliness, neglect, joint family patterns and the restrictions of the domestic space. Disappointingly, *Fire* relegates to the closet what obviously is a homosexual epistemology. In blaming love and desire between women, onto errant husbands neglectful of their wives, Mehta moves from the flagrant espousal of radicalism to both, benching a Right wing politics (though this was completely missed by the Right in its violent destruction of the cinema houses that dared a screening) as well as encoding a taut critique of domesticity.

Illustrating Mehta's critique is the figure of the widowed Mataji. Her limited authority, such as it is, is represented in the incessant ringing of the bell. She is paralysed and prefers to watch Hindu serials on the television such as the *Ramayana*. Yet she is 'forced' into a 'spectatorship' of 'indecency', by Sita's cross-dressing and by Mundu (the servant) playing porno films on the TV in her room. She does not want be a spectator in either of these deviant modes of being. In some ways, therefore, she fits the classic model of desexualised Hindu widowhood. Yet the model is complicated by her obvious symbolic and moral (rather than any real) authority in the film. Biji is thus the silenced voice of desexualised womanhood in a film, which is very much about sexual choices.

With *Earth*, Mehta moves to examine the ravages of colonisation in a society by now as much hide-bound into patterns of gender oppression as of caste hierarchies. Tracing the covetous fault lines of the symbolic order through the figure of the Ice-candy-man (played by Aamir Khan) who rebuffed in his desiring for the ayah betrays her Hindu identity to the Muslim mob. The final frame of the film, (unlike the novel), shows the ayah carried out by the men of the rioting community, as one would a lifeless body, feet first. While using as an impetus Bapsi Sidhwa's narrative of the *Ice-Candy-Man*, Mehta's portraiture differs in two significant aspects. Firstly, dispensing with the Bapsi's figure of Lenny as the child narrator and relegating her to a near mute spectator, the cinematic narrative employs not one but two points of view – that of the Ice-candy-man as also of Lenny's voluptuous ayah (Nandita Das). In focusing on the ayah's coquetry with the male coterie of admirers constantly buzzing around her, Mehta's final word lies not only with the ayah's sense of shame, concomitant upon her betrayal by those whom she thought were her friends. Rather, in exhuming the desire of the male *friends* of the ayah, Mehta points to acts of communal violence as not entirely vacant of desire but encompasses acts of extreme separatism, which the Partition of India certainly was.

However, it was with the final and last film of the trilogy *Water* that Mehta touches the raw nerves of a patriarchal society. With the figure of the widow evoking strong emotive responses – pity, awe and horror, models in literature as well as film abound. The arrival of the Christian missionaries and subsequently the reformist social movements, such as the Arya Samaj saw a virulent championing of the cause of the child bride and widow. A fecundity of literature on the topic surfaced during this period. With the missionary agenda the nation was viewed as being as badly in need of help as its women and rescuing the women therefore became synonymous to rescuing an entire nation of its obscurantism. Moreover this literature helped shore up the superiority of the white races, mainly because the writers, male, elite reformers, themselves were inculcated in the Arnoldian system of education adopted for the colony for the Macaulay government.[15] Influenced thus and in prescribing a liberal education for women, in terms of home-science, the Arya Samajists, for instance, only served to validate existing divisions of gender and domestic labour. Ashis Nandy's "colonial intrusion into Hindu society", as mentioned earlier in the essay, implies this very damning exposure to a Victorian education and ideas of feminism. A century later Golwalkar pitting of a feminised domestic sphere against individual feminine choices inadvertently voices a colonised mindset. However, it must be stated that the open legislative debate around widowhood and child-marriage in colonial India, forced into the open issues of conjugality, rendering transparent the very process of law making, even if by the white masters. This was a step towards provided woman with the space for self-determination, which as

Chen avers, gave them choices apart from the decrees of community, family or kin.[16]

The deification of Victorian norms of home, hearth and woman worked to demarcate the space of the normal.[17] In an Indian context, this stitched firmly in place the symbolic associates of Hindu widowhood. Looking at why the Hindu widow evokes such strong emotions, Chen states: "the answer lies in her symbolic power as the ultimate expression of the condition of Indian women and the Hindu social order".

From our discussion it follows that Mehta's use of a child widow as protagonist is more than a positing of innocence verses ingenuity, for it is not the latest arrival into the ashram, Chuyia, but Kalyani (played by Lisa Ray) herself who has been a child-bride and widow. Chuyia questions the system; she wants to know why there are no male widowers and why only women are subjected to this regime. Her naivety results not from the innocence attributed to the child in Victorian literature but more to the lack of a rigorous tutoring into the gender norms demanded by society. On the contrary, Shakuntala unquestioned acceptance of the *shastras*, points to a deep-rooted indoctrination that makes her passively obey and endure suffering.[18] It is Chuyia's questions and near prostitution that goads Shakuntala to breaks the stereotype of the ideal upper caste Hindu woman/widow.

Like the sati, ascetic widowhood is also symbolic of continued devotion to the dead husband's memory, and therefore a continuing symbol of martyrdom. The locale for the film is, as we have noted, an ashram populated by widows who perform the motions of life according to the dictates of a code that decrees the accumulation of *sat* (truth), the lack of which in the first place has been the cause of the loss of the husband figure. *Sat,* can be garnered only through the curtailment of worldly/bodily desires, such as those for dress, ornaments and rich food. Tonsuring, practically speaking would be a matter of exercising husbandry and hygiene. In individuating her characters, however, Mehta's focus is not on the institution per se but the empirical reality of the women identified as widows. As characters, moreover, she does not reduce her personae to archetypal carriers for her views but shows their desires as human beings in their own right. In the ashram, Kalyani, sullen and rebellious is perhaps the only one with the luscious locks but without really desiring them. While Chuyia desires the lost freedom of her childhood, as also the love and protection of her mother, for another elderly widow desire rests in the imagination of the sweetmeats she has been forced to forfeit since the death of her husband – rich food seen as a spur to lust and best avoided. Shakuntala, the educated widow having internalised *dharma*, desires to follow the path of asceticism, the Mahatma desires to teach selfhood to a slavish nation, and Narayan the male protagonist, dreams of a society shorn of hypocrisy.

The opening sequence foregrounds the gerontian desire for a youthful female body. Chuyia's marriage to a dying, old man is an attempt to resuscitate him and provide economic remuneration for Chuyia's family. It is for the satiation of similar such bodily desires that the ashram retains its economic viability, thus providing the inmates, execrated by laws of domesticity, the space to live out their shadowy existence. The irony however is that the identity scripted for the desirable Kalyani, by the pundits and their henchmen (the eunuch and the widow Madhumati (played by Manorama) serves but to encase another. The enactment of performative bodily desire, in the palace constructed by the *zamindars*, across the river, on the body of the widow Kalyani, explains this. It is significant that the class Mehta chooses to focus on is that of the brown sahibs of Macaulay's famous Minute.

Kalyani's awareness of her desire for Narayan has been interpreted, as an opportunist's need to cross into the realm of respectability, the frustrated disappointment of which prompts her suicide and the utter erasure of subjecthood and therefore all desire. The death of Kalyani, has also been read as a refusal by the author to face the volatile issue of widow/prostitute remarriage. So, the question, once again is whether Mehta, true to her Bollywood leanings, compromises on her critical insight with a "happy ending"? The argument appears flawed in the first instance because unlike mainstream, commercial ventures Mehta's film has limited box office appeal. It aligns itself more with the western category of art-house cinema.[19]

Kalyani as portrayed by the auteur, is outside of normative societal norms. Resenting her exploitation she however is unable to view it as such having been inculcated like the other inmates into denial and self-effacement to the point of non-being. She is the psychologically brutalised subaltern and in enacting her death, she refuses any further exploitation. Kalyani chooses to die and paradoxically the action staged as an extreme form of resistance is metamorphosed into a voicing of the hitherto silent and non-existent self.[20]

Moving back, the reasons prompting the violence perpetuated by the Hindu Right, seeking to ban the film appear evident. Subsequently, the movie was shot in Sri Lanka; the ban in India being lifted only after the Cannes nomination for the Best Foreign Film category. However, as a Canadian entry, *Water* is relegated to a diasporic register, a category that brings us full circle to the trope we began this discussion with.

Posing a very serious challenge to the religious establishment and her country's way of life, it does not appear that the filmmaker's sole purpose was to render exotic her native culture or package it for consumption for a white, western audience or even give them yet another crude narratives about backwardness. As she says: "I seriously wanted to break stereotypes of India, the 'exotic' India of the Raj and the princes and the mysticism. Exotic India doesn't really exist"[21]. Iconoclastic in her social defiance Mehta, rather than perpetuating, implodes images of the "Incredible India" touted by the official board of Indian tourism. Fencing similar accusations, for his book *Red Earth and Pouring Rain*, the writer Vikram Chandra defended the writer's right to choose the tropes s/he deems fit. Critiquing the 'God of Authenticity', Chandra says "the writer cannot abandon his heritage, both old and acquired, just because someone somewhere is going to find it exotic."[22]

Notes

1. Martha Alter Chen, *Perpetual Mourning: Widowhood in Rural India* (New York: Oxford University Press), 2000. p 115.
2. Tanika Sarkar. "The Gender Predicament of the Hindu Right", *The Concerned Indian's Guide to Communalism*, Ed. K.N. Panikar (New Delhi: Penguin India), 1999.
3. Popular mythological legends attribute special spiritual powers to married women. The legendary Savitri, for instance won back her

husband Satyavan from the lord of death Yama while Sita's chastity enabled her to endure the test by fire.

4. This refers to the sati of the eighteen-year widow, Roop Kanwar, during the early nineties, in the village of Deorala in Rajasthan. This was followed by heated parliamentary and academic debates and street activism both for and against the burning of widows.
5. Interview with Deepa Mehta by Richard Phillips. wsws.org/articles/1999/aug1999/meh-a06.shtml, August 6, 1999.
6. The Bollywood commercial aesthetic tends to romanticise Hindu widowhood. In *Mangal Pandey* the British army officer dramatically rescues the sati while in *Prem Rog* the Indian hero performs the rescuing, and in *Banaras* renders almost desirable the state of ascetic widowhood. For citations for the individual movies please look at the reference section.
7. For further details, see Martha Alter Chen's Introduction to *Perpetual Mourning*.
8. Julia Kristeva's theory of the realm of the semiotic as prior to the symbolic stems in opposition to the formulation of women as the 'lack' by Jacques Lacan. For Lacan the order of society is the 'Law of the Father', which he refers to as the symbolic order denoted by the power of the phallus. The 'abject' in this sense, not only defines but also challenges the symbolic order of the father.
9. The French word *jouissance*, as used by Kristeva implies a free play or an unlimited plurality or meaning leading eventually to the breakdown of the structured meaning of the symbolic order.
10. The term courtesan has an entirely different epistemology from the term prostitute, which gained currency only after 1857. Courtesans of fame such as Begum Samru or Umrao Jaan were not only skilled in the per formative arts but repositories of culture as well.
11. Prior to the imperial debates, the Tantric sects of Hindu thought clearly prohibit sati and strongly stress gender equality.
12. The point bears lucid illustration through the movie *Mandi* directed by Shyam Benegal. Owing to the hue and cry raised by the respectable people regarding the *kotha*, it is unceremoniously thrown out of the city but the narrative illustrates how the city moves and organises itself around this expunged space. This, in effect, becomes the displaced centre which truly speaking is not the city at all.
13. Ashis Nandy, *Sati: A Nineteenth-Century Tale of Women, Violence and Protest* in *Bonfire of Creeds*, (Delhi: Oxford University Press), 1999. The economic motives that Nandy emphasises for nineteenth century Bengal

appear paramount in the case of the Roop Kanwar Sati as well as the entire village of Deorala, Rajasthan, which stood to benefit from the act.

14. In 1812 the British government issued their first sati circular, making a distinction between legal and illegal sati. In 1817, the second circular challenged the religious sanction and in December 1829, the British passed the sati regulation act.
15. The Charter Act of 1835 and the establishment of Fort William College by Lord Macaulay followed by the famous *Minute on Indian Education* were the first steps towards the establishment of an Anglicist system of education. For the debate between the Orientalists and Anglicists, regarding the mode of education to be implemented in the colony, see Gauri Vishvanathan's *Masks of Conquest*. See also Terry Eagleton's *Introduction to Literary Theory*, explicating motives for the introduction of English Literature in the colony even before it was introduced in England, as part of the curriculum.
16. Feminists have decried legislative moves, insisting that they lead to little or no change in the day-to-day living conditions of women.
17. The prevalence of gender hierarchies and the demarcation of public and private space as masculine and feminine is evident not only in the wellknown poems of Lord Alfred Tennyson or Coventry Patmore's anthology *Angel in the House*, but appears in nursery rhymes as well. For instance, a popular Victorian rhyme goes: "Peter Peter, Pumpkin eater, had a wife and couldn't keep her. So he put her in a pumpkin shell and there he kept her very well.
18. Shakuntala as also millions of women before her, finds spiritual solace by aligning herself with the stories of legendary Aryan women who have suffered and endured tribulation on account of upholding the dharma. Refer to note 3.
19. While in New Delhi, India, *Water* was screened in the smaller of the PVR cinema halls usually reserved for movies with limited appeal. The same was the case in Sydney, Australia, where the movie was screened in suburban cinema hall with seating capacities of barely a hundred. The audience – besides stragglers or expatriate Indians nostalgic for home (vociferously denouncing such depictions of "home") – were mostly white students or teachers of South Asian culture. The viewing, for them, was more of an act of documenting/denouncing evidence.
20. Another film that deploys resistance in a similar manner is *Khamoosh Pani* directed by Sabiha Sumer. The film is a strong protest against religious fundamentalism; state authoritarianism and the choices women have in such circumstances. For citations, please see the references section.

21. From the Deepa Mehta's website. http://www/english.emory.edu/Bahri/Mehta.html.

22. This citation is from Ira Raja's review of Anita Rau Badami's *Can you hear the nighbird call? Book Review,* Vol.XXXI, Number 6, June 2007, p 30.

References

Banaras. Dir. Pankuj Parashar. Perf. Urmila Matondkar, Ashmit Patel, Dimple Kapadia, Raj Babbar, Naseeruddin Shah. Setu Creations, 2006.

Chen, Martha Alter. *Perpetual Mourning: Widowhood in Rural India*. New York: Oxford University Press, 2000.

Eagleton, Terry. *Literary Theory: an Introduction*. London: Blackwell, 1983.

Earth. Dir. Deepa Mehta. Perf. Maia Sethna, Nandita Das, Amir Khan, Kulbhushan Kharbanda, Kitu Gidwani, Rahul Khanna, Navtej Johar. Cracking the Earth Films Inc., 1998.

Fire. Dir. Deepa Mehta. Perf. Nandita Das, Javed Jaffrey, Shabana Azmi, Kulbhushan Kharbanda. Kaleidoscope Entertainment Pvt Ltd, 1996.

Kristeva, Julia. *Powers of Horror: An Essay on Abjection*. Trans. Leon S. Roudiez. New York: Columbia UP, 1982.

Khamosh Pani. Dir. Sabiha Sumar. Cast. Kiron Kher, Aamir Ali Malik, Arsad Mahmud, Salman Shahid, Shilpa Shukla, Sarfaraz Ansari, Vidhi Films, 2003.

Lacan, Jacques. *Ecrits: A Selection*. Trans. Alan Sheridan. London: Tavistock Publication, 1977.

Mangal Pandey. Dir. Ketan Mehta. Perf. Aamir Khan, Rani Mukerji, Toby Stephens, Amisha Patel. Kaleidoscope Entertainment, 2005.

Mandi. Dir. Shyam Benegal. Perf. Shabana Azmi, Smita Patil, Naseerudin Shah, Amrish Puri, Kulbhushan Kharbanda, Saeed Jaffrey. Blaze Films, 1983.

Namesake. Dir. Mira Nair. Perf. Irfan Khan, Kal Penn, Tabu. Fox Searchlight Pictures, 2007.

Nandy, Ashis. "Sati: A Nineteenth-Century Tale of Women, Violence and Protest", *Bonfire of Creeds: The Essential Ashis Nandy*. Delhi: Oxford University Press, 2004.

Prem Rog. Dir. Raj Kapoor. Perf. Shammi Kapoor, Padmini Kolhapure, Rishi Kapoor. R.K. Films, 1982.

Raja, Ira. *Can you hear the Nightbird call*? Anita Rau Badami. *Book Review* Vol.XXXI, Number 6, June 2007.

Sarkar, Tanika. "The Gender Predicament of the Hindu Right", *The Concerned Indian's Guide to Communalism* Ed. K.N. Panikar. New Delhi: Penguin India, 1999.

Tennyson, Alfred. *The Works of Alfred Tennyson.* London: Wordsworth Editions Ltd, 1994.

Viswanathan, Gauri. *Masks of Conquest: Literary Study and British Rule in India.* New York, Columbia University Press, 1989.

Water. Dir. Deepa Mehta. Perf. Manorama, Seema Biswas, Lisa Ray, John Abraham, Waheeda Rehman. Deepa Mehta Films 2005.

8

Gendered Subject(s) in Deepa Mehta's *Fire* and *Water*

Jayita Sengupta

In an interview with Richard Phillips, Deepa Mehta comments on her films on India: "*Fire* was about the politics of sexuality, I guess. *Earth* is about the politics of nationalism and *Water* about the politics of religion."[1] Despite such specifications, which Mehta makes, it maybe pointed out that these three films do have a common bind i.e. religion. While *Fire* and *Water* interrogate the bases of Hindu patriarchy, *Earth,* an adaptation of the novel, *Cracking India* by Bapsi Sidhwa, is about India's Partition on religious lines in 1947. Interestingly, all three titles which act as cultural signifiers have religious significations. No Hindu ritual would be complete without *yajna*, holy water and clay. Moreover fire, water and earth are the elemental things in nature, indispensable for human survival. Hence as cultural signifiers, the films are rooted in India and yet in the suggestiveness of their titles, they transgress the borders of the particular to attain universal significance.

Explaining the nature of her films, the filmmaker mentions how she has been influenced by her reading of Luis Buñuel's autobiography: *My Last Sigh,* where Buñuel talks about the importance of characters being rooted to a place acquiring universal significance because human emotions are universal.[2] To add to Buñuel's observation, the characters in the three films are not merely rooted to a place, but they are rooted in a particular tradition, culture and time. While *Earth* is about 1947, *Water* is about the condition of widows and the Indian society in 1930s, *Fire* is rooted in a postindependence middle class urban household in Delhi. All three films, chiefly, *Fire* and *Water,* in their criticism of Hindu patriarchy have raised eyebrows and embroiled Mehta in nasty controversies in India. Possibly, *Earth* is the least controversial of these three films being an adaptation and focusing on the politics of the Partition. But the ideas of the other two films are Mehta's own and are rather subversive in content and form.

The Indian reception of these two films has been that of vociferous resistance from the Hindu fundamentalists and political parties. In case of *Water*, resistance was most acute as sets were burnt, there were mass protests from Hindu fundamentalist organisations and in sum, rampant exhibitionism of cultural fascism indicating the general mentality of the people, fifty years and more after independence. Had it not been for a few intellectuals like Amartya Sen, Pandit Ravi Shankar (musician), Mahasweta Devi (writer and social activist) and a few other intellectuals who pressed their concern for the freedom of social criticism in art, *Water* would have probably remained an unscreened dream for Deepa Mehta. Mehta recalls the wave of criticism in case of *Fire* and observes how the very same political parties which had organised riots in Bombay and Delhi in 1998 had attempted to stop the shooting of *Water* in 2000. However such a political attitude is not uncommon in India. Many other filmmakers like Mani Ratnam, Shekhar Kapoor and Mira Nair have also had their share of nerve-racking experiences when their films, namely *Bombay, Bandit Queen* and *Kama Sutra: A Tale of Love* were released. The political agitators had argued that Mehta was trying to "sell" a degenerate picture of India to the West. Satyajit Ray too had had to face similar such criticism when his first film *Pather Panchali* was released. It was said then that Ray was trying to "sell"

India's poverty to the West. Notwithstanding the biased opinions of such critics and political activists, the films mentioned above have made some mark on Indian and global viewers and demand serious critical appreciation.

Though Deepa Mehta's 'India films' do foreground "women" or women's marginalisation to a large extent, she does not exclude the idea of the gendered phenomenon in Indian patriarchy which includes both the sexes. As the filmmaker points out: "Every society or traditional value, whether in the East or the West, has an incredible impact on human behaviour. So everybody ... the women, the men—confront these problems."[3] So ideas of nationalism, sexual politics and religion entwine to project the complex web of Indian society in the wake of independence and in the postindependence era. Both 'Fire' and 'Water' as religious significations in Hindu patriarchy suggest Purity. 'Fire' further has other derivative meanings, such as those of consummation, rage, passion and acts as an important device of subversion. The idea of the divine fire is common to all religions and the divinity works through human passions. 'Water' too, apart from the suggestiveness of purity, signifies sorrow, passage of time and has other implications. Mehta does not use these significations with any fixed ideas; rather the images coalesce with the context of the films and offer diverse significations. As Joy Gould Boyum states, "image and word, both 'mean', both involve perception and cognition, and both also involve what has been recently come to be known as 'decoding'". She adds: "Images in film, then, require for their decoding a certain awareness of pictorial conventions."[4] Mehta's films often use cultural signifiers as pictorial conventions for effecting the process of decoding or understanding the underlying message.

The Images of Repression and Subversion in *Fire*

The recurring motif of the dream: Fire opens with a dream, – a psycho-somatic pictorial convention, which is somewhat like an epigraph to the film as a text. It projects young Radha with her parents in a mustard field, listening to a folktale from her mother. Sharing food and feeding are acts of nurturance, which is indicated by Radha's mother's gesture in the family picnic. She nurtures Radha not only by feeding her but by attempting to offer her some pearls of wisdom through the folklore. The cosiness of the scene with the teasing nostalgic musical strains chiefly the flute in the backdrop keeps recurring as a motif in Radha's consciousness till she finds solace in her companionship with Sita. The film opens with the mustard flowers blowing in the breeze in daylight and closes with young Radha standing alone in the mustard field, brooding, till a smile lights up her face and she has found a positive answer to her mother's question. The daylight in the opening scene is replaced with a stark horizon, subtly indicating the challenge that lies ahead of Radha and Sita. The entire film is encapsulated within this framework of the folktale, following Radha's understanding of her subjectivity which impels her towards her choice of freedom. A dream, as Renee C. Hoogland analyses in agreement with Laplanche and Pontalis's hypothesis on Freud, forms a " 'heterogeneous nucleus', within a psychical reality, a resistant element, alone truly real, consisting of 'unconscious wishes' reduced to their most fundamental and truest shape .... This scheme thus leaves us with three different realities: a material, a psychological and a phantasmatic one. It is the latter which plays a critical role in the genesis of sexuality."[5] The structure of the film invokes the subjectivity of pain as a dynamic and not a passive condition, where the subjects in pain – namely, Radha and Sita, work their way out of their material, psychological and sexual repression.

The folklore about the people high up in the mountains desiring to see the sea and the aged village woman's words of wisdom, "You can see, without looking" keeps haunting Radha's consciousness. Her mother's fond question: "Radha, can you see it?" is a riddle which her mind grapples with in her semiotic consciousness. Radha is haunted by this childhood memory which returns to her in her dreams asking its meaning to be unravelled. The folklore acts as a primary fantasy which she internalises and which lies stored in her unconscious memory ready to be invoked in the process of her finding her subjectivity. As her name signifies, Radha's mind is in search of real love or passion or the life-giving force which is found wanting in her relationship with her husband. Just because she couldn't be a mother, her life only demands servitude from her. She has to work tirelessly for the hotel run by the family and cater to her husband's requirements whenever he would want her. The recurring motif in her dream or the return of the repressed desire in her subconscious mind, projects her dissatisfaction which does not find any place in her symbolic existence as the dutiful wife and *bahu* of the house.

The Motif of the Historical Romance

The newly-wed Sita too does not find her lover or husband in Jatin, who had already committed himself to a Chinese girl but who refused to marry him. He has tied the knot with Sita to appease his elder brother. Historical places of romance on their honeymoon visit to Agra fail to move Jatin emotionally. While Sita spontaneously responds to the romantic tale of the Taj Mahal, Jatin is irritated and detached. Moreover, there is a subtlety at work here which Deepa Mehta very artfully presents through the motif of the Taj Mahal. The historical monument tells the tale of romance that gets a name after the beloved's departure from this world. The Taj Mahal echoes ironically an elegiac note; it does not signify a thriving, blossoming romance, which a newly-wed couple is expected to enjoy on their honeymoon. In Indian culture, it remains a man's privilege to give love a name or to shun it in domestic cloisters. Women's passion and emotion do not require any signature, and moreover the politics of Shahjahan, in building such a monument for his departed Mumtaz, was not so much to immortalise her love, but himself as a lover. It was more of an act of self-projection than an act of nostalgia. The ironic twist to the tale of romance by the tourist guide about Shahjahan's cruelty associated with his immortal love and the architect's revenge form a comment on exploitation and self-centredness. The motif thus acts as a sort of premonition at the beginning of the film that the marriage possibly will not work. Sita's pertinent question: "Don't you like me?" to her husband is ironical. Love which is expected to blossom straightaway in an arranged marriage is interrogated here.

As the film unfolds, it becomes clear that Jatin's role as a husband to Sita is only functional limited to the consensual sexual act as a part of the marriage ritual. There is no tenderness, no affection associated with the act; only a routine practice. His relationship with Sita as one of "duty" is ironically contrasted with his relationship with Julie as that of "pleasure". However it would be wrong to judge Jatin too harshly for he is trapped in a compulsive marriage like many other Indian males, who do not want to break away from the joint family system. Jatin might grumble about the joint income etc., yet he lacks the courage to lead his own life in his way. He would rather suffer double standards and distinguish between pleasure and procreation as he is unable to derive the same from one woman. Julie exercises the right to reject Jatin as her husband and yet accept him as her lover. The Chinese label allows Julie the freedom to lead her own life which Jatin cannot. Julie taking the lead role in making choices for Jatin and herself ironically reverses the role of a woman in Indian society, where women in general have little say in such matters in most cases even today. She plays the masculine role even though she may signify the feminine pleasure principle to Jatin. Jatin is feminised by Julie and his elder brother as he has to cave in to their decisions. His lack of tenderness and demonstrative callousness through the sexual act towards his wife reveals his semiotic rage against patriarchal repression.

Cultural Signifiers

Irony and replication act as chief devices of subversion in this film. The dream scene which becomes a personal myth sets the tone of dissatisfied desire. The suggestiveness of Radha's mother's words to her, to consult one's own mind, offers a clue to a solution from the impasse in which characters find themselves. The next few scenes revealing the incompatibility of the newly-wedded Jatin and Sita and then the painful realities of Radha and Ashok's marriage explain the chasm between desire and reality or the divide between desire and the 'object of desire'. For Ashok, desire is closely bound up with procreation or else desire is 'evil'. Jatin however, revels in sensuality with Julie and can demarcate his roles. Ashok chooses strict adherence to religion and Guru-worship to find space for his pent up emotions and passions. One embraces celibacy, the other, a mistress. In sum, both Jatin and Ashok neglect their wives or fail to reciprocate their emotions and passions. Possibly, their crudeness or insensitivity springs from the kind of parvenu upbringing they have had in a typically middle class business family in Delhi thriving on a family-run hotel and a video library. The role of Biji in the house as a matriarch symbolises the impasse in which all the characters find themselves. Biji's 'expressive dumbness' – her frowns, her frustrations, her unwillingness to be fed by Mundu – demonstrate her importance and her power over the others in the household. She is the mute matriarch who sees and understands everything and holds on to the traditional codes steadfastly. Her sense of indignation and impotent rage against Mundu and her disgust at Radha, at the close of the film, signify the potency of the mute traditionalism, which has had Indian men and women in its sway, from the days of Manu. Biji's dumbness, her paralysis and yet her indignation, her control over the family, beautifully signify the baggage of traditional codes which the Indian patriarchy continues to drag on even in the twentieth and the twenty-first century.

The compulsive celebration of *Karva Chauth* to honour the husbands is another detail which Mehta includes in the film to critique traditionalism which always dishonours and subjugates the female. Jatin's reaction to the ritual shows some rationality, as he has no regard for such useless customs. Ashok, true to his 'religious' temperament, cherishes it as a necessary ritual and Biji stubbornly asserts her desire for strict adherence to the codes of the ritual. Submissive Radha gives in to the codes without a query, while Sita questions it and openly expresses her discomfiture. Ironically *Karva Chauth* does not unite the husbands with their wives; they are left alone as Ashok visits his Guru and Jatin his girlfriend. The ritual practised by Radha and Sita at Biji's insistence helps them get close and discover a new meaning in their relationship which later blossoms as a lesbian relationship.

Mundu, the servant, who represents the lower rung of the North Indian society, consciously honours the *Karva Chauth* ritual and libidinously wishes to play the role of the King who could choose between Radha the queen and Sita the "dasi". In his libidinal imagination he subverts Ashok as the holy man who introduces the *Karva Chauth* ritual, and puts Jatin in his shoes as the servant fanning the king. As Freud does not draw a clear line between conscious modes of fantasy and unconscious desire, but insists on the strong affinities between the two, Mundu's reverie can be regarded as paradigmatic of the phantasmatic process constituting a privileged moment where crude psychic materials are transferred from one system to the other.[6] The distinguishing factor between primary fantasy which Radha experiences and secondary fantasy which Mundu hallucinates, is that in the latter, the subject's position is clear and unvariable. Primary fantasy in contrast is characterised by the absence of subjectivisation, where the consciousness hovers on the "thetic".[7] Mundu's conscious subversive imagination however encourages him to gyrate before Biji in total dismissal of her presence, while watching a porno film. Even when he is caught red-handed by Radha, he can only retort with a threat of exposing her secret to the family. Further, he explains his outrageous conduct to Jatin by saying that Jatin is his 'role model'. Mundu's arrogance and subversive strategies to work his way out of his repression and find place in the household, despite his status as a servant, is further implicated by the songs which he quips from time to time suggestively such as "Bol Radha Bol" when Radha is around in the kitchen.

Mehta consciously chooses to name the two wives, Radha and Sita with their mythological connotations of illicit love and 'satidom'. She just interchanges the roles played by the two mythological women, for it is not Radha but Sita who has to suffer the test of her chastity. Mehta uses the parody of Sita's *agnipariksha* to interrogate the desirability of such traditional beliefs and codes. Loyalty towards husband becomes meaningful in a reciprocal conjugal relationship. Yet when a wife is publicly humiliated on grounds of impurity and the king accedes to the public demand for the test by fire of her chastity, the relationship suffers a jolt. The *Ramayana* is thoughtlessly swallowed by the middle class tradition-bound patriarchal system. Ashok, watches the Ram Lila performance which is almost a parody of the epic-story because of the improvisations and cross-gendering of the performers. To gather more self conviction in his mission to abstain from desire and attain nirvana he attempts to discipline his flames of passion and undertakes regular "tests" by asking his wife to sleep with him. Wife or *sahadharmini* as the *scriptures* say is an accomplice to her husband's dharma. So Ashok expects Radha to share his ideas and practise the same along with him.

Sita's trial by fire runs through the film as a recurring motif to interrogate the very bases of the codes and beliefs which repress and subjugate the Indian woman. When Mundu tries to avoid being caught by Sita in one of his moments of "recreation", he changes the porno video to the *agnipariksha* scene from *Ramayana* as if to alert Sita about her chastity. Again towards the close of the film, when Radha has the altercation with Ashok and clearly states her feelings and her deprivation, her sari accidentally catches fire in the stove lit for the morning tea. Ashok in his hurt pride does nothing to help her and sadistically watches her trapped in her sari caught in flames. To Radha's horror he abandons her to her fate and selfishly removes Biji from the bed downstairs to a place of safety. Here, one is undoubtedly reminded of Sita's trial by fire. The filmmaker imparts a new meaning to the myth through the film's subversive ending. Radha stands the test of love for the self and for her meaningful relationship with Sita. She emerges victorious in her trial with the self and can escape the flames of desire which would have burnt her out, to seek refuge in an emotionally compatible relationship.

Scenes from the *Ramayana*, which are a favourite with any cul-de-sac household, occur as a repetitive pattern in the film, to indicate how the cultural codes have had an impact on the "deep structures" of their mind. When Radha catches Mundu misbehaving before Biji, and he is strongly reprimanded by Ashok and taken to the Guru, he remains indignant. But a scene from the *Ramayana*, where Ram wrongly accuses Lakshman of secretly desiring Sita, moves Mundu to feel remorse and beg forgiveness from Ashok. It is his libidinal desire for Radha which actually makes him guilty and not really his act of masturbation before Biji. It is the repression of this desire for Radha which leads him to replace it with other diversions from porno video films. His indignant and bold retort to Radha that he has no recreation and has to work day in and day out is an honest acknowledgement of his repression. Mundu in this respect is a fine example of Judith Butler and Singer's observation on Foucault's thesis on power and sexual discourse: "We take pleasure in reproducing ourselves as sexual subjects, and in sustaining the demand for the production of the sexual discourse. As a consequence of its alliance with and construction of the sexual as that which must be represented and repeated, modern power works primarily through an apparatus of incitement rather than through the threat of repression."[8]

Butler's observation is true in Sita's case as well. Sita's changing into jeans and dancing to herself with the rhythm of the 'Indipop' on television, when she comes to the house the first day after her marriage, reflects her drive to outwit the traditional codes followed by the others in the family. Later in the film, once she and Radha have found new meaning in their relationship, she tempts Radha into a ball dance with her, where they assume lover-like roles. Sita impersonates a male, clad in trousers and with a stylish cap on her crown; Radha acts as the feminine principle. In a way Sita is quite at par with Jatin, as he too has little respect for the customs and codes followed in the house. Yet the couple never actually get acquainted with one another. Jatin underestimates Sita and thinks that a child is what she needs to occupy her. He makes it clear that he cannot love her as he loves Julie. It does not cross his mind that she may not want his love after all. It is only when Sita calls him "a pompous fool" and slaps him on his face, he is taken aback. Her arrogance rather than her submissiveness kindles his desire and he responds to his feelings at that moment by kissing her violently and by pinching her face hard. His act of sexual violence here matches with his desire to establish his hierarchical power over her as her husband. Ashok too is filled with desire and shame when he watches the lesbian couple from the chink in the bedroom door. He is even willing to forgive Radha for her "crime", should Radha fall at his feet and beg his forgiveness. Radha's arrogance and her choice make him violent and he responds to her abrogative attitude by first calling her a "whore" and then by kissing her forcefully. Not getting the desired response he could only accuse her by saying that she is not acting as a wife should and leaves her to her fate when the end of her sari catches fire from the stove. His non-action at that critical juncture or his acute callousness renders him inhuman. Ashok's sexual violence to overpower her and gratify his hurt male ego reveals his sense of shock at being decentralised in the patriarchal order of things. The myth of Sita's trial by fire is so internalised in him that he sadistically cherishes Radha's death by the accident and refuses to act. As Linda Singer and Judith Butler point out: "To the extent that women's desires are addressed to other women, men are displaced from their position of centrality, and heterosexist hegemony, and all that follows from it, is subjected to challenge, critiques, and ultimately denial."[9] Precisely, that is the *effect* of *Fire* on the general Indian society which could not accept the abrogative stance of the film on emphasising the need for "flexibility and diversity of power deployments with respect to constructing sexuality as a site for intervention into the lives of bodies and populations."[10] The 'lesbian-bodied subject' in the film represents the subversive force which has the power to destabilise the dominant cultural realities and upset the power/gender relations. Yet, lesbianism, projected here as the radical relationship between the two daughters-in-law in the same household does not stem from the biological factor, rather, from cultural repression. Radha and Sita's relationship is a realisation of the unity of 'sex, gender and desire'.[11] It is idyllic, as Radha's consciousness grasps the image of love which her mother had wished her to see in her symbiotic and semiotic relationship with her daughter. Sita's affection, her concern nurtures her desire to be "whole" again and recognise and construct her subjectivity as a woman and a human being. The film in its intensive exploration of gendered sexuality and cultural production agrees with Freud's insight that sexual desire is not an innate or biological phenomenon; it is a gradually evolving, interactive, psychosomatic process.[12]

Words, Sounds and Images of Repression and Subversion in *Water*

If *Fire* is a film on gendered sexuality, *Water* is one on repression of women, and the gratification of male desire. This film interrogates the male privilege in Hindu patriarchy, which is both marked and exercised as cultural representations which are so designed to accommodate and normalise masculine preferences and patterns of gratification. The widows' house in Varanasi replicates the order of things in the male patriarchal system, where the widows despite their subversive urges, abide and control their gratification of sensuous as well as sensual pleasures. Prostitution is a necessary evil which they yield to, for survival. Love or gratification of female desire finds no space and is strictly forbidden. The film intends to lay bare the social hypocrisies at work from Manu's days to the present. The relevance of *Water* and the resistance to its screening finds explanation in the news items recently. A recent report by the Calcutta Telegraph[13] states that the Maithil Sewa Samiti which had joined hands with Vishwa Hindu Parishad, Shiv Sena and Bajrang Dal in their destructive attempts to stop the film, has recently actually tried to push a fourteen year old into prostitution. The Samiti members who were compelling her to accept prostitution were, horrifyingly, her parents. When the girl refused, she was tonsured by the Samiti and paraded on the Varanasi streets. Alongside with such a news item is another one where a young widow was stripped in the market place suspected of a "duck theft" by a well-to-do farmer in her locality at Krishnagar, in West Bengal. Such incidents foreground the relevance of *Water* and are indicators of the cultural realities in India which have not undergone sea change in the postcolonial/global era. While the film is to be appreciated for its theme, it is also admirable for its artful presentation with its subtle suggestions, use of images, dialogues, background music and symbolic details.

Reflective Exposition

Water opens with the verses 156-161 from Chapter V of *Manusmriti,* which clearly demarcate the role of the Hindu woman in Indian society. *Manusmriti* dates back to 200 BCE – 200 CE, yet the film has for its setting the 1930s. Ages have come and gone, yet the position of women in Indian society has remained unchanged. The dawn breaks in the girl-child Chuyia's life with new and painful implications. The sun rises over a rural scene with the sitar strings setting the mood for the hour; gradually the sound of the flute in morning raga joins the sitar. The camera closes in on a pond filled with water-hyacinth leaves. It concentrates briefly on a very intricate detail on one water-hyacinth leaf. A toad hops on the leaf and crosses over to another. There are droplets of water which glisten on the leaf. Cart wheels are seen moving by the pond. Chuyia's feet are seen hanging, dancing to the music of the movement of the cart. A man walks down the village road, balancing two pitchers tied to two ropes attached to the wooden plank which he balances on his shoulders. The camera closes in again on young Chuyia gnashing sugarcane against her teeth and her mother-in-laws anxiously tending to her ill son. As Chuyia tries to tickle her husband's toe with the end of the sugarcane, her mother-in-law reprimands her with a handmade palm-leaf-fan and she grimaces. Then the mother-in-law offers water to her son holding a vessel close to his mouth. All this drama in nature and in Chuyia's family is enacted in silence. No words are spoken. Yet the silence is eloquent with symbolic implications. The toad crossing over the water-hyacinth leaf represents the ugliness of the traditional codes which are imposed on women. The pond filled with water-hyacinth leaves signifies the rottenness which has cleaved on to the society since Manu's time. The first few shots are heavily loaded with the suggestion of decay, backwardness, and stench. The river Ganges, which Chuyia's family crosses over in a boat, is the river of sorrow in Chuyia's life or any child-widow's life, and the implications are clear with the flicker of the funeral pyres in the distance. The background music comprising mainly of sitar and flute combined with other instruments, and the fine orchestration of sounds with a few western notes, subtly reveal the impending change of pattern in Chuyia's life. The silence is broken with Chuyia's father asking her if she remembers her wedding, to which the girl answers in the negative. She is told that she has become a widow to which there is an ironic rejoinder from the child: "For how long?" The girl is barely seven; yet as a widow, her life is apparently over even before it began. The drama of Chuyia being forced into the rituals of widowhood is performed in silence. The film thus provokes reflective and emotive understanding from its viewers in the first few shots through the orchestration of background music, images and carefully chosen dialogue. One notices that the dialogue here is restricted to the bare minimum to retain the impact of the mood created in the setting of the film. The exposition reminds one of Susan Sontag's observation: "Great reflective art is not frigid. It can exalt the spectator, it can present images that appal, it can make him weep. But its emotional power is mediated. The pull towards emotional involvement is counterbalanced by elements in the work that promote distance, disinterestedness, impartiality."[14] The film takes us back to the colonial past, to the eve of Independence through a distance in time; yet its relevance today enables the viewer to experience a "projective past".[15]

Names as Cultural Signifiers and the Parody of the Myth of Romance

Once the mood is set, the actual drama begins full of sound and fury when Chuyia is left to her fate by her father at the widows' house at Varanasi. As one of the elderly inmates of the widows' house point out, "Chuyia" means a mouse. Significantly, the little girl is filled with rage and resistance and uses her sharp teeth and claws to set herself free from the strictures imposed on her there. The camera focuses on a few individual widows who are reminded of their struggle and pain when they too had been dumped in that house by their relatives as children. Chuyia's resistance endears Chuyia to them as she titillates their subversive imagination. Yet they know and utter, that time tames all and it will tame Chuyia too.

The names of the other two chief characters in this film also carry significations. Kalyani to whom Chuyia is close, falls in love with Narayan. Kalyani is another name for the Hindu goddess Lakshmi, the god Narayan's wife. Lakshmi is also associated with wealth and auspiciousness. Kalyani has wealth of beauty and youth which the house sells for survival. She comes to the rescue of her inmates when one of them dies and they have not the money to carry out her funeral rites. Ironically she is more than once referred to as 'goddess' in the film for her self-sacrificing nature. Deepa Mehta's technique is once again irony in the film, for goddess and whore become interchangeable labels, which patriarchy uses to suit its purposes. As long as Kalyani caters to the requirements of the house she is a goddess, but when she seeks her own life she is loathed. Narayan's father, who had used her for his pleasure, calls her a whore. Moreover Deepa Mehta gives a very subtle ironic twist to the popular myth: 'marriages are made in heaven', through the Kalyani-Narayan episode. Having no other way out of the impasse in which she finds herself, Kalyani chooses suicide in the Ganges and drowns herself in the river of sorrow and thus aborts all possibilities of reunion with Narayan. She remains as elusive as the tunes of Narayan's flute in his imagination suggesting 'eternal deferral of desire'.

Narayan's desire for Kalyani in the film is much more than what a lover feels for his beloved. His desire for Kalyani is clearly free from the lust which his father nourishes for her. Narayan has a nationalistic desire in him to educate Kalyani and to give her an equal status in society as his wife. But as Mehta suggests, such love is too idyllic to survive in the midst of this stench of traditionalism. Subtle significations used by the filmmaker such as the *diya* which Kalyani carries with her when she goes to meet Narayan for the first time, the flute which Narayan plays against the backdrop of the Ganges with the love song in the background, the reference to Kalidasa's *Meghdoot*, are loaded with meanings which need to be unravelled. According to Hindu mythology, Krishna is the avatar of Narayan. Though Narayan may not play the flute, Krishna does in his romance with Radha. Mehta's imagination coalesces the two images of femininity, namely,

Lakshmi/Kalyani and Radha in the film. Just as Radha is caught between duty towards her husband and her love for Krishna, Kalyani is also not able to transgress the limitations imposed on her by the social codes as a widow despite her desire for a wholesome life. Death is a better option than choosing to be Narayan's father and Narayan's friend's father's prostitute. The film suggests that like Chuyia, who is made to replicate her role after her demise, she too had been led into prostitution unwittingly. But her personal codes and values do not permit her to embrace the shameful life again after she falls in love and when the gates of the widows' house close on her. Her suicide has a subversive impact on Narayan who leaves home. His love for Kalyani and her tragedy gives him enlightenment about the cultural realities in his family and society. As a young, educated Indian male who has well absorbed the syncretic strains of the Western Liberalism with Indian Classicism, he was, until his experience with Kalyani, only theoretically aware of the stances taken by Raja Ram Mohan Roy and Gandhi. His love for Kalyani becomes symbolic of his desire for action. Shakuntala who had set Kalyani free to meet Narayan, is also moved by the same desire for action. She does not want Chuyia to replicate Kalyani's fate and fall a prey to Madhumati's selfishness and social atrocities. So she thrusts Chuyia into Narayan's hands asking him to take her to Gandhi.

Shakuntala is one among the inmates who can read and write. She has a questioning mind and often puts her questions on religion and position of women in Indian society and the changing political scenario to the priest whom she serves as an attendant. Rigorous disciplining of the self makes her old before her time. Yet, when Kalyani confides to her about Narayan and seeks her advice, she is restrained. Kalyani's falling in love draws her attention to her self and that is very delicately implicated by her sudden question to Chuyia, "Tell me, how I look?" Chuyia's frank and sharp reply, "Old" sums up her tale of a life ruined by widowhood. Like the mythical Shakuntala who took her lessons from the saint who had adopted her, she looks for emancipation from the kind old priest. It is he who enlightens her about the Widow Remarriage Act, which prompts her to setting Kalyani free from the rigours of the widows' house and give her the choice of an alternative life much against the wishes of the other inmates.

Images of Love, Violence and Compassion

Just as there is certain self-righteousness in Shakuntala who can make clear cut choices by the light of her intelligence and understanding, young Chuyia is subversive from the very beginning. Her grimace when her mother-in-law reprimands her in the first scene is indicative of her personality. Chuyia's rebellion against the house's laws, her act of stomping on Madhumati, the head widow of the house, and cursing her to drown herself when she expresses horror at Kalyani's desire for remarriage, her wringing Madhumati's pet parrot's neck to seek revenge for the punishment meted out to Kalyani, are turbulent images of subversion. Passionate by nature, she responds to love with love. So instead of buying sweets for herself, she saves the *laddoo* for the old widow who often expressed her desire for tasting sweets fried in pure ghee. She would even save her paltry lunch to feed Kalyani's pet puppy, named Kallu after its silky black coat. Her love for Kalyani is transferred to her pet, just as her rage for the head of the widows' house is transferred to her pet parrot. Yet, child as she is and innocent yet of the ways of the world, she fails to match Madhumati's conceit. Ironically it is Kalyani who drowns when Madhumati refuses to take her in, and Chuyia is sent across the river to replicate Kalyani's role. The river acts as a signification of change and sorrow, the second time in Chuyia's life. She had earlier crossed the same river to embrace her widowhood, and she crosses it again to be initiated into prostitution. In both cases she is compelled to face crude realities of life and be subject to patriarchal violence, unwittingly. Madhumati's selfishness and her acts of violence on the widows especially the last one, is the ugly face of patriarchy. As a matriarch of the house, she only imitates the patriarchal stance. The film through its characterisation questions gender and sex equations. The two Seths are at par with Madhumati in their selfishness, conceit and their perversity. Child rape and widow exploitation are the two charges which are subtly levelled against the Seths or the patriarchs of the Varanasi society.

Possibly, Mehta did not wish for simplifications in the film in her critique of Hindu patriarchy. So, apart from the Seths, who have the privilege to exploit the young widows, the rest of the male characters in the film are rather compassionate. The sweet-vendor who sells sweets to Chuyia even when he had initially tried to shoo her away;

Chuyia's father's remorse and subtle shots which indicate his compassion for the young girl; the priest's compassion for Shakuntala; Narayan's love and understanding for Kalyani and his concern for the condition of the widows are some examples to suggest that the patriarchy is free of gender discrimination. Even, Narayan's friend, who surfeits himself with alcohol and romantic literature, is not averse to Narayan's Swadeshi ideals to emancipate women from the shackles of tradition. It is the play of power, economy and gender which subjugates the women in Indian patriarchy. Narayan points out to Shakuntala, after Kalyani's death, that it is chiefly economy which made the law-makers of the ancient ages demarcate such roles for men and women. Keeping a widow in the house would be expensive and would mean responsibility, so they were sent to widows' houses. Chuyia's thought-provoking question if there were such houses for widowers too, is a query which is put to the viewers for re-assessing the values and codes of the Indian society.

Conclusion

To quote Susanne Langer, film like other forms of art "creates a virtual present".[16] The two films by forcing upon us a re-viewing of our cultural codes and production give us the experience of a "projective past". The endnote to *Water* stating that there are still very many widows who continue to be exploited by the patriarchy and who live in dire conditions is to alert the masses about the cultural realities which the effects of globalisation seem to gloss over. The question of modernity prompts exploration. In *Fire,* Julie's father feels that Julie has done him proud with her New Yorker accent and her free ways of living. Jatin's observation on the issue that "We Indians are compliant" explains his case. The discussion however places the film in the context of new modernity in Asia which judges its standards by the western codes and values. Mehta's intention is to justify Sita and Radha's relationship as different from western radicalism. In *Water* too, she interrogates modernity through the characterisation of Narayan and his friend. While the former can assimilate the Western ideals with the Indian classical strains, the latter is a mimic man. The films thus explore and reassess gender roles and the individual choices of various men and women in Indian society. They indicate alternatives for a different living as against the life of repression and subjugation. Certain images of pure delight matching with the track music such as the one when Chuyia and Kalyani dance, clap and sing with the first shower of the monsoon, or when Sita and Radha dance with the 'Indi-pop', offer relief from the sustained exploration of struggle, strife and pain. Yet these scenes do not in any way detract the flavour nor are they superfluous. Rather they are the images of delight even as images of subversion.

As art films, both *Fire* and *Water* spatialise time and present a very sophisticated handling of narrative organisation, with an orchestration of words, sounds and images which forces on the viewer the tension between inner reality and the social mask. They represent subversive elements capable of profoundly destabilising the existing patriarchal system of power/gender relations. But as the Indian reception of the films signifies, subversive elements are not in themselves sufficient to generate social change. To conclude with Judith Butler's observation,[17] subversive potential must be actively mobilised in the construction of all modes of reality: material, psychological and phantasmatic, which the films attempt to do through artful presentation.

Notes

1. Deepa Mehta in an interview with Richard Phillips, 6 August 1999 published in *WSWS: Art Films,* from the internet.
2. *Ibid.*
3. *Ibid.*
4. Joy Gould Boyum, *Double Exposure: Fiction into Film* (New York: Universe Books, 1985), p.25.
5. Renee Hoogland, "First Things First: Freud and the question of primacy in gendered sexuality", *Journal of Gender Studies, Vol.8,No. 1*, p.46
6. *Ibid*, p.47.
7. The "thetic" phase marks a threshold between two heterogeneous realms: 'the semiotic and the symbolic'. See Kelly Oliver, *Reading Kristeva: Unraveling the Double Bind,* (Bloomington & Indianapolis: Indiana University Press, 1993), p.40.

8. See, "True Confessions: Cixous and Foucault on Sexuality and Power", in *Erotic Welfare: Sexual Theory and Politics in the Age of Epidemic*, edited by Linda Singer, Judith Butler *et al*, (New York: Routledge, 1992), pp.146-162.
9. *Ibid.*
10. *Ibid.*
11. Judith Butler states in *Gender Trouble: Feminism and Subversion of Identity* (New York: Routledge, 1990), p.22, that "The metaphysical unity of three (sex, gender, desire) is assumed to be truly known and expressed in a differentiating desire for an oppositional gender – that is in a form of oppositional heterosexuality."
12. See Sigmund Freud, "The Dissolution of the Oedipus Complex" in *On Sexuality: Three Essays on the Theory of Sexuality*, edited by A. Richards, The Pelican Freud Library (Harmondsworth: Penguin, 1977)
13. See *The Telegraph*, Calcutta, Monday, 2 July, 2007, p.6.
14. See Boyum, p.27.
15. This is a term used by Homi K. Bhabha in *Location of Culture* (London: Routledge, 1994) to suggest that the continuous process of remembering empowers one to tell difficult stories and to have a meaningful existence, individual as well as collective. The films by Mehta provoke re-thinking and remembering in order to call into question the gender binaries and to bring about change in the Indian social system.
16. See Joy Gould Boyum, p.33.
17. Judith Butler, "Gender is Burning: Questions of appropriation and subversion", in *Bodies That Matter* (New York: Routledge, 1994).

9

Female Bonding/Female Desire

Deepa Mehta's *Fire*

Bandana Chakrabarty

It is but natural that a film, which was released in 33 countries and went on to win 14 International Awards, should cause a furore. This is exactly what happened when Indian Canadian director, Deepa Mehta's film *Fire* was released in 1996. It was received with wild enthusiasm in the west and violent criticism in India turning *Fire* into a highly controversial film. This paper proposes to look at female bonding vis-à-vis female desire in Mehta's film. The way Deepa Mehta asserts female desire outside of the marital bonds and the methods through which she validates female sexuality in a society, which regulates it through religion and other socio-cultural constructs, is the focus of this paper. Female bonding is the formation of a close personal relationship between women. It is a term that is used in etiology to describe patterns of friendship, attachment and co-operation in women. Though the expression and representation of desire in Indian culture is ancient, in the present day political reality "we are made to believe that 'desire' is a dirty word" (Bose 2002).

Desire as the feeling that accompanies an unsatisfied state is too limited a definition. The meaning of desire extends beyond the desire for material things or pleasures of the sense. It also includes the desire for life, the desire for fame, the desire for emotional states, the desire for knowledge and the desire for freedom. The articulation of female sexual desire remains completely contained within a larger patriarchal order. Exploring sexuality in women is still a taboo.

The film *Fire* is about two Indian women, who are entrapped by marriage, religion and patriarchy, each of which binds them to their joint family household rules and regulations. Mehta uses contrastive images to prove her point. Set in India, the plot of *Fire* revolves around two sisters-in-law, Radha (Shabana Azmi) and Sita (Nandita Das) living in a joint family. Radha's husband, Ashok (Kulbhushan Kharbanda) accuses her of being barren, so he takes a vow of celibacy that lasts thirteen years, while Sita's husband, Jatin (Javed Jaffrey) has a long time Chinese mistress and is not at all emotionally involved in his new marriage. Jatin's marriage had been arranged by his elder brother, Ashok, primarily with the purpose of continuing the lineage. Radha seems resigned to her loveless life. It is Sita's arrival as a new bride, which disturbs the quiet equilibrium of the house. Both women are oppressed in their marriages. They turn to each other and come closer together in ways neither imagined nor visualised. They finally come out of the very oppressive patriarchal structures which had initially brought them together.

The opening scene of the film depicts a verdant field blooming with bright yellow flowers where sits a happy family of mother, father and daughter. This scene recurs throughout the film. Soon we witness a family, which is devoid of passionate love. Immediately the scene shifts and we are taken to Agra where the Taj Mahal is being shown around to some foreign tourists. They are being told the story of Shahjahan's eternal love for his beloved wife and that he built the Taj in her memory. Sita and Jatin, newly married and on their honeymoon, are as far away as possible from love and reciprocation. The symbol of love, that is, the Taj Mahal is juxtaposed with their loveless relationship. Mehta captures this scene beautifully by showing the couple in a dark silhouette as contrasted with the Taj in its full splendour The tourist guide goes on to narrate how the emperor got the architect's hands cut off, and how the architect made a hole in the roof of the Taj so that "the symbol of eternal love has been flawed." The message that Mehta sends in the very beginning of the film is that there is already a trace of coldness and aloofness on the part of Jatin in his behaviour towards his new wife. Sita has been forced to define her own womanhood in a way that compels her to question her own attractiveness. Catherine McKinnon observes, "What defines woman as such is what turns men on,"[1] and Jatin's distance undermines her belief in her own youth and womanhood. When she asks her husband, Jatin, at the Taj, "Don't you like me?" it is the sexual appeal that is framed to which Jatin's cold response is matter-of-fact, "We've been married only three days." In a society where heterosexuality is the norm and women are under control, this definition is imbibed and internalised by women. Indian films go a long way in putting a stamp on heterosexuality and romantic love. Sita has been indoctrinated by the ideal of romantic love. Heterosexuality has been glorified in movie after movie.

Gayatri Spivak in her essay, "Can the Subaltern Speak?" says that "the ideological construction of gender keeps the male dominant," a process that Deepa Mehta contests in her film showing how Indian women "caught in the constrictive web of familial commitments, arranged marriages and notions of duty" are trying to maintain an equilibrium between all the three. An Indian girl, from her childhood, is deliberately trained in how to be a good woman and hence through "conscious inculcation of culturally designated feminine roles," she is taught docility and submissiveness. Radha, who has grown up from the little girl in the opening scene of the film, loved nature deeply, believed in her potential, and dreamt of freedom, has by now become a typical Indian woman who is expected to perform her duties and conform to rules without questioning, Conscious of a sense of duty, she is 'a good woman.'

Religion exerts a great pressure on Indian women who are taught to adhere to the ideal of womanhood as exemplified by Sita in the *Ramayana*. It exercises control over women and their sexuality. Sita has been "transformed into a cultural icon that has for centuries assisted in the validation of various ideological forms of oppression [of women]", (Pandit 116). Women are weighed down by the Indian scriptures and they are supposed to be pious and dutiful all the time. The notion of duty is forced and re-inforced in the film through shots of the *Ramayana* where Sita is shown as the pious and dutiful wife of Rama. Sudhir Kakar is of the view, "It is through recitation, reading, listening to or attending to dramatic performances of this revered text (*Ramayana)* that a Hindu re-asserts his or her cultural identity as a Hindu and obtains religious merit."[2] Ashok, in keeping with his Indian upbringing, demands of his wife, "You should be touching my feet."

Similarly, in the other wellknown religious epic of the Hindus, the *Mahabharata,* Markandeya tells Yudhishthira of "wives restraining all their senses and keeping their hearts under complete control....By serving their husbands only can they win heaven" (Roy 488). The husbands are regarded as gods and Kakar points out, "This is the ideal, purveyed over and over again, in numberless myths and legends, through which the Hindu community has tried to mould the character and personality of its female members."[3]

On returning home after the honeymoon and after finishing with the usual rituals like touching the feet of Biji, the matriarch of the home, and invoking her blessings, Jatin immediately leaves the house on the pretext of a meeting with the video people and Ashok, the elder brother-in-law, dismisses the recent arrival of the newlyweds with "All good things must come to an end. Back to work," suggests all is not well in the joint household.

The family owns a food joint – a take out – and also a video rental store. Only Jatin and Mundu, the servant, have access to the video store whereas the two sisters-in-law are relegated to the kitchen at the back of the store. In showing customers buying food and renting pornographic films, Mehta connects oral desire and visual gratification. In another scene Radha tells Sita about a saying she had learned from her mother, " The way to a man's heart is through his stomach" whereas she discloses to Sita that she likes plain boiled rice. Her liking for the insipid boiled rice indicates the insipidness of her life. The close association between men, sex and food, is emphasised by Mehta. In the Indian consciousness, food and sexuality are closely linked. As A.K. Ramanujan points out, " The words for eating and sexual enjoyment have the same root, *Bhuj,* in Sanskrit."[4] Sex and food go hand in hand in the male world making women the economic and sexual slaves of men. Rosalind Coward in *Female Desire* writes that this association has sadistic overtones since, "there's a language of devouring, gobbling up, feasting with the eyes, a language which suggests the desire not only to eat but perhaps to destroy the loved object."[5] Julie, Jatin's mistress is a "liberated" woman who refuses marriage. However she desires to act in Kung-Fu films and this speaks volumes about her desire to objectify herself. Julie does not want to get married because she does not want to be fettered by the rules and regulations of a joint family. She knows very well that in marriage, duty has an upper hand over pleasure and desire. Heterosexuality gives men direct control over women and it also binds women to the home and away from other women.

Both the sisters-in-law are left alone in the evenings. Sita's husband passes his time paying obeisance to his mistress whereas Radha's husband devotes his evenings to his Swamiji. Mehta uses contrasts and irony recurrently in the film. In one scene Jatin is shown caressing and kissing Julie's foot and, in another, Ashok is shown massaging the Swamiji's feet and he expects his wife to touch his feet! A scene in the film, where Radha and Sita meet on the terrace of the house, to get a breath of "fresh air" – depicts a space free from oppressive marital duty. They watch a marriage procession passing in the street below, a common sight in India. Mehta suggests that our lives are so obsessed with films and film music that they become part of the marriage ritual. The dreary life of these women is juxtaposed against the noisy and merry marriage procession.

In the very next scene when Sita is crying and Radha comes in to comfort her, Sita kisses her on the mouth. They have transgressed male space as the room shows posters from Kung-Fu films. It is "the beginning of Radha's and Sita's relationship" says Irina Negrea, marked by the contradiction between happiness and joy that the wedding song expresses and the grim reality of their marriage (Negrea, online article 2004). Mehta's critique of Hindi movies, which distort reality, goes hand in hand with her own portrayal of the cracks in the system. Hindi films depict marriage as a fulfilling relationship based on reciprocated romantic love. When marriages do not work, Mehta is of the view that men always have choices, whereas women have none. They can only suffer in silence. The choice left open to Radha and Sita is to enter into a lesbian relationship that is mutually fulfilling and that does not involve power struggles or notions of 'duty.' Ashok has never acknowledged

Radha's needs and desires because she is barren. He has refused her all physical and emotional contact for thirteen years. He's taken a vow of celibacy and he is testing his desire by having the object of his desire, that is Radha, lie near him until temptation subsides. When Radha asks him –"How does it help me?" Ashok replies, "By helping me, you are doing your duty as my wife". For Ashok, "Desire gives pain" to which Radha's retort is, "Without desire, life is not worth living."

What bonds Sita and Radha in the first place is what Adrienne Rich has described as the, "breaking of a taboo and the rejection of a compulsory way of life". It is also a "direct or indirect attack on male right of access to women" (Rich 192). Deepa Mehta shows two parallel scenes where both Sita and Radha refuse their husbands' desires. In the picnic scene the two women are shown exchanging loving looks and Sita massaging Radha's feet. They are both sitting and facing each other and this sets them both on the same level. The irony is that they are exchanging loving looks under their husbands' eyes. These are silent moments of mutual understanding, which neither husband understands. Ashok comments, "I'm lucky to have such a loving family." It is ironical that the loving family is completely out of joint. Soon, when Ashok discovers that Radha and Sita are fulfilling each other's desires, he gets enraged and is himself overcome by desire,. The film shows Ashok sitting on the steps and imagining the two women making love – a satisfaction he has consciously denied himself. His posture is one of helpless impotence and a jealousy which he has lost the right to express. All along he has striven to build up hierarchical models, expecting subservience, not love.

Lillian Faderman in her book, *Surpassing the Love of Man: Romantic Friendship and Love between Women from the Renaissance to the Present,* observes that the word lesbian describes:

> a relationship in which two women's strongest emotions and affections are directed towards each other. Sexual contact may be a part of the relationship to a greater or lesser degree or it may be entirely absent. By preference the two women spend most of their time together and share most aspects of their lives with each other. (17-18)

This 'coming out' is the rite of passage through which the lesbian establishes and affirms herself. The film establishes the point that one is not born a lesbian but becomes one. Sita makes Radha aware of the limitation of her role particularly as a wife and daughter-in-law. She does not want Radha to respond to tradition like "a trained monkey." As Ruth Vanita and Salim Kidwai have commented, "The film uses tropes of female intimacy such as oiling each other's hair, tropes of marriage such as exchanging bangles, feeding one another cardamom, and pressing each other's feet and explores in a masterly fashion the eroticism of exchanged glances" (214).

It is true that most homosexually and bisexually inclined people in India are married at some time or the other in their lives, live ordinary lives, move about in their workplaces and neighbourhoods and look indistinguishable from heterosexually inclined people. Romantic attachments between men and between women have been considered as perfectly compatible with marriage and procreation. For instance, a person may be a perfect spouse or parent but his or her emotional attachment maybe to a person of his or her own sex.

Deepa Mehta establishes a parallel between the narrative of the film and a scene from the *Ramayana* in which Sita is asked by Rama to walk through fire to prove her purity and chastity. This scene comes up again and again as part of a film, as part of a TV serial and as part of an enactment at a local Ram Lila, which is being witnessed by Ashok and his Swamiji. Like Sita in the epic, Radha in the film, undergoes a trial by fire when she discloses to Ashok that she is leaving him for Sita. She says, "I desire her warmth, her compassion, her body. I desire to live." She is no longer the passive Radha. Frenzied, Ashok forces himself upon her and shoves her into the burning gas stove. As Gairola points out, " Ashok attempts to impose a nonconsensual act of sati on Radha" (Gairola 2002). At this point of the film, Mehta enforces, visually, Rene Girard's notion of mimetic desire thus: "Even within the ritualistic framework of marriage ...sexuality is accompanied by violence and as soon as one trespasses beyond the limits of matrimony to engage in illicit relationship – the violence and the impurity resulting from this violence grows more potent and extreme" (qtd. by Gairola 35).

Radha's white sari catches fire and as she is struggling in her burning sari, Ashok carries away his mother, averting his eyes. Radha manages to come out unscathed and is proved to be pure. It is desire that brings her "back to life." Radha finds comfort and solace in a love in which "a patriarch is not the lowest common denominator of desire" (qtd by Gairola). Deepa Mehta's film opens up new avenues of representation that offers woman the option of finding companionship and love with another woman.

Fire thus breaks the patriarchal code and creates breathing spaces for women through female bonding, which in this case actualises itself as lesbianism.

Notes

1. See Irena Negrea's article, " Now There's Two Heroines in one Kitchen: Lesbianism and Me(h)tafilmic Discourse in Deepa Mehta's *Fire.*" *Portals* Vol.2. Spring 2004.http://userwww.sfsu.edu/-clsa/2004/negrea.html.
2. Sudhir Kakar, *The Inner World: A Psychoanalytic Study of Childhood and Society in India.* Delhi:OUP, 1981.pp.63-64.
3. *Ibid.*, p.67.
4. Sudhir Kakar. *Intimate Relations: Exploring Indian Sexuality.* New Delhi: Penguin,1989, p.91.
5. Rosalind Coward, *Female Desire: Women's Sexuality Today.* London: Paladin,1984, pp.13-16.

References

Bose, Brinda, ed. *Translating Desire: The Politics of Gender and Culture in India.* New Delhi: Katha, 2002.

Faderman, Lillian. *Surpassing the Love of Man: Romantic Friendship and Love between Women from the Renaissance to the Present.* New York: William Morrow and Co., 1981.

Fire. Dir. Deepa Mehta, Prod. David Hamilton, Perf. Shabana Azmi, Nandita Das, Kulbhushan Kharbanda and Javed Jaffrey. 1996.

Gairola, Rahul. "Burning with Shame: Desire and South Asian Patriarchy from Gayatri Spivak's 'Can the Subaltern Speak?' to Deepa Mehta's *Fire*" *Comparative Literature*, Fall, 2002. http://findarticles.com/p/articles/miqa3612/is_200210/ai_n9091637/

Kakar, Sudhir. *The Inner World: A Psychoanalytic Study of Childhood and Society in India*. Delhi:OUP, 1981.

—*Intimate Relations: Exploring Indian Sexuality*. New Delhi: Penguin, 1989.

Negrea, Irena. "Now There's Two Heroines in One Kitchen: Lesbianism and Met(h)filmic Discourse in Deepa Mehta's *Fire.*" *Portals*, Volume 2, Spring 2004.

Pandit, Lalita. "Patriarchy and Paranoia: Imaginary Infidelity in *Uttararamacarita* and *The Winter's Tale.*" *Literary India*. Jaipur and New Delhi: Rawat Publications, 1997.

Rich, Adrienne. "Compulsory Heterosexuality and Lesbian Existence," *Signs* 5. No.4. (Summer 1980): 648-49.

Roy, P.C. (trans.) *Mahabharata*. Calcutta: Oriental Publishing Co.Vol.3

Spivak, Gayatri. "Can the Subaltern Speak?" *Colonial Discourse and Postcolonial Theory: A Reader*.(Eds.) Patrick Williams and Laura Chrisman. New York: Columbia University Press,1994.

Vanita, Ruth and Salim Kidwai, eds. David, eds. *Same-Sex Love in India*. New Delhi: Macmillan, 2000.

10

Looking for Ways of Representation

'Looking' as a Trope in *1947–Earth*

Sudha Shastri

At the conclusion of his eloquent essay on the 1984 anti-Sikh riots in Delhi, Amitav Ghosh raises a question that has become, sadly enough, increasingly urgent in the world today: the problem of giving literary expression to violence.[1] His concern over the reconciliation of the artistic representation of violence with a writer's responsibility is arguably the most significant part of his essay, and one that could perhaps work well as an investigative tool for reading texts (books and films) that portray violence.[2] It is from this point-of-view that I am going to look at Deepa Mehta's movie on the Partition, *1947–Earth* (1998).

The second of Mehta's much-touted trilogy of films (*Fire, Earth* and *Water*), this is possibly her least controversial film. It takes its inspiration from Bapsi Sidhwa's novel, *Ice-Candy-Man*, published in 1989. My paper will focus on the role of mediation in cinematic representation, to ask if and how cinematic mediation can achieve the thing that Amitav Ghosh hopes from fictional representation of violence. Although Ghosh speaks of (only) the writer, his articulation of the issue is large enough to include the filmmaker in its purview: the issue, after all, is representation.

Background

In August 1947, India achieved independence from her coloniser, the British. What should have been cause for triumph, following from a moral victory, was to become a painful timeline etched in the lives and memories of Indians on both sides of the 'national' border, drawn into the Punjab in the West and Bengal in the East. Migrating Hindus and Muslims, unable to withstand the agony of leaving their roots for an alien place they now had perforce to call 'home', gave expression to their emotions in violence: a violence that has been graphically described in story after story; from fictionalised accounts like Khushwant Singh's *Train to Pakistan* (1956), Manohar Malgonkar's *A Bend in the Ganges* (1964), Bhisham Sahni's *Tamas* (Hindi original 1974, English translation by Jai Ratan 1988), Chaman Nahal's *Azadi* (1975), and the pointed, poignant stories of Saadat Hassan Manto, the more famous of which are "Toba Tek Singh" and "Open It", to the factual, detailed account provided by Collins and Lapierre in *Freedom at Midnight* (1975), or the more recent non-fictional record of Urvashi Butalia's *The Other Side of Silence* (1999).

A look at the publication dates of these works reveals that the decades following the partition continued to engage the creative imagination of writers, who tried to make sense of an epoch marked by senselessness of a disastrous order. In 1986, Govind Nihalani turned Sahni's novel into a stark and powerful television film also called *Tamas* that, in turn, triggered violent reactions, pointing, rather ominously, to the interdependence of reality and fiction. The reverse direction of influence, from fiction to life, while perhaps counter-intuitive, is also interesting, because it presupposes the writer's responsibility in her portrayal of sensitive issues. In particular this is true of film, a medium of more immediate reach than the text.

Before I go on to look at *1947–Earth*, it may be relevant to consider the highlights of Sidhwa's novel *Ice-Candy-Man/Cracking India*. It was the first novel on the Partition to come from a Parsi perspective (and that too one located in Pakistan), and therefore significant with respect to the question of neutrality. It was a narrative point-of-view that aligned itself with none of the communities that were implicated in mutual violence. To that extent, it is empowered by being capable of an objectivity (in theory at least) that could redeem the 'story' from implied biases. By being a Parsi, the narrator is loyal equally to Hindu, Muslim and Sikh – or to rephrase, loyal to none at the expense of another.

At the same time, the novel has another trump card in favour of impartial narration: the narrator, Lenny is a little girl, aged eight, and her child-narrator status endows her account with reliability that the most sophisticated of adult narrators would be hard put to achieve.[3] Those matters that are beyond the comprehension of a child (which is where the child narrator typically distorts information) are taken care of by the adult narrator whose voice-over at the end clinches in a nutshell the meaning of the ending of the story of Shanta.

In an interview with Julie Rajan, Sidhwa remarks on the highlights of the movie: "The movie stands on its own. But it has the voice of the child and it has the spirit of the book – it has objectivity and it has the story". In the same interview, Sidhwa explains the change of title from *Ice-Candy-Man* to *Cracking India*. One of them is to do with sales:

> There are so many books published in America each year, that unless the title says something about the book, it can fall through the cracks. My American publishers felt that at least people interested in India would buy the book. The title *Ice Candy Man* would mean nothing to an American. I think they're right.

Another, more pertinent reason has to do with presenting the image of India as a riddle to crack:

> ...like a nut, like cracking open a nut. Riddle also fits the title because the complex mix of religions and the interwoven fabric of family and community life in India are confounding to the uninitiated – the novel attempts to explain that.[4]

Sidhwa goes on to explain the difficulty of representing violence (the difficulty identified by Amitav Ghosh) and claims the hurt of memory to be one of the reasons why so little (sic) has been written, according to her, on the Partition.

1947–Earth

I propose to look at some of the main scenes/sequences in the film, at the ways in which the relationships between Lenny, her ayah Shanta, Shanta's admirers and history – or perhaps History – evolve as the story unfolds. I shall focus in particular on those scenes where Lenny remains a character and at the same time becomes a viewer whom, we the audience, are enabled to watch. My point is that when we see events and watch Lenny, also seeing them, these events become filtered by a focalising consciousness and such mediation creates a distance between the events and us, the audience. Lenny is a focaliser of many events in the film[5], but her focalising role is highlighted in such a way as to encourage self-reflexivity; as Lenny watches, we see her watch, and are thereby reminded of our own role. Self-reflexivity, typically, encourages distance for the spectator.

Does this distance prevent us from emotional involvement with the story? Does this twice-distanced visual mode equip the spectator with an understanding (following detachment) that a direct identification with Lenny or any character, can preclude? These questions tie in with the issue raised by Amitav Ghosh about (among other things) the role of spectacle in the portrayal of violence:

> When I now read descriptions of troubled parts of the world, in which violence appears primordial and inevitable, a fate to which masses of people are largely resigned, I find myself asking: Is that all there was to it? Or is it possible that the authors of these descriptions failed to find a form – or a style or a voice of a plot – that could accommodate both violence and the civilized, willed response to it?[6]

The question whether this kind of distancing is a way whereby the filmmaker can address Ghosh's anxiety, is one that I shall leave the reader of my essay to decide for herself.

While speaking of focalisation, Manfred Jahn points out that

> The basic concept in focalization theory is focus, and this term refers to *two* intricately related things: 1) *the position from which something is seen* – in narratological terms, this is the spatiotemporal position of the focalizer; and 2) *the object seen 'in focus'* – this is the focalized object or 'centre of attention'. Consequently, in film analysis, we will often ask two questions:

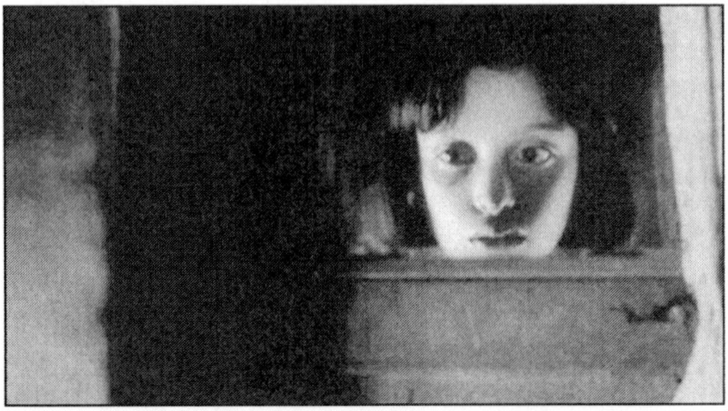

A child's curiosity: The gaze shot

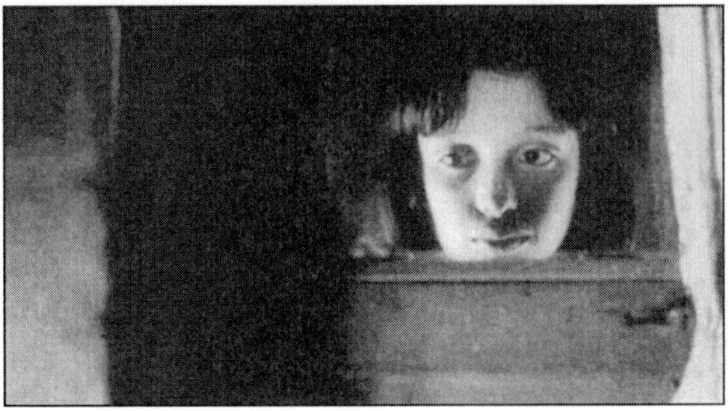

The unseen observer

> 1) Who sees?, i.e. Who is (in the position of) the focalizer? And 2) What is the object (thing or human being) that the focalizer focuses on?[7]

Jahn identifies strategies by which the camera can approximate a character's point-of-view, and gives us a vocabulary: one of these, the eye-line shot, which is a gaze shot (showing a character looking at something) followed by a point-of-view shot (the camera assuming the position of the character and showing the object of her gaze), is reversed in instance 12 that I shall delineate in the succeeding section, *Scenes and Sequences*. Here, we have an instance of a gaze shot following a point-of-view shot when Dil Nawaz looks at Shanta and Hassan making love. At the same time he is himself the object of Lenny's gaze, who is also presented in a point-of-view shot and then in a gaze shot, presumably to increase suspense. However, since these technical terms help clarify rather than analyse the focalizing phenomenon in *1947–Earth*, and they are applicable to the film notionally rather than literally, I shall not use them in a definitive sense in my paper.

The following quotation from Chatman, quoted in Jahn, is more lucid:

> [T]the [film] director has two options. The actor can be so placed in the frame as to heighten our association with him. For example, his back or side profile may appear on an extreme margin of the screen. As he looks into the background we look with him. The other (or "montage") convention uses a simple match-cut: if in the first shot the character looks off-screen, to right or left or front or back, and there follows a cut to another setup within his eyeshot, we assume that he has in fact seen that thing, from that perceptual point of view. And we have seen it with him. (Or vice versa: we may see the thing first and secondly cut to the character looking at it.)[8]

In instance 4, the kite-flying, described in the following section *Scenes and Sequences*, we have an inversion of the position suggested by Chatman: Lenny who is watching Shanta and Dil Nawaz is situated at the far right corner while the lovers romance away in the foreground. In such a positioning, our identification with Lenny is not complete. She is also watching what we are watching. This is one of the ways in which her focalising role is heightened (a point I have made at the beginning of this section).

Scenes and Sequences

To recapitulate in approximate sequence the main narrative units[9] of *1947–Earth*, we have:

(1) The beginning: with a voice-over in the background, the child Lenny is colouring with crayons a map of undivided India; as an opening scene it is similar to the opening credits of *To Kill A Mockingbird* (1962), a film that resembles *1947–Earth* in many interesting ways. Harper Lee's novel turned film also has a narrator recollecting the events of a time long past, with an initial voice-over. Like Lenny's, Scout's memory too traces events fraught with violence, a violence that does not, however, touch her in too personal a fashion. But the most visually arresting resemblance between the two movies is the beginning where the respective children are busily

drawing pictures of the events that they are going to narrate. Lenny, as I have already said, is colouring the map of India, while Scout, humming to herself, is drawing a mockingbird before she carelessly tears the picture in two, foreshadowing the callousness with which Maycomb town will destroy their innocent mockingbird, Tom Robinson. This is echoed in Lenny's gesture, coming soon after the colouring scene, when she takes a plate and drops it so that it crashes, wondering as she does what it would be like to break a country into two.

While Lenny's initial narratorial role, established with the voice-over, is not conspicuously picked up later on, it is impossible to ignore that she is present in almost every narrative unit that I am going to consider. This raises a related question about thresholds of control: how distant and unaffected is she by what she views? This query becomes weighted when we move on to instance 12, where she is clearly overwhelmed by the violence she witnesses from the terrace of Ice-candy-man's house.

(2) The dinner hosted by the Sethnas for the British and the Sikh couple, a 'party' that wavers between open altercation and tense undercurrents. The Sikh and the Englishman are literally at each other's throats, while the hosts soothe their ruffled feelings. This scene begins with Lenny and her cousin sitting below the table, identifying the guests for our benefit from their shoes – and what of their clothes they can see below the table. Thus as early as here, the presence of Lenny as a viewer-commentator becomes a significant element in the movie's representation of the events of the Partition as it happened in Lahore.

(3) The park scene. Lenny and her ayah Shanta go to the park where Shanta is surrounded by her admirers, including Hassan the masseur and Dil Nawaz the Ice-candy-man of the book's title; although there is 'Hindu-Muslim' talk, at this point, the men's religious identities are all subsumed by their common identity as male. This idea is reinforced in the way the male gaze operates, as all eyes stare at Shanta's generously displayed cleavage while she chats with the men. Lenny's presence registers itself in the scene simultaneously; as the men fall silent, drinking in Shanta's curves, Lenny looks around at all of them in puzzlement over their response.

Lenny, at this juncture, is an innocent presence, and has not yet begun to process the information she receives. The pornographic content of this scene is, I believe, significant, since this uninhibited gluttonous viewing is not too different from the response aroused by violence made into spectacle: the pornography of violence.

(4) The kite-flying: while Dil Nawaz and Shanta indulge in flirtation while flying kites, the camera also shows Lenny who is flying a kite herself, turn around once and watch the two of them. This character as viewer is thus, a recurring feature.

(5) Hassan and Shanta: Lenny's role as spectator becomes a little more sophisticated here as she, with another little girl, watches Hassan take Shanta on his bicycle for a ride. Lenny giggles as she watches, a possible indication that she is aware of the sexual undertones in the interaction between the two adults, even if she is too innocent to understand their import.

(6) More dalliance: Shanta is having her palm read by Dil Nawaz, who swiftly kisses her hand, at which she draws away in mock-anger. Lenny, watching this by-play, smiles too.

(7) The Sethna family goes out driving, and narrowly escapes being hurt in an anti-India demonstration. Lenny is sitting in the back seat, a position that underscores distance.

(8) A unit I have chosen for the facet it shows of Dil Nawaz: he comes as a Sufi and 'fools around' for a while in the park, when a quarrel threatens to brew which is Hindu/Sikh versus Muslim in character. He acts quickly to prevent a fight from brewing. Although not precisely a peacemaker at this point, he is definitely not the active participant in violence that he eventually proves to be.

(9) Altercation again when Lenny, Shanta and her admirers are all eating: Dil Nawaz sees Hassan and Shanta exchange glances.

(10) The kissing scene: Shanta goes with Lenny to a deserted place to meet Hassan, and there he kisses her. What is remarkable about this scene is that Lenny figures almost centrally as a viewer. She first stays with Shanta, then she goes away a little distance, and from there she turns around and watches the two of them kiss. The camera clearly shows her watching them, so that to us, the audience of the film, her presence is registered. We are reminded of this scene later when her cousin kisses Lenny on her birthday, and she remarks

that "Maalishwaala can kiss ayah better" – reminding us of what she has seen.

(11) Probably the most critical part of the plot, in its potential for generating horrific consequences. The long-awaited train comes in from Gurdaspur, bearing corpses, some still bleeding; even as we watch the gory scene, we also watch Dil Nawaz looking at the scene in utter shock. Again, viewing is foregrounded, our viewing is mediated.

(12) Another unit significant for the way in which viewing is foreground. The three adults Dil Nawaz, Hassan and Shanta are standing with Lenny on the terrace of Dil Nawaz's house, from where they get an unobstructed view of the violence erupting in the city below them. The police, ostensibly trying to douse flames with water, are discovered to have thrown petrol on a building for communal reasons. A man is tied to two jeeps and then torn apart as the two vehicles move in opposite directions. The violence assumes frighteningly huge proportions, but most remarkable is the effect it has on Lenny's impressionable mind.

The connection that the film makes between watching and being affected by what you watch, is tellingly demonstrated when Lenny imitates this act of violence in a 'game' a little later. Ordering her cousin to hold one side of her doll, she pulls it from the other side so that it tears into two. "Pull", "Pull harder, you fool", admonishes a tearful Lenny, even as her cousin wonders why she is being "so mean if [she] can't stand it".

(13) A brief conversation on the ethics of neutrality: according to Lenny's mother, "we're letting down our neighbours". But is loyalty so easily definable? Who do they owe their loyalty to when they have Hindu, Muslim, and Sikh neighbours? Her husband clinches the conversation by stating that the neutral position was the best position, and if the Swiss could do it, they, the Parsis could do it as well.

(14) Lenny's birthday, barely registered in her household, from her father to Imam Din immersed in the newspaper. When her cousin comes, they go up a flight of stairs to watch a group of refugees who have gathered there. It is noteworthy that in this case as well as in instance (12), Lenny's view is from the top, and from a distance. Lenny hears that one of the women there is a 'giri hui aurat' (meaning

'fallen woman') (her cousin corrects, 'raped') and they converse with this woman's son.

(15) Lenny watching the love-making of Shanta and Hassan. The voyeuristic nature of this scene is emphasised in the way she peeps through a crack in the wall instead of going back home as asked to by Hassan. Her gaze is ironically conflated with Dil Nawaz's gaze from another side of the same room, also from outside, But his is not a curious gaze, like Lenny's; it is full of emotional intensity.

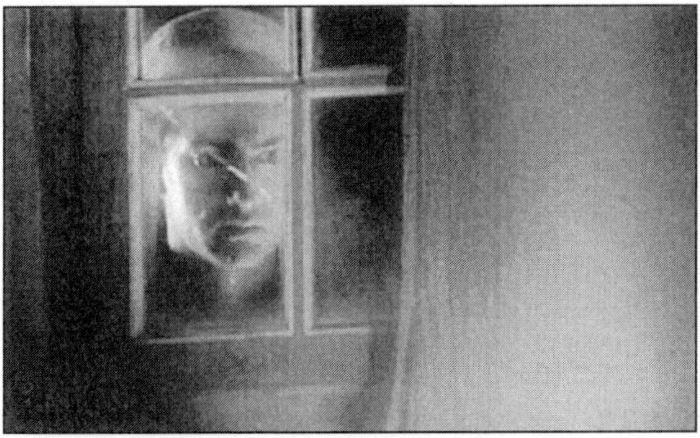

Through the glass

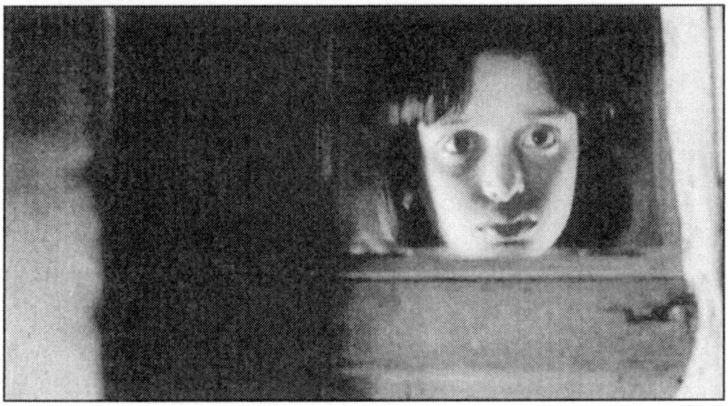

Shifting the look: The other watcher

For us, this scene is thus filtered through at least two viewers. In the hierarchy of viewing with knowledge, Lenny comes right after us, by having the advantage of Dil Nawaz, who has only seen Shanta and Hassan, and not seen Lenny peeping in on them.[10]

(16) Lenny finally becoming a player in the game from being a viewer: unwittingly, in her innocence she betrays Shanta to Dil

Nawaz. Her feeble though valiant attempts to retract are rendered futile by the howling mob, which storms the Sethna household and drags Shanta away to her doom.

(17) The ending, with the voice-over: it is fifty years since the incident, and the older Lenny is describing how in ignorance she betrayed her ayah Shanta, and how she never set eyes on her afterwards, though rumours continued to circulate about her.

Summing Up

To go back to the question with which I began my essay, (how) does *1947–Earth* find a way for a 'responsible' portrayal of violence?

As I have endeavoured to show through the middle section of my paper, the way in which the viewing of events becomes a simultaneous presence with the representation of these events, goes a considerable distance towards establishing a perspective on these very events. Rather than being caught up in the cathartic impact of the plot, we are encouraged time and again to position ourselves away from the plot, either by watching Lenny or by watching what happens to characters who are watching what we are also watching.

If we were to test some of the more central narrative units of *1947–Earth* against Jahn's proposition that there are distinctive techniques that draw attention to both focalisers and focalised objects, we will (as I have pointed out earlier in this paper) find that the camera singles Lenny as an observer in units 3,4,5,6 and 10. In units 12 and 15, her role as observer assumes greater significance, though with different effects. In the former case, she succumbs to the power of the violent spectacle, and imitates it without wholly understanding its import. In the latter, her viewing lacks comprehension in a contextual sense. In both cases she becomes a victim of what she sees, by being manipulated by her emotions in the first case and by Dil Nawaz in the second.

In my attempt to show how *1947–Earth* employs techniques to distance the viewer, I have reasoned onward and ahead – to connect its impact with the larger question of artistic responsibility. I have also tried to look for the threshold over which the viewing is no longer detached, and the viewer succumbs to what she views. In more than one case in the film, it appears that when violence becomes spectacle (whether it is Dil Nawaz watching the corpses in the train, or Lenny watching a man torn in two by rioters), the viewer cannot resist being engulfed by what she sees, whether in a displaced fashion like Dil Nawaz's, who takes revenge on Hindus who have nothing to do with the carnage on the train, or in a literal fashion like Lenny, who re-enacts the tragedy she has witnessed by tearing her doll apart, despite hating every minute of it.

What we want, then, is distance without the 'indifference' that Ghosh mentions. It is possible to argue that the impact of the story is more poignant because we *see* Lenny fall victim to the violence. The danger of violence is that it is contagious, and *1947–Earth* makes this point in such a way as to both disengage us emotionally and enhance our awareness of the import of an event by endowing us with that most rational gift: perspective.

Notes

1. It is difficult to choose from this brilliantly lucid essay "The Ghosts of Mrs Gandhi" (1995), to make my point, but the following excerpts are perhaps most relevant to the issue:

   "When I went back to my desk in November 1984, I found myself confronting decisions about writing that I had never faced before. How was I to write about what I had seen without reducing it to a mere spectacle?"

   "The riots were generated by a cycle of violence, involving terrorists in Punjab on the one hand, and the Indian government on the other. To write carelessly in such a way as to endorse terrorism or repression, can add easily to the problem: in such incendiary circumstances, words cost lives, and it is only appropriate that those who deal in words should pay scrupulous attention to what they say. It is only appropriate that they should find themselves inhibited…But there is also a simple explanation. Before I could set down a word, I had to resolve a dilemma, between being a writer and being a citizen. As a writer, I had only obvious subjects: the violence. From the news report, or the latest film or novel, we have come to expect the bloody detail or the elegantly staged conflagration that closes a chapter or effects a climax. But it is worth asking if the very obviousness of this subject arises out of out modern conventions of representations: within the dominant aesthetic of our time – the aesthetic of what Karahasan calls 'indifference' – it is all too easy to present violence as an apocalyptic spectacle, while the resistance to it can as easily figure as mere sentimentality, or worse, as pathetic or absurd" (http://www.amitavghosh.com/essays_html_indv.php?essay_no=20).

2. It is useful to look at Ghosh's interview to Sheela Reddy in August 2002: To the interviewer's comment that "You talk in your recent book about the 'aesthetics of violence' – how in writing about violence, writers sometimes sacrifice truth and goodness for the spectacle", Ghosh responds with "I think it's a real problem when you have an aestheticization of violence. As writers we have to resist the temptation to make violence seem heroic. When you just hold up a mirror to violence, all you see is more violence" (http://www.worldpress.org/Asia/754.cfm).
3. Strictly speaking, the narrator is actually a remembering narrator, speaking from the advantage of hindsight as an adult, but the acts remembered have happened in childhood, and one takes the narrator on trust that the events are reported as the child saw them. In *1947 – Earth*, the distinction between the two narrators is established by means of the voice-over. When the older Lenny comments, the voice-over takes over.
4. All quotations are from Julie Rajan's interview of Bapsi Sidhwa in (http://www.monsoonmag.com/interviews/i3inter_sidhwa.html,© Monsoon Magazine 2000.
5. See Manfred Jahn's comprehensive analysis of film: (http://www.uni-koeln.de/~ame02/pppf.htm#F4) "focalization The ways and means of presenting information from somebody's point of view. Focalisation can be determined by answering the question *Whose point of view orients the current segment (track, channel) of filmic information?* Or: *Whose perception serves as the current source of information*"
6. This question is raised by Amitav Ghosh in his thought-provoking essay, See Note 1, "The Ghosts of Mrs. Gandhi".
7. The excerpt quoted is from Jahn's work on the analysis of film, also the source of note (http://www.uni-koeln.de/~ame02/pppf.htm#F4)
8. This quotation is also from Jahn's analysis of film (159) (http://www.uni-koeln.de/~ame02/pppf.htm)
9. I am using the phrase 'narrative unit' with more caution than precision, since in some cases (as in instance 1) the units I am describing can be limited to just one scene – by which I mean, one 'shot' – while in some others the unit may be a sequence of shots that add up to a meaningful inference. Also, while I have found Jahn's terminology useful for my description, I have not resorted to its application in toto. More exciting to me is the way in which the import of Lenny as a viewer – irrespective of the angle from which she is presented a viewer – affects the content of the film.

10. It is arguable that Lenny gains any significant knowledge after seeing Dil Nawaz look in on the lovemaking couple. That Lenny has not understood the import of Dil Nawaz's gaze, or at least not until the mob drags Shanta out, seems to me reasonable speculation.

References

Ghosh, Amitav. "The Ghosts of Mrs Gandhi". http://www.amitavghosh.com/essays_html_indv.php?essay_no=20 11th June 2007.

Ghosh, Amitav. "Writing through Turmoil". Sheela Reddy, *Outlook*, (independent weekly), New Delhi, India, Aug. 19, 2002 http://www.worldpress.org/Asia/754.cfm 11th June 2007.

Jahn, Manfred. 2003. A Guide to Narratological Film Analysis. *Poems, Plays, and Prose: A Guide to the Theory of Literary Genres.* English Department, University of Cologne. Version: 1.7. Date: August 2, 2003. This page: http://www.uni-koeln.de/~ame02/pppf.htm Project introductory page: http://www.uni-koeln.de/~ame02/ppp.htm 11th June 2007.

Mehta, Deepa, dir. *1947–Earth.* (1998), Writers: Deepa Mehta, Bapsi Sidhwa. Perf. Aamir Khan, Nandita Das, Rahul Khanna, Maia Sethna.

Sidhwa, Bapsi. "Cracking Sidhwa". Interviewed by Julie Rajan. (http://www.monsoonmag.com/interviews/i3inter_sidhwa.html). 11th June 2007.

11

Re-Presenting the Partition of India

From Bapsi Sidhwa to Deepa Mehta

Somdatta Mandal

The Text

Among the scores of narratives dealing with the theme of the partition of India, *Ice-Candy-Man* is the first novel written from a non-partisan attitude by a Parsi who did not belong to either of the two communities that perpetrated mayhem on each other.

Born in Karachi, raised in Lahore, living for some time in India, and now residing in America, Bapsi Sidhwa's writings are a reflection of lived experiences, told in a form that is at once simple and delicate. Conscious of her triple identity as a Pakistani, a Parsi and a female writer, she wrote her third novel *Ice-Candy-Man* in 1988 and it was published in the United States three years later in 1991 as *Cracking India.*[1]

Ice-Candy-Man is told through the eyes of an eight-year old Parsi girl, Lenny. Though, like the writer, Lenny has had a bout of polio and has had to undergo several operations, Sidhwa insists that it is

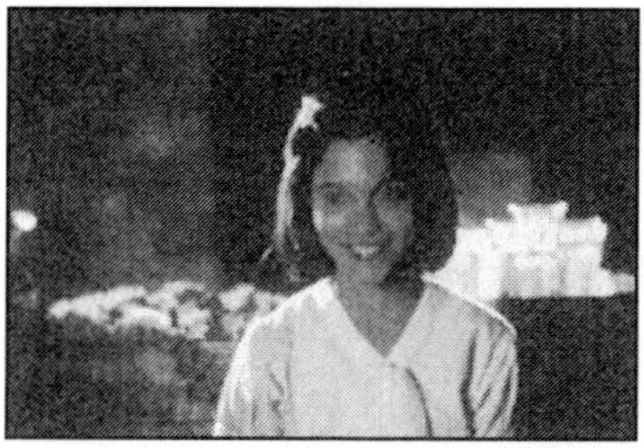

Lenny : the young observer

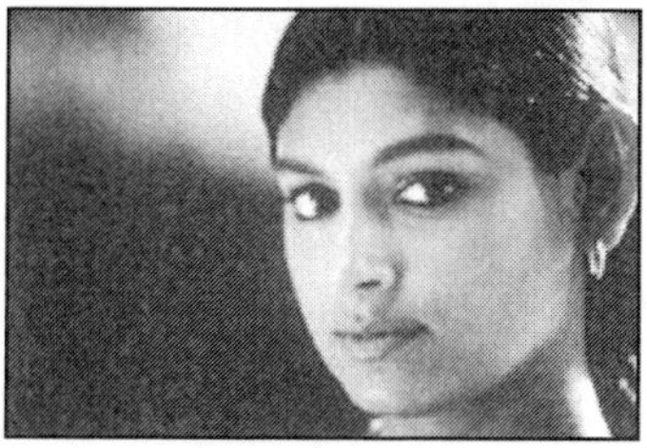

Ayah : the centre of the group

not a self-portrait. The decision to make her narrator a child allows Sidhwa to restrict her world to a very small geographical area of Lahore The narrative is about Lenny's comprehension about the turbulent events during the partition of the Indian subcontinent into India and Pakistan but the compressed world of a child's vision is populated by a relatively small group of people which provides a useful microcosm through which Sidhwa can convey the wider history of the period. Most of the narrative centres upon what happened to her beloved ayah, the maid who looked after her. When the story begins, ayah is surrounded by many admirers that include a Hindu, a Muslim, a Sikh, a Pathan from the mountains, a Jat from the plains, who together are representative of the population mix of Lahore prior to Partition. Among them is the character Lenny calls "Ice-candy-man," a seller of treats.

Besides the local people, the British Raj enters Lenny's little world too, when Mr. and Mrs. Roger come for dinner, and her tutor Mrs. Pen is an Anglo-Indian. As the Partition nears, and the breakup of the Indian subcontinent becomes imminent, Muslims and Hindus become enemies. In an attempt to save themselves, some Hindus convert to Christianity, others to Islam. Some Hindus leave Lahore. Ayah is Hindu, but she assumes that as a member of a Parsi household she will be safe. Dil Nawaz or the Ice-candy-man, who has not received any special favours from her, arrives with a group of

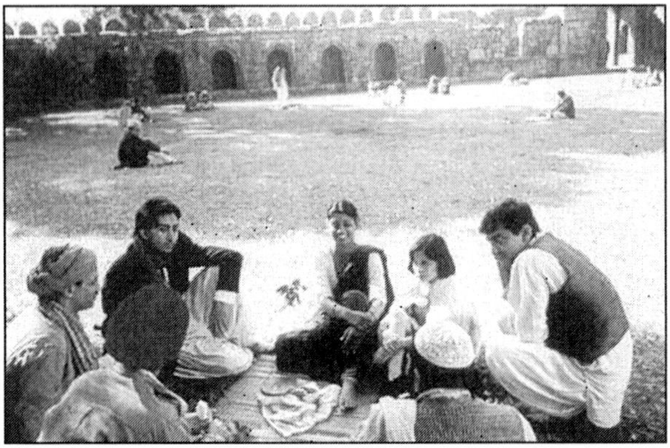

Friends and lovers

fellow Muslims and abducts her. The narrative follows ayah to Hira Mandi – the red-light district of Lahore – where Ice-candy-man has ensconced her, and then goes on to describe her rescue and subsequent departure for India.

An important aspect of this novel is the present tense narration of the story and Sidhwa's deliberate use of an unreliable or apparently unreliable narrator. But if we are to agree with the critic Aamer Hussain,[2] there is more than this. Writing in the grand tradition of the progressive writers on both sides of the border, scrupulously fair to all parties concerned, approaching politics with the empathy and compassion of a humanitarian feminist, the point of view that Bapsi Sidhwa adopts is one of the novel's most successful ploys. We believe we are witnessing the events of the partition through the eyes of an innocent child, but strategically placed flashforwards signal, in a subtle manner, that the adult Lenny is actually reliving the past in order to make sense of the events that baffled her when she was too small to comprehend; simultaneously, she restricts herself to the experiences and sensory perceptions of the child she was. Thus we are given a double – even dialogic—perspective that layers innocence on experience.

Lenny's unreliable narration proves, after all, to be reliable in its own way and causes us to question the British and Indian versions of the truth that have hitherto been accepted. The sickening violence of the period (revealed in all its enormity in the great set-piece story that Lenny's young friend Ranna tells of his own escape from the slaughter that overtook his village) which is difficult for a child

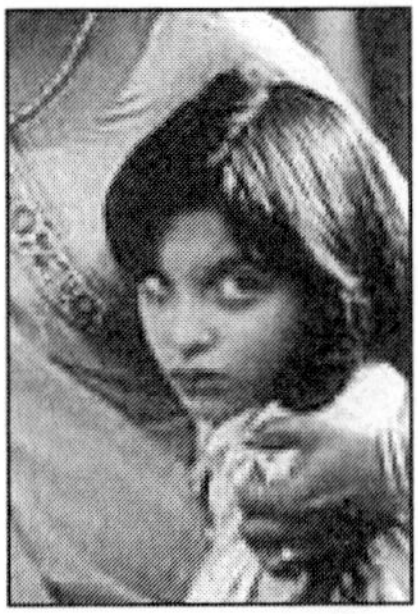

A look of fear and bewilderness

(Lenny or Ranna) to understand is paradoxically seen more clearly by the reader through the uncomprehending eyes of a child. It is the innocence and disbelief of the children in this book – Lenny, her brother Adi, Cousin, Ranna – together with the humanity of people like Lenny's mother, who smuggles rationed petrol at great personal risk to help her Hindu and Sikh friends escape Lahore, and some wonderful, deft, comic moments, that save the novel from an all-consuming bleakness and provide hope for the future. As Ralph Crane[3] rightly points out, this essential humanity, this innocence, this indistinctive understanding of the need for restraint, is apparent too in other Partition novels, in Khushwant Singh's *Train to Pakistan,* in Chaman Nahal's *Azadi,* and in Manohar Malgonkar's *A Bend in the Ganges*.

The Film

After developing the filmscript herself, the Toronto-based, Indo-Canadian director Deepa Mehta adapted the novel into film and *Earth–1947* was released world-wide in late 1999 as part of her projected trilogy called *Fire, Earth* and *Water*. These three different films are according to Mehta herself "about elements on one level that nurture and destroy us. They are very tangible elements. *Fire* is about the politics of sexuality, *Earth* is about the politics of nationalism and *Water* is about the politics of religion."[4] Like most adaptations, it is needless to say that there are several differences between the novel and the film. Focusing primarily on the theme of Partition, Mehta omitted several parts of the story, especially the humour, the humdrum activities of ordinary people in Lahore, and several subplots. She sifted through the book, amalgamated the characters and combined different elements to make it cinematically viable. Lenny's polio, which forms a significant early narrative thread, is sidelined as are the changing relationship between Lenny's parents, the murder of a British official, the child marriage of the much-abused daughter of one of Lenny's family servants. Also missing from the film are characters like the slightly crazy Slavesister as well as the young cousin who attempts incestuous relationships with Lenny.

The purpose of this article is not to highlight individual differences between the novel and the film, but certain facts need to be stated to point out the reason for such differences. This pertains primarily to the fact that the novel is a verbal medium whereas the film is visual. Geoffrey Wagner in his book, *The Novel and the Cinema* (1975) divides film adaptation into three 'modes': the *transposition*, in which a novel is directly given on the screen with a minimum of apparent interference; the *commentary*, where an original story is taken and either purposely or inadvertently altered in some respect; the *analogy*, which must represent a considerable departure for the sake of making another work of art. In this case, Deepa seems to be following the second path and the subtitle of the film reads: "An Epic Romance Set against the Blood Stained Canvas of Partition." Speaking about the problems of adaptation, another critic Joy Gould Boyum states:

> I've already suggested that a film might be considered faithful to its source to the extent that its implicit reading remained within the confines of that work's interpretative possibilities, to the extent that it neither violated nor diminished them.[5]

Though there are several historical elements like communal violence, the British snobbery, the flight across the border for the millions who were rendered homeless by the events of 1947, *Earth* is best viewed not as a historical drama, nor a political fable. It steers clear of being a movie about the events of the Partition only; rather, by concentrating on its effects upon a small group of friends and how it affects their friendships and relationships, it shows the soul of Partition.

At the same time, *Earth* is not a traditional Bollywood movie either. It is funded only in part with Bollywood money and has many links, in terms of style, with western cinema. The whole film was wrapped up in forty days and comprised of an international unit comprising British, American, German, French and Indian members. Though it gracefully established the beauty of peace and crudely depicted the tragic loss of it during the Partition, and concluded with the idea that the most painful kind of betrayal is that which occurs within the family, *Earth* also utilised several aspects of Bollywood cinema. For example, Ice-candy-man is played by Aamir Khan, one of Bollywood's biggest young stars.[6] The director highlights the passionate love between the Masseur and Shanta – a Muslim and a Hindu – they want to go to Amritsar and marry. Though Mehta does

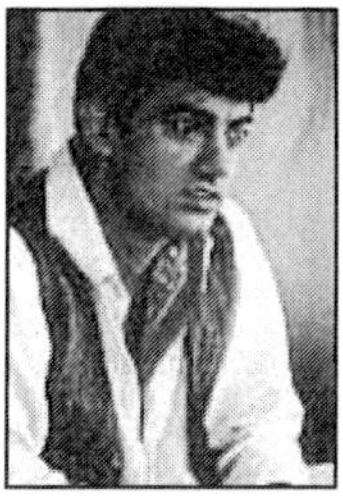

Dil Nawaz

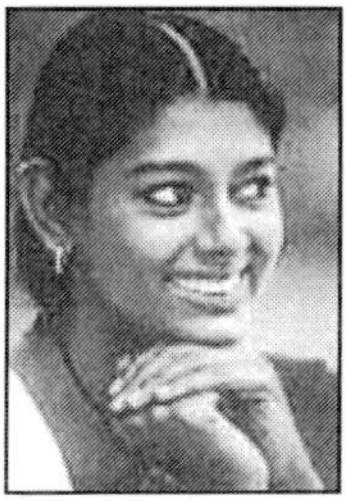

Shanta

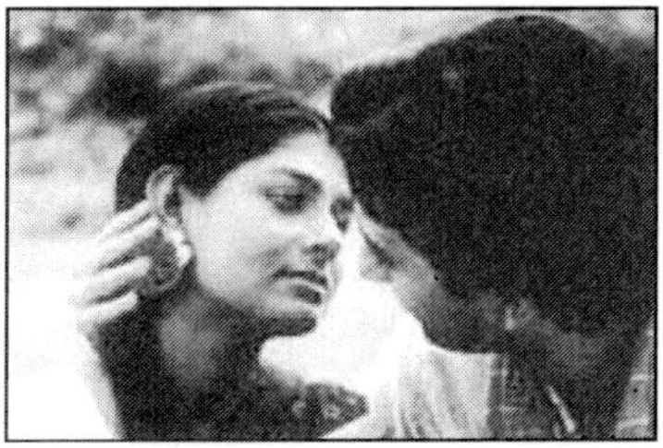

Shanta and Hassan

not show too many intimate scenes, the love triangle and the revenge motif – staples of mainstream commercial productions – also make their presence felt in the film. The integration of several art forms – singing, dancing, and music – also a trait of the "Bollywood style" – is witnessed, especially in the scene where ayah rides with Masseur on his bicycle. Here the extended use of a song to replace dialogue (the lyrics to the songs in *Earth* were written by Javed Akhtar, one of India's most prominent lyricists/poets) gave the sequence a particularly romantic feel. The music provided by A.R. Rahman was also fascinating. So Mehta's film can be called a crossover production, catering at the same time to the global and the local.

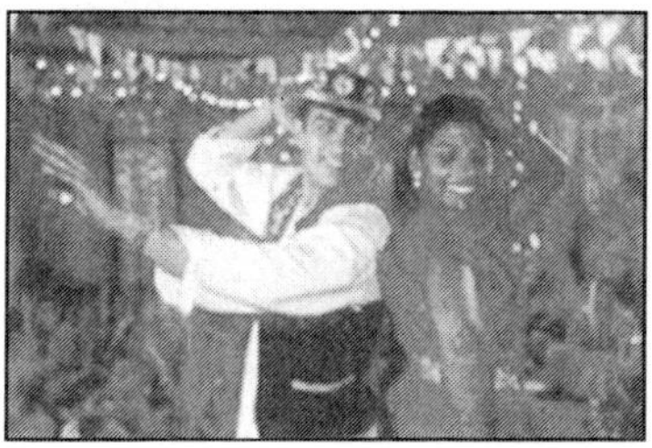

Framing festivity

The reception of the film has been more or less positive. While most critics have praised the wonderful performance that Deepa extracted from her actors, C.J.S. Wallia criticised the movie downright stating that Mehta's rendering of the horrendous tragedy of the partition of India is "a simplistic treatment of a complex history."[7] He also states:

> Mehta manages to distort the complex history of the partition and in the process depicts the role of the Hindus and Sikhs falsely and negatively. The film's weak storyline, its limiting viewpoint, its poorly developed characters, and the distorted roles of the different Indian religious communities and the British produce a dismal picture of the complex background-events of the partition....Mehta's film viciously distorts the historical role of the Sikhs in the freedom struggle and during the partition of India to convey the strong impression that they initiated the riots.

The Director's Reaction

When Richard Phillips asked Mehta about some background to *Earth,* why she made the film and why there have been so few films made by western filmmakers about the partition of India, Mehta's reply was candid:

> The partition of India was like a Holocaust for us and I grew up hearing many stories about this terrible event. Naturally I was attracted to the subject. I have my own theory about why there has been such a silence about this tragedy by western filmmakers, and it is just a theory. I think it is bound up with a number of attitudes that prevail in the western countries about India....There is firstly the spiritual India – a place where you can go and find nirvana. Secondly, there is the conception that India is entirely poverty-stricken, with a permanent kind of begging bowl attitude. There is India of the Maharajas, princes and queens, and the India that comes from nostalgia for the Raj. And there is always the prevailing pressure that people should feel superior to some other place: look how bad India is with all the beggars, aren't we lucky to be better off.
>
> It is uncomfortable and difficult for some filmmakers to produce works that destroy these perceptions. India brings specifically

> fixed images in many western minds, and the minute you start de-exoticising that, you have to deal with Indians as real people, and there is pressure not to do that.[8]

On how the film *Earth* came about, Deepa Mehta explains to another interviewer how she became fascinated with Sidhwa's book:

> I was hooked. The tumultuous period surrounding the British division of India into two separate countries, Independent India and a newly created Pakistan, had always held a sort of dark fascination for me. India, after years of struggle, finally gained its Independence from the British Empire in August of 1947. However, for most Indians, that 'Independence' is synonymous with its 'Division' or 'Partition', as it is known on the sub-continent. The announcement made by Viceroy Mountbatten, declaring the boundaries which would divide India into two, began a sectarian strife that would wreak havoc for the next fifty years.
>
> My father and his family were some of the eleven million people that were uprooted from their homes during Partition. I grew up hearing stories about... the carnage, the rapes and the mindless acts of violence that people who had lived together in relative harmony for centuries, committed against each other – all in the name of religion and nationalism.[9]

Deepa also added that Bapsi's *Cracking India* was a highly personal account of the Partition as seen through the eyes of an eight-year-old girl living in Lahore during that crucial time. What made it totally fascinating for her, was that Lenny, the protagonist, belonged to the minority sect of Parsis who had remained neutral and non-aligned, while the Hindus, Muslims and Sikhs single-mindedly massacred each other. Lenny's was an entirely unique perspective. It

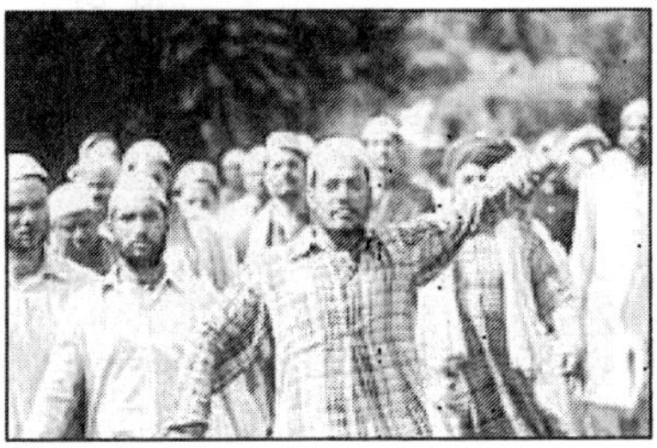

Blood thirsty mob

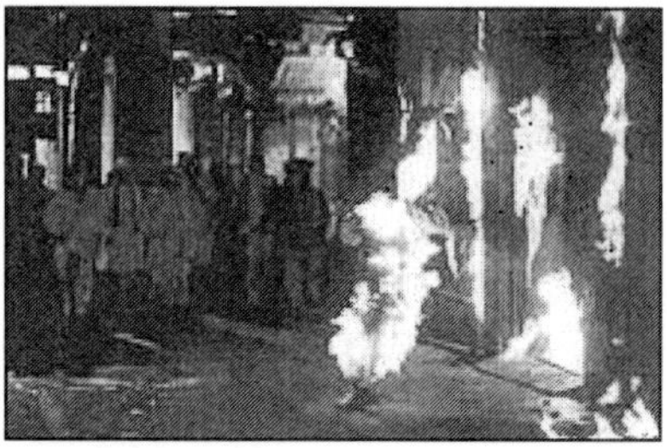

All ablaze

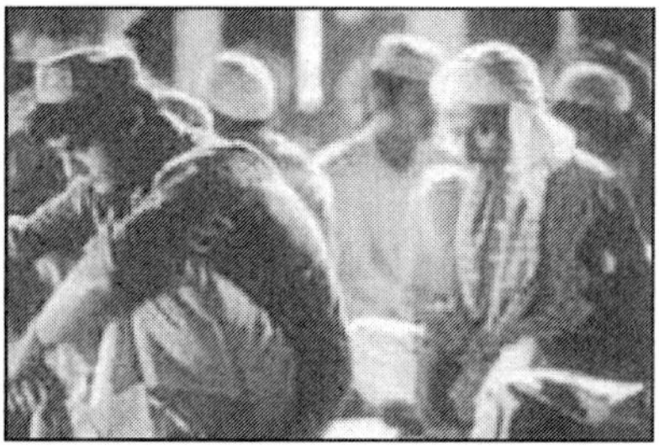

Waiting for the ghost train

came from within an impartial community, but was also the point of view of a child, who learnt about love, war, destruction and betrayal within a span of a few months.

Bapsi Sidhwa's novel is written in English, and although she wrote the screenplay in English as well, Mehta decided to make the film in Hindi titled *Earth*. "Most of the characters in *Earth* are working class people and the thought of them speaking English in 1947 felt ludicrous, though some relevant scenes remain in English." Mehta also adds that she was lucky that Bapsi understood her position that a book and a film are different mediums. She also reiterated the fact that her film is a direct statement against nationalism and separatism, not just in India, but everywhere. To Maya Churi she confides:

> The enemy really divided and ruled and then left. There is no nostalgia for British Raj in this film. The reason I wanted to do a film about the partition of India into India and Pakistan was that also it is an exploration about what happens with sectarian war whether its Rwanda or Kosovo or which ever country has been colonized and where the colonizers left, the way the French left Vietnam, they've always left a country that's divided. 52 years later, for us, we are still struggling with the same boundary issues. As in Ireland or Kosovo.[10]

At the question and answer session after the screening of *Earth* in Melbourne, Deepa also rejected the idea when someone made a comment that Muslims and Hindus had their own homeland, why should not the Sikhs. She categorically stated:

> The issue of separation comes down to a socio-economic platform where religious fervour is used, or misused, by politicians for their own ends. Today it is basically the dollar that drives the demands for separation. The British first perfected it through the method of divide and rule...Film is a powerful medium and my hope is that *Earth* will produce a dialogue and force people to think more deeply about the cost of such divisions. If people want to separate they should understand what it would really mean. I know that there will be some dialogue or some debate. I hope that *Earth* will put this into perspective. I think I have made a film that shows the futility of sectarian war, a film that is anti-war.[11]

Towards the end of the same interview Deepa also declared that the film was also "a period of self-expression" for her. It was not just a question of making an anti-war film, but a constant challenge.

The Author's Reaction

The response of writers to the adaptation of their work into film have varied from person to person and have ranged from total rejection to full support. So we get writers like Ernest Hemingway who sold the maximum number of stories to Hollywood producers and yet clearly stated that the only way to interact with them was to drive up to the California state line – "you throw them the book, they throw you the money, and then turn and drive back fast the way you came." This was his tacit way of stating that after he sold his book, he was not bothered with what the director did to it. On the other hand we also have writers like Bernard Shaw who was spellbound with the infinite possibilities that the cinema could afford and who also stayed in the sets to watch how his plays were adapted.

In the case of Bapsi Sidhwa, we find the writer herself appearing in person in the last scene of the film from which it can be assumed that she has full support of Deepa's production. She told an interviewer how in Hollywood, as soon as a book is optioned, they don't allow the author near the sets. But here, Deepa wanted her participation throughout the making of the film. In part, this was because there was so much Parsi culture in it. She did not interfere too much because "it was Deepa's vision." In a very humble way Sidhwa also stated that she accepted Deepa's generosity in having her around the sets. "I did have a part in the film though."

Though she agreed that the film stood on its own strength, Sidhwa only wished that Deepa had "retained the original title. It would have helped the book."[12] They tried "Cracking the Earth," but it sounded like a documentary by a farmer. Eventually Mehta chose "Earth," and in India, "Earth–1947." When Julie Rajan further asked her how Deepa decided to make her novel into a film, the author explained in details:

> I got a call from Deepa Mehta one morning. She was very excited having just read *Cracking India* and said she had been searching for me. Deepa loved the book and talked about it for a long time. She asked if she could make the film. She is also from Punjab; when we talked, I felt that she understood every nuance of the novel. She understood what was very important – the importance of the Parsi child and her passionate perspective. I told her to go ahead and make the film, and she said, "But what if somebody else calls you tomorrow and offers you more?" I said, "Look, nobody's offered me anything in four years. I don't think anybody's going to call me tomorrow." I think she was carried away by the book, and, in the heat of that, wrote the script even before the contract was signed – this is exactly how I wanted it to be: that she should love the book enough.[13]

Again, Sidhwa has also been very forthcoming about the changes made to her story and she candidly explained to her interviewer:

> The movie stands on its own. But it has the voice of the child and it has the spirit of the book – it has objectivity and it has the story. A movie is only a two-hour affair. A book is spread over a wide expanse of time. Deepa had to get rid of many incidents and characters. I hated the fact that every time I saw the script it was shorter. Then when the film was made, scenes were thrown out until something that seemed very bare to me was left. I realize now that the film works so excellently because of the cuts.

Asked whether the movie would do justice to her overall purpose for the novel, Sidhwa replied in the affirmative. She understood that the screen exerts its own dramatic demands and that the film had to end the way it did otherwise the impact would have been weakened. She was aware that the movie has a totally different audience, a different way of seeing things. But the film widens the audience for the original story. The purpose for writing the story is to reach an audience, so through the film, that goal was further achieved. "This wider *Earth* audience may, in turn, learn from the historical tale told in *Cracking India*."[14]

In a much later controversy that cropped up with the filming of Deepa's last film in the trilogy, *Water*, Bapsi Sidhwa not only wrote a novel based on the script but also sent a letter to *Hindustan Times* defending Mehta against the virulent attacks of the Hindu extremist organisations seeking to prevent the production in India of the said film. A copy of the same letter that she also provided for publication on the *World Socialist Web* site reveals how Sidhwa gave a lot of moral support to Mehta and stated that she was being punished for deflating the egos of some people. Praising her for her professionalism and her commitment to her art, she pointed out how Deepa was caught up in a grotesque Kafkaesque landscape only trying to make a film which was a love story beset by the kind of injustices and misunderstandings that hound the path of true love in the time-honoured tradition of tragic storytelling. In the same statement she reiterated her stand on the earlier film adaptation:

> I wish to make myself clear on another score, as well. I love *Earth,* the film adaptation of my book *Ice-Candy-Man.* Novels are notoriously difficult to adapt to the screen, and this was perhaps the most difficult of my novels to make into a film. The task would have daunted a lesser filmmaker, or one less courageous. Deepa had to jettison many characters and subplots to give shape to her cinematic vision of my book and fit it into a two and a half hour movie. But the film stands firmly on its own, as a work of art, apart from the book. It has its own intrinsic integrity and logic.[15]

Though it can be argued that a cinematic adaptation of any work of fiction at least helps the less perceptive reader/viewer to understand and appreciate that particular work of art or *oeuvre* of the novelist better, it would be appropriate to conclude the eternal debate of adaptation by quoting from Joy Gould Boyum once again:

> In assessing an adaptation, we are never really comparing book with film, but an interpretation with an interpretation – the novel that we ourselves have recreated in our imaginations, out of which we have constructed our own individualized 'movie', and the novel on which the filmmaker has worked a parallel transformation. For just as we are readers, so implicitly is the filmmaker, offering us, through his work, *his* perceptions, *his* visions, *his* particular insight into his source. An adaptation is always, whatever else it may be, an interpretation. (61-62)

Thus Both Sidhwa's and Mehta's interpretations of the Partition remain equally engrossing.

Notes

1. Bapsi Sidhwa, *Ice-Candy-Man.* (London: Heinemann, 1988); republished as *Cracking India.* (Minneapolis: Milkweed, 1991). The recent edition of the book published by Penguin India has the title *Ice-Candy-Man* on the cover and as a subtitle which reads, "now filmed as 1947 – a major motion picture by Deepa Mehta." A black and white picture of a distraught looking Aamir Khan as Ice-candy-man also features on the cover, thereby lending some sort of authenticity to the cinematic adaptation.
2. Aamer Hussein, "Bapsi Sidhwa, Storyteller." Introduction. *The Bapsi Sidhwa Omnibus.* (New Delhi: Oxford University Press, 2001).
3. Ralph Crane, "A Passion for History and For Truth Telling: The Early Novels of Bapsi Sidhwa." www.bapsidhwa.com
4. Maya Churi, "Deepa Mehta's Elements, from "Earth" and Beyond." Interview.
   http://www.indieware.com/people/int_Mehta_Deepa_990914.html
5. Joy Gould Boyum. *Double Exposure: Fiction into Film.* (Calcutta: Seagull Books, 1989).
6. In a Rediff On The Net interview, 3 June, 1998, Aamir Khan tells Alpana Chaudhary that he liked his role in the film very much:

   "It has amazing graph, that of the transformation of an innocent, lowly but charming rogue faced with the atrocities of partition. Being an average human being, he is shaken to his roots and loses all control over his actions....I have a dialogue that gives you an insight into his behaviour and which goes something like this, 'It's nor a question of Hindu, Muslim or Sikh. All of us are like caged beasts waiting for the cage to open. And when that happens only God is the *Maalik!*" It's not a role you interpret in absolute black and white terms."

7. C.J.S. Wallia in *India Star Review of Books*. www.indiastar.com/wallia22.html
8. "If people want to separate they should understand what it would really mean." Interview by Richard Phillips, 6 August, 1999. http://www.wsws.org/articles/1999/aug/1999/meh-a06_prn.shtml
9. Deepa Mehta's Earth. http://www.filmeducation.org/secondary/Earth/index.html.
10. Interview by Maya Churi.
11. Interview by Richard Phillips.
12. "We don't need to carry on with the Partition any longer." Interview in *Mumbai Mirror*, 10 October, 2005:10.
13. Julie Rajan, "Cracking Sidhwa." http://www.monsoonmag.com/interviews/i3inter_sidhwa.html
14. *Ibid.*
15. *Ibid.*
16. Bapsi Sidhwa, "They are punishing Deepa for deflating their egos." 19 May, 2000. www.wsws.org.

12

Wounded India in Deepa Mehta's *1947–Earth*

Neelam Raisinghani

Deepa Mehta's *Earth* is a painful and horrifying tale of the partition of India and its aftermath. Its technical accomplishments alone make it worthy of attention: an economic and imaginative use of colours, sound, sophisticated cross-cutting, editing and graphic compositions which are sometimes as detailed and evocative as paintings. Because of these accomplishments *Earth* will probably always appeal to the audiences of different generations and from many countries. But for the purpose of this paper, Mehta's film is most intriguing as a reflection of the turbulence in Indian society in the forties. Whether consciously made or not, the film seems to work as a mirror image of the rise of communal frenzy, hatred and violence in India, but in reflecting that rise the film may be most important as an attempt to expose it to the Indian audience that was so involved in this frenzy.

The film has at its heart the year 1947 when India was decolonised, accompanied by its partition into two countries – a Hindu and Sikh dominated India and a Muslim controlled Pakistan. What made this Partition and independence a singular event was the large scale ethnic violence and mass migration that accompanied it. In the nine months between August 1947 and the spring of the following year, by unofficial counts, at least 18 million people – Hindus, Sikhs and

Muslims – were forced to flee their homes and become refugees; at least a million were killed in ethnic violence. Another feature of this violence was the large scale abduction of over 1,20,000 women by men of the other community. Despite the scale and nature of violence involved in this partition, making it one of the most violent events in the history of nation-formation, and indeed the world's biggest mass migration, very little attention has been paid to the critical impact of this violence and mass migration on Indian minds. Unmemorialised institutionally, the collective memory and social effects of the 1947 violence and migration can be apprehended in the literature and films that inhabit the public sphere. In particular, the film illuminates the contours of the complex relationships amongst rhetorics of ethnicity, masculinity and femininity in nationalist ethnic violence.

During partition religious fanaticism played a major role in driving people apart. But unfortunately none of the communities saw any positive results that they thought that partition would bring to them. Communal violence which shook the very foundations of the Indian society is resurrected through memory in Deepa Mehta's film *Earth*. Derrida in his essay "Theatre of Cruelty", Ann Kaplan in her essay "Can Cinema Mark Trauma" and Gyanendra Pandey in his recent work *Remembering Partition: Violence, Nationalism and History in India* have all commented on the unrepresentability of violence. But Jasbir Jain in her *Reading Partition/Living Partition* argues that though it is true that violence cannot be represented as such, "literature goes beyond the empirical reality, beyond treaties and wars and probes the silence of the human mind" (4). Many creative writers and cinematographers have depicted the partition of India and the associated bloody riots in *Garam Hawa, Hey Ram, Gadar Ek Prem Katha, Khamosh Pani, Pinjar, Train to Pakistan, Tamas, Midnight's Children, Ice-Candy-Man* and *Azadi*. These depictions relate to the massacres, ghost trains, conversions, ruined economies, wagon loads of corpses and no established experienced system of Governments. To move to the contested site at once, here is the opening section of the archetypal partition novel *Train to Pakistan* (1956), by Khushwant Singh.

> The summer of 1947 was not like other Indian summers. Even the weather had a different feel in India that year... There was no rain. People began to say that God was punishing them for their sins.

> Some of them had good reason to feel that they had sinned. The summer before, communal riots, precipitated by reports of the proposed division of the country into a Hindu India and a Muslim Pakistan had broken out in Calcutta, and within a few months the death roll had mounted to several thousand. Muslims said the Hindus had planned and started the killing. According to the Hindus, the Muslims were to blame. The fact is, both sides killed. Both shot and stabbed and speared and clubbed. Both tortured. Both raped. From Calcutta, the riots spread north and east and west: to Noakhali in East Bengal where Muslims massacred Hindus, to Bihar where Hindus massacred Muslims. Mullahs roamed the Punjab and The Frontier Province with boxes of human skulls said to be those of Muslims killed in Bihar. Hundreds of thousand of Hindus and Sikhs who had lived for centuries on the Northwest Frontier abandoned their houses and fled toward the protection of the predominantly Sikh and Hindu communities in the east. They travelled on foot, in bullock carts, crammed into lorries, clinging to the sides and roofs of the trains. Along the way at fords, at crossroads, at railroad stations – they collided with panicky swarms of Muslims fleeing to safety in the west. The riots had become a rout. By the summer of 1947, when the creation of the new state of Pakistan was formally announced, ten million people – Muslims and Hindus and Sikhs – were in flight. By the time the monsoon broke almost a million of them were dead, and all of northern India was in arms, in terror or in hiding. (9-10)

And here is a description of Hindu women being paraded naked through the streets of Narowal (Sialkot), from the 1977 Sahitya Academy Award winning novel *Azadi* by Chaman Nahal:

> They were all stark naked. Their heads were completely shaven, so were their armpits. So were their pubic regions... They were all crying, though their eyes shed no tears. Their faces were formed into grimaces and they were all sobbing. Their arms were free, but so badly had they been used, so wholly their spirits crushed, their morals shattered, none of them made any attempt to cover themselves with their hands. (296)

And this one is from *Ice-Candy-Man* (1989) by Bapsi Sidhwa; thirty two years after *Train to Pakistan* and forty one years after partition:

> A train from Gurdaspur has just come in. Everyone in it is dead. Butchered. They are all Muslims. There are no young women among the dead ! Only two gunny bags full of women's breasts. (149)

The changing nature of India's partition history comes through, especially when turning to the most recent works concerning the memories and experiences of witnesses and their narratives and being produced by scholars situated (or schooled within) western institutions of learning or as part of the globalisation of academic discourse emerging with Subaltern Studies Project, where interests revolve around witnessing trauma, subjectivity and history.

Bapsi Sidhwa situated in USA wrote her novel *Ice-Candy-Man*, on which Deepa Mehta, situated in Canada based her film *1947–Earth*. She portrays the abhorrent reality of violence. Mehta conceived of her film in dramatic terms placing domestic settings and familial images within the larger social and political systems that are exposed in the narrative as corrupt and repressive. History and memory have been used to facilitate a more complex reading of the film that represents intense human sufferings within the framework of a love story or personal drama. The narrative framing of the film inscribes the function of an impressionistic history based on personal experience, rumours and gossip put together through the agency of an eight year old crippled girl. Lenny is neither Hindu nor Sikh nor Muslim but one of the neutral Parsis. She makes an ideal choice to be cast in the role of a narrator both professedly neutral and objective. Her child-like innocence combines with the non-political viewpoint of her religious background. Moreover she stands in as a symbol for the truncated India trapped in its violence.

In the opening scene the theme of the film is introduced as Lenny smashes a plate on the floor and asks her puzzled mother "Can you break a country?" Although her mother tries to allay her fears and tells her to ignore the rumours, the film goes on to show exactly how the cracks have started appearing. We can identify many key scenes in the film that work to strengthen her fears. Most of the film takes place before the violence explodes in the region, but the ominous signs of the approaching violence are audible. Turning to the scene of Lenny's parents' dinner party near the very beginning of the film, one's attention is drawn to the intriguing camera work – the way it roves around the room – and also to the many racial comments and the positioning of the neutral Parsis between warring sides in this case Mr. Singh and the English Inspector General of Police, Mr. Rogers. The camera does not fix on any individual until the conflict ensues. Its constant movement provokes an anxiety and ruptures the simple composition of the scene. The point of fixity (when a real argument breaks the light banter) aligns with the moment when each individual character is finally framed by the camera and labelled with a particular stereotype. Mr. Singh becomes the militant Sikh while Mr. Rogers becomes the imposing and treacherous white man. The Sethnas prefer to remain invisible and call themselves chameleons.

Another scene which if viewed superficially gives the illusion of an idyllic situation but it has deep connotations of the approaching storm. Lenny's nurse Shanta daily meets her admirers either in the Queen's Garden or the *dhaba*. Each of her friends represents a different religion. Their everyday jokes and games are replaced by bickerings and harsh remarks over religious and family bloodlines. The differences, once unimportant to friendship, end up dividing the friends as they are shaken out of their familiar moorings. The group of friends obviously represents microcosms of India's ethnic mix and Shanta can be seen as the surface harmony imposed by British rule. Their overt Hindu, Muslim and Sikh biases are clearly visible. Partition further aggravates these biases. Almost overnight the landscape of Lahore is fragmented into religious enclaves. "People shrink dwindling into symbols of religion". They are divided into Hindus, Sikhs, Muslims and Parsis. The debates about the fate of India and Pakistan including a litany of stereotypical fearful opinions and hateful feelings become more and more heated. Leaders of the religious and ethnic groups begin jockeying for positions within the new order being established by the departing British authorities.

There are then a number of double images or double reflections in the film that seem to muddle the question about a society in crisis. Where does the crisis originate? Where is the order and where is the disorder? Which is the nightmarish dream and which is the reality? This double image and the questions it provokes are most apparent in the claims made by the politicians and the communal violence that picks up steam with independence acclaimed as a great day by the politicians. One particularly noted moment, the midnight hour of

August 14-15, sees the film's characters listening to a radio broadcast by Pandit Nehru who declares "At the stroke of the midnight hour, when the world sleeps, India will wake to life and freedom" (138). These hopes appear to be meaningless in the face of the dislocation. Hari feels "Independence from the British will be soaked in our brothers' blood" (138).

The earlier period of colourful kites flying from rooftops fades and gives way to the ghastly nights of frenzy-stricken, bloodthirsty mobs seeking vengeance. A Muslim man is drawn and quartered apart by a pair of police vehicles; and Hindu tenements are set aflame by gasoline dosing fire trucks. The people watch Sikhs slaughtering Muslims, Hindus butchering Muslims and Muslims burning Hindus alive, helplessly. The savagery is thrust into Lenny's idyllic world. The massacre sets into motion events that turn her world upside down. Though Shanta attempts to shield her young charge from this communal violence, but by now all innocence has been shattered. Traumatised Lenny repeats the horrific scene symbolically at home by ripping apart her rag doll.

Rising tensions are inflamed with reports of murder, rape and rioting mobs wrecking homes, shops, temples and mosques. Communal frenzy and hatred are further provoked by the arrival of the train at the station in Lahore. The train, as modern machinery and transporter of death, arrives and the sounds of screaming witnesses to the travesty overwhelm the background music. From the bodies piled up and aesthetically arranged in the train, to the use of colour and lighting that draw the eye's attention to the bodies' surfaces, and once again the insertion of a dramatic score with a pulsing beat, where the train and its impending arrival signal horror and the "path towards certain death" for its passengers.

The majority of the population in Lahore is Muslim but most of the businesses are owned by Hindus, so each group initially has reason to hope that Lahore will end up in the country most favourable to their own interests. When it becomes evident that Lahore will be part of Pakistan most of the Hindus and Sikhs pick up and leave. Those that decide to stay behind soon find themselves in great jeopardy. The only alternative to flight or death for the Hindus and Sikhs is quick conversion. Fear compels Hari to convert to Islam, and the sweeper's daughter Pappoo is married off to an elderly midget and her family converts to Christianity.

The once charming Ice-candy-man, vying for ayah's affection, is inexorably drawn into the communal rhetoric and hatred. The loss of his sister and the trainload of the dead drag him to the lowest possible stage of human life. He admits: "Hindu, Musalman or Sikh, we are all bastards. All beasts, like that caged lion which scares Lenny Baby lying in wait for the cage to open" (136). Lenny in the end asks him "Who's guarding the lion"? He replies "Nobody" (136). This is symbolic how no one has any control over the bloodshed and communal frenzy.

Within recent partition historiography, particularly those works that focus on the abduction and rape of women – the very drama around which *Earth* revolves – finds a moment of its dramatic climax. There is an attempt to reveal how women's bodies can be made the contested ground, the very territory upon which notions of subjectivity and communal frenzy are constructed during such turbulent times. Mehta has depicted how women are constructed as signs and symbols of the nation or ethnic/cultural community in nationalism. Their bodies have been shown to bear the symbolic burden of signifying culture and tradition, community and nation. She strives to bring women's issues of the subcontinent into public discussion.

Lahore, a border city of Pakistan, was promptly flooded by hundreds and thousands of refugees. Many thousands of these were victims of rape and torture, with nowhere to go and no hope of restoration to respectability. These 'fallen' women were sent to rehabilitation camps. Victory was celebrated on a woman's body; vengeance was taken on a woman's body. Mehta recalls the chilling shrieks and moans of recovered women and draws out the most damaging effect of the Partition, the symbolic desecration of women on both sides of the conflict. In this dark narrative of the cross-religious abductions of women, their pain is evident in these lines by Amrita Pritam:

> Today I call Waris Shah
> To speak out from the grave
> And open afresh a new page
> From the book of love.
> A daughter of Punjab
> Had wept once
> And he wrote a million dirges

Today a million daughters weep
And look up to you Waris Shah
Rise ! O narrator of the grieving; rise I look at your Punjab Today.

("Aj Akhan Waris Shah Noo")

Earth is the story of thousands of hapless women who were caught in the rapacious battle between the two ethnic communities. Rape and sexual violence have been invisible issues. They are often dismissed as private acts, the ignoble conduct of perverts and regrettable excesses of communal violence. Recent analyses, however, have focussed attention on the fact that far from being an isolated act, rape and sexual violence have often been used as strategic weapons of war.

The partition of India points to this fact that sexual violence was a central instrument of terror especially in campaigns that involved ethnic fratricide or nationalistic orthodoxies. In addition rape and violence have been used to assert dominance over ethnic enemies. Since women's sexuality is seen being under the protection of the men of the community, its defilement was an act of domination asserting power over the males of the other community or group that was under attack. Sexual aggression has long been regarded as an act of domination in anthropological literature. Susan Brownmiller's *Against Our Wills* chronicles in detail the use of rape as an act of domination since pre-historic times – not only domination against women but also against the men who are expected to protect them.

In the film, Mehta has made an attempt to reveal that Shanta's body becomes the contested ground, upon which notions of subjectivity, agency and national prejudices are constructed during the times of ethnic violence. Shanta's sensitive lover Hassan, the only voice of reason, is not allowed to sustain a fragile relationship between a Muslim and a Hindu. He is butchered by fanatic Muslims and Shanta becomes a token of Hinduism for her erstwhile Muslim admirers and friends. She is raped in retaliation for the trainloads of dead Muslims and bags full of the breasts of Muslim women cut off by Hindu men. She is abducted by Muslim hoodlums and the Ice-candy-man pushes her into the profession of prostitution.

Rape and sexual violence are also used in ethnic wars to pollute and defile the other side. Violation of chastity is an aspect that has been recorded in modern wars where racial and ethnic purity are valued. In describing violence against women in ethnic conflict – during the Partition in India – Kamala Bhasin and Ritu Menon argue, "economic factors though important cannot sufficiently account for the brutality... part of the explanation lies in cultural, psychological factors and in the abiding nature of prejudice"(39). Communities, have a historical memory of warring with each other and their enactment of this violence makes it central to the definition of self and community. In fact Benedict Anderson in studying nationalist myths comes to the conclusion that the history of violence and suffering and its memory bond communities together more than the positive, non-violent acts of nationalist history.

Bapsi Sidhwa's novel focuses on and elaborates upon the question of raped women and their future lives. She does it through the Muslim women of Pir Pindo. These women are forced to gather together in a house and, in case of attack, burn themselves alive rather than taint their family honour. Those who survive live with a sense of guilt for a long time. This survivor's guilt paralyses them and they look like skeletons. Shanta suffers from this guilt after she is discovered by her Parsi benefactor in a brothel. The ethical issues related to the whole idea of the recovery of abducted women and the reluctance of their original families to accept them back, are presented and debated in Sidhwa's novel, but this aspect is not the concern of Mehta's film.

Another strength of the novel comes through in its recognition of 'plain economics' as one of the originary impulses in partition violence, but it is lacking in the film. Material greed of erstwhile neighbours and the compulsion of refugees to earmark a property or house as prospective shelter, the logistics of the attack and the information network, the planning and the loot and the whole refugee mindset of vengeance are there in the novel. The perception of material gains to be had played a major motivating role in partition violence. The bare fact is that the violence, very often, was directed against enemy property rather than the body of the enemy, and the body as the custodian of that property – material or human (women and children) – becomes the target.

However, the film is silent about certain concerns, which leave a gap in the partition film. These concerns have been eloquently and competently documented by Urvashi Butalia in her *The Other Side of Silence*. Butalia's feminist credentials make her work raise the woman question of 'honour', which reveals the inability of the film to engage and probe the gaps and silences of official history, the silent complicity of those who did not actually kill, the almost racial nature of the pogrom, the comparison with the Holocaust, the placing of partition violence in a global perspective, and above all its continuity with violence in independent India.

The recent reservation and anti-reservation movements by Gujjars and Meenas in Rajasthan prove Butalia's assertion that there is a definite continuity between partition and the recurrence of the communal violence in post-1947 India. Although Amitav Ghosh does not fit into the definition of the partition novelist, but his reference to the communal violence in 1964, over the disappearance of the Prophet's sacred hair from Hazratbal in *The Shadow Lines*, talks of this silence:

> Every word I write about those events of 1964 is the product of a struggle with silence. It is a struggle I am destined to lose – have already lost – for even after all these years, I do not know where within me, in which corner of my world this silence lies... It is not the silence of an imperfect memory. Nor is it a silence enforced by a ruthless state... this silence must win, must inevitably defeat me, because it is not a presence at all; it is simply a gap, a hole, an emptiness in which there are no words. (218)

Urvashi Butalia apropos partition violence remarks:

> I began to understand gradually, that the silences of partition are of many kinds. If, at one level, we are faced with a kind of historical silence, at another this is compounded by a familial silence, in which families have colluded in hiding their own histories, sometimes actively, sometimes simply through indifference... for many people there was also a sense of resignation. (358-59)

The film simply refuses to grow up and its tendency to luxuriate in dark descriptions of savagery and melodrama leaves it hamstrung when it comes to dealing with the profound psychosocial and moral issues that lie beyond the romance and carnage. An insight into human behaviour is almost absent from the film *Earth*.

But one is astounded by the caressing fluidity of the camerawork; the uncommon beauty of cosmopolitans, especially indoors, where the muted earth or glowing yellow colours of the décor and the warm household scenes and a brownish amber to catch the vast beauty of the countryside are shown in sharp contrast with reds and purples to express the blood-curdling scenes of Lahore under siege. Violent scenes are either shockingly graphic or horrifyingly suggestive like the inert leg of a Muslim peeking from the corner of camera after he is ripped apart by two jeeps. It is noteworthy for exploring in detail the destruction of innocence and the arbitrary splitting up of the earth, and how people get caught up in the emotional frenzy of hatred and how difficult it is to hear the voice of reason.

If *Earth* is, then, like other Indian films an indirect reflection of an Indian society in communal crisis, a maddening society where friends become enemies and are seen prepared to kill each other, it is also more than a simple reflection. Combining melodrama with trauma, it makes nightmares real and reality a nightmare in a manner far more disturbing than most other Indian movies of the time. Perhaps this is why the Pakistani authorities refused to allow Mehta to film *Earth* in Lahore and banned it in Pakistan and it was significantly censored in India also, because its political sensitivity exposes the ugly scars of a wounded India.

References

Anderson, Benedict. *Imagined Communities: Reflections on the Origins and Spread of Nationalism*. New York and London: Verso, 1983.

Bhasin, Kamala and Ritu Menon. *Borders and Boundaries: Women in India's Partition*. Delhi: OUP, 1993.

Butalia, Urvashi. *The Other Side of Silence: Voices from the Partition of India*. Delhi: Penguin Books, 1998.

Corrigon, Timothy. *A Short Guide to Writing About Film*. New York: Harper Collins College Publishers, 1994.

Derrida, Jacques. "The Theatre of Cruelty and the Closure of Representation", *Writing and Difference*. Translated by Alan Bass. London: Routledge and Kegan Paul, 1978.

Ghosh, Amitav. *The Shadow Lines*. Delhi: OUP, 1995.

Hassan, Mushirul. *India Partitioned: The Other Face of Freedom*. 2 vols. (1995) Delhi: Roli Books. Enlarged edition 1997.

Jain, Jasbir. *Reading Partition/Living Partition*. Jaipur: Rawat Publications, 2006.

Kaplan, Ann. "Can Cinema Mark Trauma", paper presented as part of the Joan Carlisle-Irwing Lecture Series. Vancouver: University of Columbia, 2001.

Mehta, Deepa, dir. *1947–Earth*. (Film based on Bapsi Sidhwa's novel *Ice-Candy-Man*) Producer David Hamilton, Perf. Aamir Khan, Nandita Das, Rahul Khanna, Maia Sethna, Kitu Gidwani.

Nahal, Chaman. *Azadi*. Delhi: Arnold Heinemann, 1975.

Pandey, Gyanendra. *Remembering Partition: Violence, Nationalism and History in India*. Cambridge: Cambridge University Press, 2001.

Pritam, Amrita. "Aj Akhan Waris Shah Noo", *Ek Muthi Akshar*. Delhi: Hind Pocket Books, 1994.

Sahni, Bhisham. *Tamas*. English translation New Delhi: Penguin Books, 2001.

Sidhwa, Bapsi. *Ice-Candy-Man*. New Delhi: Penguin, 1989.

Singh, Khushwant. *Train to Pakistan*. Delhi: Orient Longman, 1956.

13

Readings, Misreadings and Fundamentalist Readings

Reflections on the Making of Deepa Mehta's *Water*

Uma Mahadevan

The story of the making of Deepa Mehta's *Water* has been one of multiple displacements of time and space. The film was originally planned to be made in India in 1999, but after some religious fundamentalists in Varanasi protested against its making, destroying the sets and threatening more violence, the project was shelved. *Water* was eventually filmed in Sri Lanka four years later. Based on the shooting script itself, during the attempt to film in India, Mehta had been accused of having plagiarised her plot from Bengali novelist Sunil Gangopadhyay's novel *Sei Samay*, translated into English as *Those Days*. The plagiarism charge was immediately appropriated by some religious extremists as a supposedly valid reason to pre-censor the film; meanwhile, the plagiarism case itself was finally settled out of court (Indrani Roy Mitra, Rediff, 2005). *Water* has now been made in Hindi, with English subtitles, with financial support from the Canadian government. After its resounding commercial success in North America, the film was submitted as Canada's official entry for the 2007 Academy Awards under the category of Best Foreign Film. At the time when this paper was being presented, the final winner was yet to be announced; paradoxically, the film had its limited release in India even later, in March 2007. In every way, *Water* appears to be a success of Canadian multiculturalism.

Not only the creative process but also the personal journeys of the film's maker and the writer who later novelised the film, have involved displacements. Mehta is an Indian-born filmmaker now based in Canada; Bapsi Sidhwa is Parsi, of Pakistani origin, now based in the US. Mehta's second film in the Elements trilogy, *1947–Earth*, based on Sidhwa's novel *Ice-Candy-Man*, was originally planned to be filmed in Lahore, where the story was set; but for want of permission from the authorities, the film had to be made in Delhi. Following their successful collaboration on *1947–Earth*, Sidhwa was asked to produce a novel based on the film *Water*. According to Sidhwa, she was given a period of three months for the novelisation, to time it with the release of the film in the US (Sidhwa 2006). The selection of Sidhwa for the novelisation is a curious decision, given the fact of the film's setting and plot. Nevertheless, as diasporic artists, based in and working from one place, setting their work elsewhere and filming in yet another location, inhabiting and being inhabited by the worlds in which they move, Mehta and Sidhwa occupy positions where it might be especially possible for them to trace connections between the First World and the Third, between the West and the East, between the magnified self-image of a nation and its complex realities. In reading their work, one may examine the extent to which they are able to do so.

There is a third text, a meta-narrative of sorts, that records the process of the film's making: and that is Devyani Saltzman's memoir *Shooting Water: A Mother-Daughter Journey and the Making of a Film*. Saltzman recounts how, after meeting Canadian filmmaker Paul Saltzman in Delhi, Deepa Mehta emigrated to Canada in 1973. The couple divorced some years later when their daughter Devyani was eleven years old. Asked to choose between her parents, Devyani chose to live with her father (Saltzman 4). This decision caused a rift between mother and daughter that would find resolution only during the filming of *Water*. In that sense, it is a way of coming of terms with personal history. An interesting and slightly odd back-story that I discovered while reading for this paper is that Devyani's grandfather, a Ukrainian Jew who emigrated to Canada and maintained an online journal until his death in his nineties recently, had expressed violent disagreement with his granddaughter's representation of his life story in her memoir. This was only discovered after his demise and the relevant paragraphs were then expunged from the online journal by his sons. The reason I bring this up is because it seems to me to be one more instance of the fraught nature of the creative journey, with progressive underminings of every telling, which creates a difficulty in terms of belief and raises questions about the nature of representation itself, about how we read, and about trust and responsibility.

Different texts appear within the film as well as the novel. Apart from the passages from the *Ramayana* that the priest recites to the widows, the line from the Gita that Kalyani quotes, and the story from the *Mahabharata* that Shakuntala reads to Chuyia in the novel, there are also snippets of Byron and Shakespeare that the colonial-educated young men quote to each other. We are shown different forms of "setting right the text" – in the novel, when Rabindra misquotes Byron, Narayan corrects him for accuracy; when Rabindra is taking liberties with a Schiller aria, Narayan stops him by putting his hand over his mouth – in effect, silencing him in a playful kind of censorship. When Shakuntala says, after Kalyani's death, that according to the sacred texts, all this is an illusion, maya, Narayan replies bluntly that Kalyani's death is no illusion, thereby questioning the given wisdom directly. Earlier this is shown to us literally when he scribbles a note to Kalyani, tearing out the title page of the volume of *Meghdutam* that he is reading: texts are repeatedly being questioned, revised, interpreted, and even literally having pages torn out of them. At the same time, poetry remains the vehicle for a powerful expression of emotion – as we see when Narayan quotes poetry to Kalyani – as well as the way to thought and understanding. Not surprisingly, it is Shakuntala, who can read and who is seen constantly reading the old texts, who discovers sustenance and strength from this process of thoughtful reading.

At this point, however, we must dwell on the opening and closing texts in the film itself. The opening text contains three verses from the *Laws of Manu* which are in the nature of injunctions to widows or women in general:

> A widow should be long suffering until death, self restrained and chaste.
> A virtuous wife who remains chaste when her husband has died goes to heaven.
> A woman who is unfaithful to her husband is reborn in the womb of a jackal.

The film closes with the following words:

> There are over 34 million widows in India according to the 2001 Census. Many continue to live in conditions of social, economic and cultural deprivation as prescribed 2000 years ago by the Sacred Texts of Manu.

Endings leave us at a certain point in the narrative and point to a message. Among other things, one effect of this ending is that it takes a narrative set in 1938 and fast-forwards it into the present day. The opening and closing texts frame the film narrative, compelling us to look at the plight of a small group of widows in one ashram in one small town in northern India as the situation of many of the "over 34 million widows" of the country. How many is many, we wonder; besides, there is no single code of conduct for widows in different parts of the country, and India is in any case not one monolithic entity. The ending also brings us up against the question of scale, as if India's sheer vastness compels its stories to be narrated on a vast scale, as if the individual story, the particular narrative, has no other way of encompassing it all.

The closing text also raises the important question of why the film is set in 1938 at all. The final scene on the railway platform, with the train pulling out – a familiar film convention – and Shakuntala's act of entrusting Chuyia to Gandhi's care, suggest that Gandhi's leadership will lead to freedom not only from British rule but also from the strictures of orthodox patriarchal religion. Since the closing text states that many of India's widows still live in similar conditions, we may wonder whether we are encouraged to critique the ways in which Gandhi and the Gandhian version of nationalism led the country, or whether is it a gratuitous use of Gandhi as an icon, appearing almost as a *deus ex machina* at the railway station to create an optimistic and acceptably uplifting ending for the film by replacing colonial patriarchy with another kind of patriarchy based on nationalism. Not least of all, because Gandhi's words themselves have already appeared earlier in the film as lines repeated by Gulabi the eunuch to Madhumati, almost as gnomic utterances whose full meanings have not yet percolated to the ordinary people.

It is also relevant, with the film being set in 1938, less than a decade before the country was to become independent, to look at the film's portrayal of orthodox Hinduism vis à vis the British colonialists. "The British don't treat their widows as we do," says Narayan to Kalyani as they go on a buggy ride around the bright, sunlit and orderly façades of the British Cantonment, as opposed to what we have already seen as the dull, grimy interior of the ashram, the narrow lanes of the Indian quarter of the town, or the lamplit, exoticised temple scenes.

Without arguing for a moment that orthodox Hindu practices such as forced tonsuring of widows are not discriminatory or unjust, one may also keep in mind that the portrayal of the colonial presence as a benevolent, civilising mission ignores the very real effects of colonial oppression that led to the further impoverishment of Indian families, the brunt of which was borne by the women, especially the widows in those families. Further, it is difficult not to remember that the ostensibly "civilising" mission of the British colonialists in India, which included the effort to better the condition of the oppressed Indian women, were also used as part of a larger justification for the entire colonial project. This irony, however, is absent in Mehta's narrative.

Sidhwa's novelisation begins two years before the film begins, in 1936, and ends with the train scene – leaving out both the opening and closing texts of the film. The novel begins with Chuyia as a little wild child growing up in a village on the border of Bihar and Bengal, eating copious amounts of gooseberries and playing with her clay dolls. It also brings in an important character, that of Chuyia's mother Bhagya – important because when Chuyia's father brings news of the marriage proposal for their little daughter, including the matched horoscopes (also, by the way, an instance of texts read unquestioningly and uncritically), it is Bhagya who tries to argue with her husband that her six-year old daughter is just too young to marry a widower in his forties. Bhagya is of course made to fall silent after her husband brings on the combined authority of the scriptures, gods and ancient sages – but not before she has blazed with protest at the injustice and raised the question of a woman's sexuality. The novel also adds nuances and layers to some of the scenes in the film – for example, when Narayan's mother asks him about the girl he wants to marry and whether she is fair. In the film, Narayan simply replies that yes, she is fair; in the novel, before telling his mother that the girl is fair, he asks whether fair skin is the only thing that matters.

Like the film, the novel also mentions the markers with which people read each other – the sindhoor, bangles, white saree, tonsured head – as well as the silent ways in which husband and wife can read each other's faces, on which are nevertheless written the confusion, protest and anguish that cannot be spoken. One of the poignant scenes in the film, appearing also in the novel, dwells on this cruel shorthand. When Chuyia meets Narayan she tells him, with childlike naivete, "I am a widow." Narayan replies, "Yes, I know." (Sidhwa 62). Another interesting moment in the film is when Narayan fixes a picture of Gandhi on his bedroom wall; for in the novel, we have already seen Bhagya asking her husband to get her a picture of this "holy man from far away" to add to her prayer table where she has her pictures of gods and goddesses – thus suggesting that Gandhi, even in the form of his picture, could be a bridge, in these times, between Chuyia's family and Narayan's wealthy house (Sidhwa 11).

The novel dwells on the sustaining power of poetry and the lessons contained in the epics – for example, when Narayan recites Kalidasa to Kalyani, she comes back to the ashram and teaches the same words to Chuyia. We also see Shakuntala reading the story of Dushyanta, Shakuntala and their son Bharat, the story of Bharatavarsha, and what is interesting is the way in which the widow Shakuntala draws an unusual and yet entirely appropriate lesson for Chuyia from this story. She reminds Chuyia that this is a young boy growing up alone in the forest, and yet growing up brave and strong. What we make of a text through our active, thoughtful reading, is often as important as what the text itself contains.

Some of the concerns I had about the film, especially my reservations about the casting of Lisa Ray and John Abraham as Kalyani and Narayan respectively, were reinforced when I read Saltzman's memoir. She writes about the casting changes made by Mehta for the 2004 filming (64). One of the conditions of getting back the script from the person who held the rights, as well as the Indian distribution rights, was apparently that Shabana Azmi, Mehta's original choice for the role of Shakuntala, should no longer be cast in the film: the fear was that among other things, Azmi's identity as a "political activist" would scare off the Indian distributors. As for the role of Kalyani, which was originally to have been done by Nandita Das, Saltzman writes about Mehta's meeting with Das in Delhi: "It had been four years since Benares, and although she was still an unequivocal beauty, she no longer possessed the deep innocence needed for the character of Kalyani, the beautiful young widow" (Saltzman 164). This emphasis on fragile beauty, vulnerability, innocence does suggest that the question of how Deepa Mehta engages with issues like fair skin and feminine vulnerability need further scrutiny.

The mainstream reviews of the film in the western press have been almost unilaterally appreciative for its portrayal of (what has been presented as) the general plight of Indian widows at the mercy of a fundamentalist religion – and I am not sure if the film does not, to a certain extent, support this kind of reading. One of the popular mainstream reviewers in the US, Roger Ebert, even has this bizarre comment to make: "The character name 'Narayan' is a reminder of R. K. Narayan, the novelist whose works are delightful human comedies about life in India."

On the other hand, another group has seen the film as "drenched in colonial benevolence." According to Kamal Arora, Saydia Kamal and Usamah Ahmad, writing in *Seven Oaks Magazine*, "Mehta's film does nothing to challenge this inherent tension in representing and perpetuating notions of victimised Indian women lacking any agency or means of resistance within the context of past and current imperialism."

Both these positions are extreme, and not entirely accurate. To read the film as depicting only passive victims is as much of a misreading as to see it as depicting the condition of all Hindu widows. We do see life changing, directly, for at least four of the widows – Bua dies after eating a laddoo and, we hope, goes straight to heaven; Kalyani kills herself when she discovers the identity of Narayan's father; Chuyia is handed over to the care of Gandhi and, we hope, a new and progressive India. And what of Shakuntala, who has cared for Bua in her last moments, who has helped Kalyani in her quest for a new life – who has now ensured that Chuyia rides on Gandhi's train of change? Shakuntala's is the strongest and most intriguing character in the film. She demonstrates agency, solidarity and courage. And although I did wonder whether the film could have ended differently, whether instead of the rather unsatisfactory device of the closing text bringing us to the present, we could perhaps have seen where Gandhi's train took Chuyia – for me it was actually the moment of Shakuntala's turning to look at the camera that was the more powerful closing for the film. Because when she turns, Shakuntala seems to gaze directly at us across the years, compelling us to reflect, among other things, on the peculiar indignity of our own situation and the sadness of it: because wherever else that train did lead, it would eventually come to an India where, at the cusp of the new millennium, a film set in India, telling an Indian story, was not allowed to be made. It is particularly poignant that Saltzman's memoir, too, begins inside a train: one that will bring her to Varanasi for a shoot that we know will not happen there. We can only read, after all, when we are free to read.

References

Arora, Kamal, Saydia Kamal and Usamah Ahmad. "*Water*: Drenched in Colonial Benevolence". *Seven Oaks Magazine* (October 5, 2005) 5 February 2007. <http://www.sevenoaksmag.com/commentary/81_comm4.html>

Ebert, Roger. "Water". RogerEbert.com Movie Reviews. (May 5, 2006.) 5 February 2007.<http://rogerebert.suntimes.com/apps/pbcs.dll/article?AID=/20060504/REVIEWS/60315003/1023>

Gangopadhyay, Sunil. *Sei Samay*, trans. Chakravarti, Aruna. *Those Days*. Penguin Books, New Delhi : 1997.

1947–Earth. Dir. Deepa Mehta. 1998. Perf. Nandita Das, Aamir Khan, Rahul Khanna, Mala Sethna, Kitu Gidwani. 1998.

Roy Mitra, Indrani. "Deepa Mehta to Settle Plagiarism Case". Rediff.com (November 10, 2005) 5 February 2007. <http://www.rediff.com/movies/2005/nov/10sunil.htm>

Saltzman, Devyani. *Shooting Water: A Mother-Daughter Journey and the Making of a Film*. New Delhi: Penguin Books, 2006.

Sidhwa, Bapsi. *Ice-Candy-Man*. South Asia Books. 1989.

Water: A Novel Based on the Film by Deepa Mehta. New Delhi: Penguin Books 2006.

Water. Dir. Deepa Mehta. Perf. Lisa Ray, John Abraham, Seema Biswas, Sarala. Canadian release September 2005. Indian release March 2007.

14

Characterisation of Space as Home in Mehta's *Water*

Shamini Shanker-Jain

> "...how we inhabit our vital space... how we take root... in a corner of the world."
>
> Bachelard

A home is generally defined as a locus of love, embodying the sense of free spirit, emotion and empathy where life becomes secure and warm. I believe in Henri Lefebvre's recognition of a space as not merely a "preexisting void endowed with formal properties alone.....a container waiting to be filled by a content – i.e. matter, or bodies – a space that is fundamentally produced by and through human actions, and which is thus constituted neither by a collection of things or an aggregate of sensory data, nor by a void packed by a parcel with various contents...."(qtd by Wegner 181). Phillip Wegner elaborates upon this in his essay "Spatial Criticism" at length and expands upon Bachelard's view that, space is not static: it is openended and complex, many times also conflicting and contradictory in its relationships. It is a process in which we are the agents of continuous intervention, change and exchange.

I look at Mehta's visual characterisation of a widows' home in *Water* as the subject of an enquiry into the sense of place as home. A widows' ashram represents a community of women who are forced to make a home away from home after a compulsory exile from their homes. It is an environment of forced confinement where married women, on the death of their spouses are left faceless members of a society, with no choice but to leave their marital or parental homes at whatever uncertain age it may happen. In Mehta's *Water* this environment of rejection is duly represented as a dark, sullen and confining enclosure where dreams are starved and the human spirit is deadened. This representation of a confined space may be synonymous with the atmosphere prevailing in an oppressive present-day prison setting or a mental asylum. Analogically, it can be said that within an existing social fabric of a city, the widows' home is akin to a highly public theatre of punishment that is located in a ritualised and defined arena and distant from an everyday existence. There exists within this enclosure, a complex structure of relationships demonstrated by the powerful versus the weak, the existence of an hierarchy like Madhumati at the helm of the ashram's affairs down to Chuyia while women like Bua, Shakuntala, Kunti and Kalyani build their own recognisable spheres of influence within the ashram's confines. Human relationships within such structures are constantly under threat, surveillance and manipulation and many times the hierarchical order gets shaken – as one vividly observes in Chuyia's defiance of Madhumati at their first meeting, "I don't want to be a stupid widow! Fatty!' (Sidhwa 42).[1] Kalyani's defiance of Madhumati when she walks out of the widows' home hoping to regain that lost magic in marital bliss with Narayan, and Shakuntala's defiance of Madhumati when she opens the door of Kalyani's locked room in the attic all fall into the same category.

Yet, in spite of the constant efforts from outside, in this case society itself or from the other widows' who desensitise their environments, Mehta's story reflects the resilience demonstrated in a handful of individuals whose human spirit transcends the strict confines of their surroundings, ultimately finding a new togetherness and trust.

In the process there is that unconscious momentum that helps build a new community order from within. Bachelard's view is once again of importance there. His view that "All really inhabited space bears the essence of the notion of home. [Here] memory and imagination remain associated, each one working for their mutual deepening.....The house is one of the greatest powers of integration for the thoughts, memories and dreams of mankind.... Without it man would be a dispersed being."[2]

Background: 1938 Colonial India

Mehta's *Water* portrays both space and substance in the widows' home through the story of Chuyia, the child widow who is compelled to abandon the warmth of her family home and banished into the cold and calculative precincts of a widows' ashram in Benaras. Home no longer is with people of the same blood. Chuyia feels extreme estrangement and alienation. Her sense of home begins to see many locations which enable her to see changing perspectives and experience it as a place where she discovers new ways of seeing reality and the frontiers of difference, a place where she also develops new surrogate kinship patterns.

Mehta's imagery of a home and its 'parts' is particularly unique. She portrays in her story a powerful spatial imagery which is invested with a sense of home through a combination of imagination, sweet reminiscences, sorrowful memories, dreams and reflected human values. Each of these characteristics is subtly embodied in space with the right tones of colour, light and shade in order to reflect a sense of being and well-being. Linda McDowell has discussed the specificities of home with reference to gender and foregrounds memory and imagination as two main constituents of home. Falling back, on Bachelard's work in the *Poetics of Space,* McDowell elaborates no matter however dreary and gloomy the place one is forced to inhabit, past experiences and memories combined with the ability to imaginatively project into another future enable the development of a sense of home (McDowell 71-72). In the film the presence of women like Shakuntala, Bua and Kalyani add a sense of meaning to Chuyia's life through their demonstrations of love, caring and bonding. Each one seeks with every passing day, a strength in her beliefs that someday a sense of emancipation will arrive. "You must say the japa, Jai Shree

Krishna 108 times a day and you will soon fly away home", Kalyani advised Chuyia (Sidhwa 54). And then there are those resigned to their fate, like the old Bua who continues to sustain herself through past memories, "I was so fascinated with... plump, juicy rasagollas, piping hot gulab jamuns, kaju barfi, yellow laddoos dripping in ghee." (Sidhwa 83). Even for Bua there are some sweet memories. "As Bua slowly masticated the laddoo with her toothless gums she relived the best part of her life: her acceptance by her prosperous new landowning Brahmin family and the kindness shown by her mother-in-law, 'You are our little Lakshmi'" (Sidhwa 101).

Home alternates between being a mere inhabited space with fluctuations in priorities, a constant shift in relationships and in ways of communication pointing out to the specific oneness people feel with their home. Bachelard states that inhabited space "is not an inert box", it transcends "geometrical space" (Bachelard 47). A related question is: can this feeling be reproduced in confined spaces like prisons and asylums that contain and control space. The process of reconciliation and acceptance, in itself, is a complex one.

Chuyia's life of widowhood begins with the innocuous act of crossing the ashram's threshold. The dictionary meaning of threshold is the 'part' defined as "the floor at the entrance of a room or building". The threshold, both architecturally and figuratively, is of significance in the film. It is one of the spatial tropes that carry the burden of temporal struggles both of the individual and the nation. Architecturally, the threshold is always given a special spatial presence by the "elaboration and enrichment of its structure" through porches, arches, mullions and jambs to name a few (Cirlot 341). It also symbolises a transition in time and space: an act of bridging two separate worlds say, outside with an inside and can be related analogically to all forms of duality. According to Heidegger, a boundary may also be understood as a threshold, that is an embodiment of a *difference*.[3] In a building, a threshold serves the purpose of simultaneously separating and uniting an outside and an inside, that is, what is alien and what is habitual. "It is a gathering middle where an outlook on the world is opened up and set back on earth" (Norberg-Schulz 46). Heidegger upholds the view that boundary and threshold are constituent elements of place. They form part of a figure which discloses the spatial reference in question. In

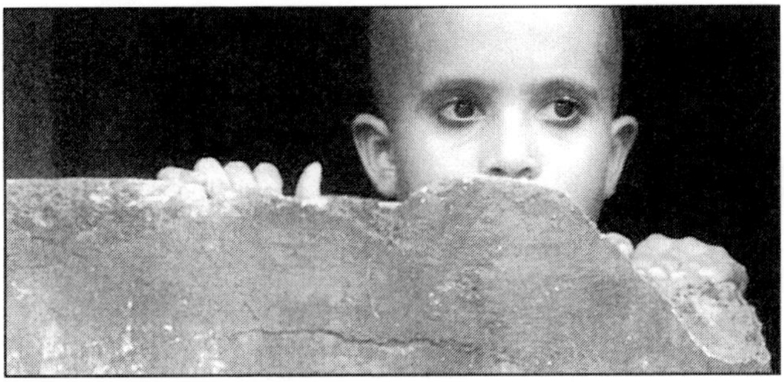

From the outside

the widows' world the boundary and the threshold of the ashram were physically one and in Chuyia's world, the first step across marks the beginning of a new journey of life from the security of a parental home to a new adopted home, adapting to the strange ways of the women in white. The simple act of crossing the threshold symbolises Chuyia's relocation in a split second into an exclusively "reserved" womens' domain – a widows' ashram – their 'dwelling', 'sanctuary' and 'refuge', where society has relegated them to *be*. "In our shared grief, we're all sisters here and this ashram is our only refuge", said the mighty Madhumati to the little Chuyia over their first meeting in the central courtyard (Sidhwa 41).

'Sanctuary' is defined as "an official protection given to someone by a place that is safe for them" and 'refuge' as a "place you go to protect yourself from something dangerous and threatening"[4]: two loaded words and terms not generally associated with a sense of home and dwelling. Significantly, it needs to be noted, no male member is allowed to cross the ashram's *threshold.* For all practical purposes it is a closed world, formidable in its barriers and isolated from all normal festivity. But the outside world enters it through Gulabi, the eunuch, who introduces the dreaded name 'Gandhi' to Madhumati; and the entry of new widows like Chuyia who bring newness from beyond and across the threshold, or through the priest Sadanand who guides them in their religious beliefs. On the other hand is young Kalyani, demure and sensual, and allowed to grow her hair. (The other widows were made to shave their heads and with their long, stern faces some looked like men. They were not permitted to adorn themselves with jewellery and had ash smeared on their foreheads). She was chosen to 'overstep' the ashram's *threshold* and surreptitiously allowed to cross the *threshold* into rich

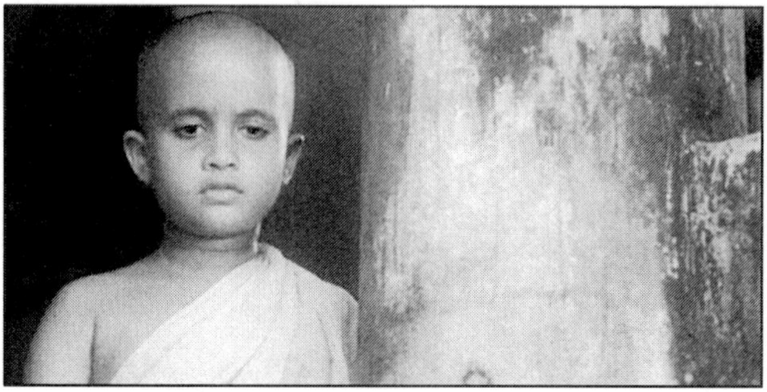

Forlorn and hesitant

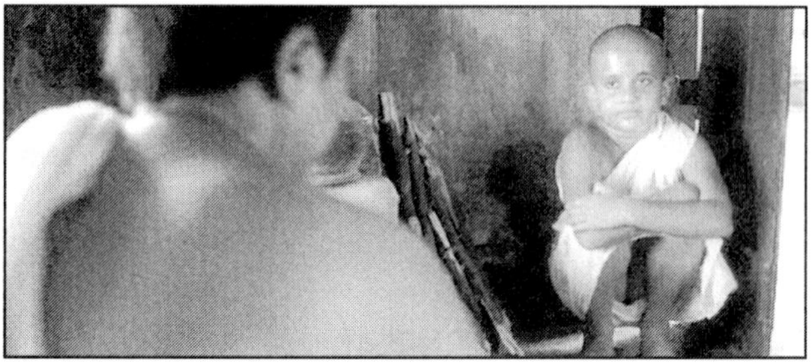

In the presence of a proactive other

households of the gentry to fulfil their desires. So easy was it for 'them' to alter destinies at will. The threshold upholds this concept of duality and transition with its one side recognising a sense of 'being forbidden', to the other side of 'being accepted'.

Chuyia's introduction to Shakuntala, her mentor and "stern visaged saviour", is by chance. She crosses the *threshold* of Shakuntala's room after a defiant moment with Madhumati, chased by Kunti and two others. At this point, a noticeable transformation appears in Chuyia's general disposition – from the threat of adversity on to hope, from a sense of insecurity to security, from the aggressive other to the proactive other.

The *threshold* to Shakuntala's room is a mute witness to a number of interesting and intense moments. Chuyia stands on a threshold between Shakuntala's room and the rest of the ashram demonstrating her childish arrogance, "Reluctantly, Chuyia left the 'sanctuary' of Shakuntala's room but not before she impishly stuck out her tongue" (Sidhwa 44). Kalyani stands at the *threshold* of Shakuntala's room waiting for Narayan's note to be read. The

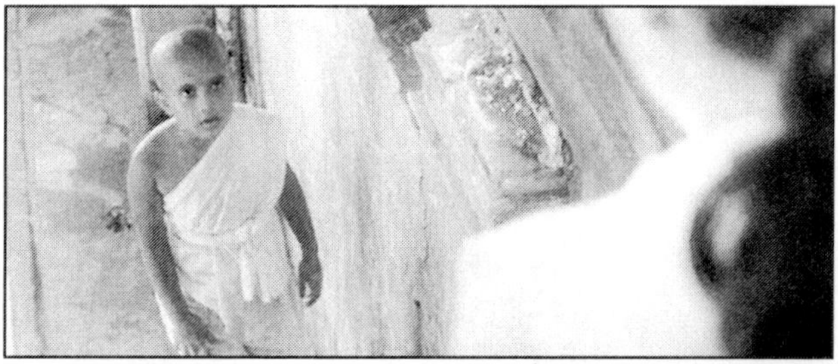

Who's there ?

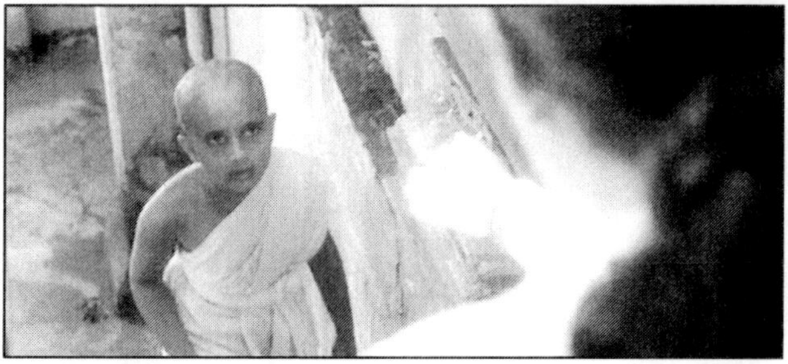

Kalyani reaching out in friendship

implications of this act are significant: Shakuntala recognises a deep, dangerous and forbidden love between a member of the "gentry" and the widow. It marks the beginning of a slow turmoil where Shakuntala questions the practiced social taboos through a deeper understanding of the religious texts.

Chuyia's introduction to the rest of her new surroundings begins with the curious gaze of her "sisters of all ages, shapes and sizes", occupying their exalted positions in the sun drenched central courtyard of their home. Each to their own devices, the central courtyard is the heart and soul of the widows home. The widows need to conglomerate, seek companionship and build up collective strength in their forced isolation made this central place all the more meaningful. The rough grey floors, the column lined periphery and the visible sky of an imaginary ceiling, had all the dimensions of an outdoor cosy living room. "They sat companionably close; the one all angular and withered with age, the other in the bosom of robust childhood... similar in their innocence and vulnerability, they completed a circle" (Sidhwa 45). The courtyard though rectangular, recognises the presence of a 'centre'. The old and the young found their places together. Pillars, trees and corners offered the widows a choice to choose the extent of their participation in activities related

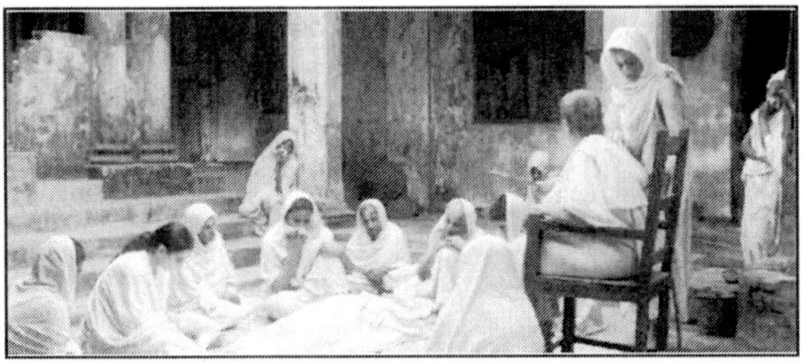

Hierarchy in mourning

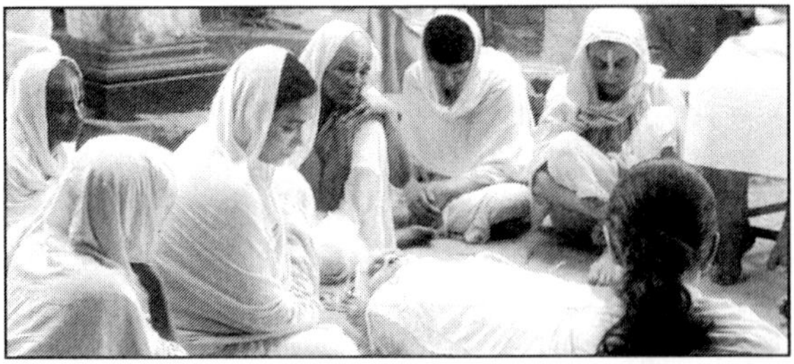

Sisters in sorrow

to the ashram. Their various activities ranging from daily chores, stitching, grinding spices, religious discourses and celebration of festivals transformed this space into a kaleidoscope. "Shakuntala left Kalyani to her internal debate and wandered to the courtyard. She needed to be by herself. She sat quietly, a little apart from the singing widows finding a quiet space for herself in that noise" (Sidhwa 120).

Beyond the strong, grey, weathered columns were dark and dingy rooms painted in depressing shades of grey. They were meticulously arranged around the periphery of the courtyard. Their quiet presence was in great contrast to the humdrum of the spaces outside. The widows' private spaces seemed cold and distant and offered very little hospitality to the outside, save for the balcony located at the first floor level which was their open window to the 'free' world.

The judiciously placed doors and fenestrations along the walls allowed for good ventilation, satiated their intense curiosity and fulfilled their need for connecting and communicating. A circumambulatory passage was their only means of connection with an all-in-one exit and entry – their private sacred realm on the one side and the more public, collective face of the ashram on the other. Only the privileged eunuch Gulabi was allowed to exercise the right to walk down the passage with access to the threshold of their private domain.

The room in which Kalyani was further isolated, allowed her to nurture her dreams of Lord Krishna and Narayan. These images gave her immense strength and will to live and were subjects of her focus and inner desires. Chuyia becomes Kalyani's companion and sounding board. It was through Kalyani, and the room she occupied close to the sky, that she experiences immense joy in Kallu, the black pup. Vivid memories of Tun Tun her pet pariah, make her feel more concerned about Kallu's security and illegal status in the widows' home. It was here that Chuyia watched the rain and Kalyani introduced her to the magical powers of Lord Krishna.

The house and the body are interlinked. The home is an extension of the person, like an extra skin; it serves as much to reveal and display as it does to hide and protect. House, body and mind are in continuous interplay, the physical structure, furnishing, social conventions and mental images influence the activities and ideas which unfold within its boundaries. In essence, a space becomes meaningful only if it is endowed with the necessary human indicators which facilitate growth, memories and one's imagination.

We do recognise the fact that the state of our physical and emotional well-being directly impacts our physical surroundings and vice versa. The two are not mutually exclusive of each other and each contains the possibility of surprise. Lescure's firm view is that "an artist does not create the way he lives, he lives the way he creates". Bachelard in *Poetics of Space* focuses on the poetic image, a concept I have transferred to the spatial image. Bachelard's writes, "It becomes evident, then, that a man's work stands out from life to such an extent that life cannot explain it."[5] Art has or ought to have the capacity to surprise life. Lescure applies this quality of art to painting, where the colour is expected to throw up the unexpected. For a moment this idea of the 'ability to surprise' has to be expanded to the act of living that can take us beyond our course; the unyielding space that begins to yield a homeliness; and in this case also the film itself that responds to new perceptions that can lead us to the discovery of new possibilities.

The walls of the widows' home were draped in shades of depressing grey. Does characterising a life of self-denial and pain mean painting a sordid picture of their physical and spatial well-being? Isn't there any other means of characterising hope in misery? We always seek spatial references and props in our environment that could uphold a positive will to overcome adversity:

maybe a widows' home with clean sparkling walls, a dash of colour, a happy portrait could uplift one's senses at a time of resigned fate? Chuyia finds momentary happiness in an "oval portrait on a wall of a pink cheeked English girl clasping a bouquet of flowers in her white hands. She has luxuriant brown hair crowned by a flaming red cap" (Sidhwa 46). Yes, perhaps the presence of colour in little Chuyia's imagination: pink, brown, red and white, a child clinging to little strands of her imagination in her spatial surroundings in order to keep her spirits alive. Isn't it necessary for Chuyia and her sisters to demonstrate a super human resilience and a strong will to survive such adversity – small measures that allow them to seek happiness and make the best of their surroundings?

The red in the portrait with the English girl – the colours of intensity and passion – are perhaps used in the film to characterise the intensity of their suppressed desires, the intensity of their dreams and of their hopes, aspects that society forbids them to nurture or display. The presence of red in the visual frames of the film is notional and its effects enhanced to intensify the settings and the performance of its strong characters. The only undisputed presence of red that was accepted in their surroundings, was from the colour of the flames of the midnight lamps, the vermilion on the forehead of Lord Krishna, the flaming red cap on the portrait on the wall and the tobacco stained walls of Madhumati's grimy surroundings. In contrast, the colour white signified purity. Society's recognition of white, the colour of the skin of the English girl is in stark contrast to the colour white draped on a widow's brown skin that identified with her persona. The harder they prayed to atone their sins, the whiter their souls and clothes, while the colour of their skin and their circumstances remained unchanged. At one point Rabindra comments on the difference in the perception of widowhood in the two cultures co-existing in a British Colonial India!

But contexts become another way of resisting enclosures, they encroach from the outside, the outsides which enters this closed world through poetry and romance. When the two unequally matched girls play with each other, recite poetry or talk about Lord Krishna, the outside creeps in through emotions and aspirations. A different world is created, temporarily indifferent to the harsh surroundings. This interplay between space and emotions when connections with dreariness are snapped in order to create a microcosm of their world, not by widows who scold and carry tales, but by Kalyani, Chuyia, Kallu, Lord Krishna and the poet Kalidasa as the cloud messenger is talked about, become the means of transcending the hostility of the environment. Besides this, language as poetry and as the written word, penetrates through the barriers – first through the scriptures, then through *Meghdoot* and finally through law. The underlying movement is towards an emphasis on the act of interpretation: how does one interpret language, symbols, scriptures, law and social change? The push is towards contexts both for the characters and for the viewer. Mehta thus, through an interaction between time and space, characterises a widows' home with all its limits, bleakness and negativity as a home that moves outside them.

The knowledge of the law on widow remarriage opens out other possibilities and Gandhi's influence in a changing India becomes Chuyia's ultimate passage to freedom. Yet again, a new chapter begins in the journey of life for the child Chuyia as she is thrust into the arms of people who care. The ashram as a building typology dissolves from the existing social fabric of the city, giving rise to newer cities with a new socio-political order thereby justifying the metaphor of the threshold. By the end of the film, each one of the characters is a different person – Chuyia, hurt and chastened; Kalyani who descended from hope to despair and is now a memory, Shakuntala who discovers her hidden strengths, and Madhumati who stands deprived of power. The threshold of change has long-term implications as we see the counterpoint in the disintegration of the family structure in Seth Dwarkanath's home where the balance is no longer in his favour; Narayan leaves home and his mother is now much more sensitive to Narayan's stand. Having been brought face to face with her husband's immoral rapacity she too has moved out of her passive enclosure of willed ignorance. Neither the widows' ashram nor Seth Dwarkanath's house are ever going to be the same.

In spatial terms the film *Water* starts with its greyness and stone walls that characterise the widows' home, but in emotional terms it creates crevices, openings and exits – through death, assistance and self discovery. Even as the relationship between the four women is explored – Madhumati, Shakuntala, Kalyani and Chuyia – it is the process of reconciliation between environmental space and emotional space that becomes an important indicator in community formation as well as a source of sustenance in itself.

Notes

1. All quotations referring to the dialogue are from Sidhwa's novel *Water* (New Delhi: Viking Penguin, 2006). Sidhwa's fictional work, as it is based on the film, reverses the process of transferring a text to an image to one of transferring an image to a text and thus is free of authorial interventions. It translates the visual image into language. I have used the novel for my quotations from the dialogue and have quoted only such dialogues as occur in the film.
2. Gaston Bachelard quoted by Linda McDowell in *Gender, Identity and Place: Understanding Feminist Geographies* (Cambridge: Polity Press, 1999), p.72.
3. For more details refer the essay "Heidegger's Thinking on Architecture" by Christian Norberg-Schulz in *Architecture: Meaning and Place: Selected Essays* (New York: Electa/Rizzoli), p.46.
4. Refer Macmillans Dictionary. Also Shorter OED (2 vols), which defines "sanctuary" as a holy place, a consecrated ground and a place where 'immunity is secured.' 'Refuge' is defined as a 'shelter or protection from danger or trouble, a place of safety and security.'
5. Refer Bachelard's "Introduction", *Poetics of Space,* Translated into English by Maria Jolas (Boston: Beacon Press, 1964) xxix.

References

Bachelard, Gaston. *Poetics of Space* (1958). Translated from French by Maria Jolas. Boston: Beacon Press, 1964.

Cirlot, J E. *A Dictionary of Symbols.* Translated from the Spanish by Jack Sage, London and New York: Routledge, 1962.

McDowell, Linda. *Gender, Identity and Place: Understanding Feminist Geographies.* Cambridge: Polity Press, 1999.

Norberg-Shulz, Christian. *Architecture: Meaning and Place.* New York: Electa/Rizzoli, 1988.

Sidhwa, Bapsi. *Water.* New Delhi: Viking, Penguin India, 2006.

Water, Dir. Deepa Mehta, Prod. David Hamilton, Perf. Seema Biswas, Sarala, Lisa Ray, John Abraham, 2005.

Wegner, Phillips E. "Spatial Criticism" *Introducing Criticism in the 21st Century.* Ed. Julian Wolfreys. Edinburgh: Edinburgh University Press, 2002.

15

Exteriority, Space and Female Iconography in Deepa Mehta's *Water*

Vijaya Singh

That Deepa Mehta had to pull out of Benaras and shoot *Water* in Sri Lanka is now part of the history of the film's making. Her daughter Devyani records the entire sequence of events leading to the abandoning of the film in India and its subsequent shooting in Sri Lanka in her book, *Shooting Water: A Mother-Daughter Journey and the Making of a Film*. The book documents both the making of the film and her own difficult relationship with her mother. Inadvertently, it seems to me just as the book is a chronicle of Devyani's difficult if rewarding relationship with her mother the film too is a testimony of Deepa Mehta's own difficult if rewarding relationship with India, her home country. Devyani, confirms in the book how her choice as a child to live with her father continues to haunt not only her relationship with her mother but also everything else in her life. For me, Devyani's troubled relationship with her mother is a metaphor for Deepa Mehta's own troubled relationship with India, her country of origin. I suppose it is not entirely unproblematic to read a film by overstretching a personal conceit. It relegates all the political, cultural, and social critiques to an emotional, nostalgic, sentimental realm even while critically looking it. There are however interesting parallels in Devyani's relationship with her mother and that of Deepa Mehta's relationship with India, a country, she chose not to live in but which haunts her imagination.

I realise that in using the emotionally fraught binary of mother and daughter to explain the diasporic relationship with the country of origin I am reducing the entire diasporic debate to that of a family drama where if Deepa Mehta is the daughter, India is the Mother and patriarchy, the father. In fact, in this drama there is a very real father figure, namely Bal Thackerey, jealously guarding Indian culture and tradition, then there is Canada the tolerant and reasonable foster parent. Actually, these terms of reference are provided for by Devyani's book and the back cover of the film themselves. Even as the book laments the undemocratic rightist forces in India it brings to light the laudatory effort of the Canadian government in providing funding for the film, in a telling comment she points out:

> In the end it was the Canadian government, through Telefilm Canada, a film funding body, that provided the largest investment in the project. This decision to support *Water* was the beginning of a new way for Canada to support its artists. ...Although they required that we shoot an English version of the film alongside the Hindi, they supported *Water,* a film set in India, beginning to embrace a new definition of what it meant to be Canadian. (151-152)

Indeed, how innocent is the advertisement of "the beginning of a new way for Canada to support its artists" by the Canadian government. As Uma Parameswaran points out in her essay, "Contextualizing Diasporic Locations in Deepa Mehta's *Fire* and Srinivas Krishna's *Masala*", "Look at it this way there is a neo-imperialist ploy in Canada to encourage diaspora writers to occupy the safe space of the original homeland, and to roughshod over the few who choose to talk negatively about the here and now. Write about India, negatively if possible, and you win kudos and awards; but write negatively about immigrants' life in the new world, and you are sent to stand in the corner with a dunce cap on your head"(290).

So much so for the autonomy of Mehta's herculean efforts in making *Water!* Theodore Adorno categorically exposes the politics of such undertakings:

> The purposefulness of pure works of art which denies the utility and instrumentality that rein in the world outside art, is premised on commodity production. The 'autonomy', the freedom from external purposes of pure works derives from their being produced 'privately' and not on demand for a particular customer. (10)

In Mehta's case, as we are all aware, her unquenchable thirst for the representation of the plight of widows in India in *Water* is patronised by the Canadian government. It is not enough for Mehta to champion the cause of the Indian women, she also projects herself as the defender of freedom of speech and the powerful enemies she has made in her crusade for the rights of the downtrodden. It is not for nothing that the back cover of the DVD of the film *Water* outlines the travails of Deepa Mehta in India and specifically points out that Shiv Sena leader Bal Thackeray "one of the most powerful right-wing Hindu fundamentalist groups in India" is rumoured to hate Deepa Mehta "the most in the world". It goes on to add, "...one must wonder what it is that Mehta did to raise the ire of the man...the answer is simple: she made films which questioned the interpretations that current Hindu leaders were giving to the sacred texts and in particular as they related to the treatment of women". One may smile at the facile, self-important explanation but the key words 'interpretation' and 'treatment of women' point to a debate much larger than the immediate, contingent demands of shooting a controversial film. Both the events of abandoning the film shoot in India, its subsequent shooting in Sri Lanka and the issue of interpretation of sacred texts point at the struggle over the meaning of India itself and the literal distance between the diasporic filmmaker and the investment of her creative imaginary in the country of her origin.

Arjun Appadurai in his *Modernity at Large: Cultural Dimensions of Globalization* identifies, "media and migration" as the two most influential components in the emerging dynamics of the present world. Migration which gives rise to a diasporic population is also the crucible for a politics, which implicates both the new and the country of their origin. The anxiety of the diaspora to not lose affiliation with the country of origin left behind and at the same time the desire not to antagonise the new country often leads to a duplication of uncritically examined attitudes of the country of new residence. Appadurai uses the trope of displacement of the cabaret dancers in Mira Nair's film *India Cabaret* to stress the deterritorialised mobility of the diaspora which he says is at the "root of their problems" and goes on to show how the "tension between global and local that drives cultural production today" (63). He further stresses "...the need to incorporate the complexities of expressive representation (film, novels, travel accounts) into our ethnographies, not only as technical adjuncts but as primary material with which to construct and interrogate our own representations"(64).

I wish to stretch the above argument further and present a case for examining not only the politics of representation but also to point out how the aesthetics of diasporic films themselves may be structured in response to the politics of the global and local. To elucidate this point I use the concept of "exteriority" as elaborated by Edward Said in *Orientalism* to analyse the " text's surface" and "what it describes"(20). I, however, use the term exteriority, not just to examine the use of external space in Mehta's film but also as a useful indicator of contemporary diasporic existence which moves with tremendous ease between and through different spaces, willfully re-creating the denied space – in this case the Ghats of Benaras in Sri Lanka. Cinema itself as an art form is notorious for creating illusions of reality and filmmakers are known to construct sets ranging from the real to the fantastic. Mehta's film thus is not unique in creating a set of the substitute Benaras, Rawalpur in Sri Lanka, a country as she says in an interview "without any ghats." What is however remarkable is the juxtaposition of these two illusory spaces: of cinema and the sets in Sri Lanka in Mehta's *Water*. This space that Mehta creates in her film is inside a void that she has been forced to hollow out from the inability to film in Benaras. She collapses an irreducible site upon this void and generates a text that creates as Foucault would tell us a "heterotopia...of compensation" (*Diacritics* 16, 1986: 27). A space both concrete and abstract at the same time. In the same essay he goes on to say "...and I wonder if certain colonies have not functioned somewhat in this manner"(1986: 27). The invention of this space thus creates a power discourse that allows Mehta, a privileged diasporic filmmaker with the funding and backing of the "first world" to generate an India outside of itself and position herself not only as the champion of the rights of the oppressed and voiceless as against the powerful patriarchs who desire the continual subjugation of Indian women but also as the defender of freedom of speech. As Devyani notes in her book in various passages:

> ...Before leaving, my mother looked at the officers.
> 'It's a dark day for democracy', she said...(87).

> Mom snapped back. 'This is about freedom!' (90)

And then she refers to Pawan K Verma's view: "All nations indulge in a bit of myth-making to bind their people together," and asserts "Someone had gone to great lengths to ensure that *Water* didn't challenge that myth" (91). Devyani ends the first section of the book by including a mail she wrote to her father on her last day in Benaras:

> A sad day in Indian history and a sadder start to the twenty-first century. *Water* has been shut down by the state government... but I also know that this film *will* be made at some point, but maybe not in this place. For a city I love so much...it is hard to see it in anything other than darkness. (93)

Darkness thus becomes the engaging metaphor for India and this is evident in the use of external and internal space in the film as well. All that is creative, loving and free is outside of the closed confines of the ashram. Even the feisty and wise Chuyia is reduced to a screaming and agitating brat inside the ashram. The dark, constricted space of the ashram is where freedom is curtailed, its inmates forced to live in fear and self-abnegation. Any attempt to escape the threshold of the ashram is severely punished as in the case of Kalyani the beautiful young widow. The inmates are kept inside either by a willful suspension of their rights and freedom as human beings or by physical force and manipulation as in the case of Chuyia. So where the internal space of the ashram is symptomatic of India, the external represents the new world the diaspora has managed to escape to. This is not to say of course that the external is devoid of any conflict. It has its dilemmas and difficulties but it is a fecund world, full of possibilities. It is the space in which romance flowers, where plots of minor rebellions are crafted, where women learn of the new ways of the new world, where water is not forced into limited containers but flows untrammeled. Inside is, old age, death, darkness, unhappiness and eternal bondage. Outside lies freedom, new ideas, the possibility of choice and love.

Kalyani (played by Lisa Ray), Chuyia (Sarala) and Shakuntala (Seema Biswas) are the only women in the ashram to traverse the internal and external space. All three embody three different states of being; Kalyani's youth and beauty are prostituted for the sustenance of the ashram, she therefore has some claim to a freedom of movement; Chuyia's defiance and childhood too allow her some mobility and Shakuntala's self-imposed asceticism and stoicism, which permit her to examine the prevailing tradition and custom sanction her an intellectual mobility. But all three mobilities are eventually trounced in the film. Kalyani who has allowed herself to be prostituted finds the muck climbing up her lotus petals. As she tells Narayan (John Abraham), quoting from the Gita that her life is like the lotus, which even though it grows in sludge is above it. In finding out that Narayan is the son of Seth Dwarkanath, her client, she decides to return to the ashram from where she is turned away and eventually drowns herself in the Ganga. It is here, in projecting herself as representing the 'treatment of women' in India, that Mehta ties herself in knots and is seen legitimising the burden of spiritual trusteeship and incest taboo in the refusal of Kalyani to marry Narayan. The shift from a regulated body to a resisting body ends for Kalyani in suicide. Interestingly, even this rebellion is predicated on Shakuntala finding out, that a new law has come into being which allows widows to remarry, from the Brahmin priest who is projected as the good keeper of tradition along with Gandhi – whose name he invokes as the man who alone listens to the voice of his conscience – versus the fathers of both Narayan and Rabindra who exploit and interpret the Brahminic tradition for their own selfish motives. The agency for acting out their desires comes hence not from the female quarter but male quarters. Only when widow re-marriage has been accepted in the public domain does Shakuntala allow Kalyani to leave the ashram to marry Narayan and hands over Chuyia to Narayan to be placed in the custody of Gandhi.

Interestingly, the ghats that Mehta invents in Sri Lanka are a space in which it is not unusual to see a newly-wed couple, a widow, a dead body burning on a pyre all collapsed in a single frame. I am referring of course to one shot in particular in which Shakuntala is seen filling her small container from the ghat; she is framed on her right by a newly-wed couple, on the left by a burning pyre, behind her beyond the scenic space is her ashram and in front is the wide, open river. Centring Shakuntala in that shot is both symbolic of how a widow's life is framed by marriage and death on either side; selfdenial and an unknown, uncharted territory behind and in front of her. The scenic space of the film is so constructed that it itself disallows any space and mobility for the widow. Of course the water in front opens out the space but those who do venture into that space are scarred and condemned to either a life of indignity or suicide. Both Kalyani and Chuyia who venture into that territory are violated hence forced back into the dark pit of unexamined tradition except of course Chuyia who is rescued by Narayan.

Female sexuality in the film is legitimised only within accepted social domains and not outside of it. The only salvation for Kalyani lies in her marriage to Narayan. If she had only been a widow she could still have been rescued but she is also a prostitute – even if forcibly. A deviant sexuality such as hers, is silenced in the film through her eventual suicide. The passive Rabindra of the comprador class who professes to like the English and their ways quotes an allegedly ancient saying, "*raand, sand, seedhi, sanyasi inse bache to bhoge Kashi*" on seeing Narayan surveying the silhouette of Gulabi (Raghubir Yadav) the procurer of widows for the rich and powerful. Kalyani's death validates the above saying and liberates Narayan from committing both a social as well as a spiritual death. In Kalyani's death is Narayan's freedom.

Significantly, none of the characters turn tradition on its head. Narayan on learning that his father is responsible for the ruin of Kalyani, shames and rejects him by saying, "Ram has condemned those Brahmins who interpret the scriptures for their own selfish ends" and leaves Benaras to pursue his practice of law in some other place. Narayan brings a superior understanding of the scriptures to shame his father. He rejects the old law of his father and chooses the new law of the British, which confers dignity to the women of India. In the film Narayan tells Kalyani, "the British do not treat their widows as we do". Indeed, it is the new British law that the Brahmin priest is referring to when he tells Shakuntala of the new law permitting widows to remarry. Mehta for all her anti-colonialist rhetoric in the film is seen sanctioning one of the British rationales for ruling over India: to rein in the inhumane and crippling traditions of India, which have kept women in a state of perpetual bondage. An example of which is found in James Mill's *The History of British India*:

> The condition of women is one of the most remarkable circumstances in the manners of nations... the history of uncultivated nations uniformly presents the women in a state of abject slavery, from which they slowly emerge as civilization advances.... A state of dependence more strict and humiliating than that which is ordained for the weaker sex among the Hindus cannot be easily discerned. (445-47)

Upendra Baxi in his essay "The State's Emissary: Law in Subaltern Studies" proves the lie inherent in the liberatory discourse of the British and says:

> Protection and promotion of the basic human rights of the subjects was no *explicit aspect* of the ends of colonial governance.... It is doubtful that the colonial law in either its home-grown or its export variety has any aspiration towards the liberation of women.... Its 'abstract legalism' only testifies to colonial law's distinctive ways of leaving subject women 'betrayed and bleeding', and 'soiled and humiliated'. (253)

Mehta fails to expose the colonial ideology of the British. As a matter of fact she perpetuates such an understanding. In fact, in projecting both Narayan and Gandhi as saviours of Indian women, she rescues them from Manu and places them squarely in the hands of Gandhi – granting them no agency of their own.

Indeed, it may be argued that Gandhi, his philosophy, his allegiance to truth, his theory of passive resistance inform the underlying narrative of the film and establish him as the conscience of the nation and the saviour of Indian women. It is worth noting how Mehta brings a number of disparate elements, a young widow, who is also a prostitute, a child widow, a Gandhian idealist, in the city of Benaras together in the cinematic space of the film but fails to resolve them adequately, especially with reference to Gandhi and Indian women, more so because Gandhi occupies a liberatory space in the film. 'Passive resistance', is a term that is bandied about casually in the film. Narayan is enamoured of the concept and wonders if

Rabindra may not want to join the Congress. Gandhi who subverts the masculine logic of British imperialism by bringing the feminine notion of passive resistance into the public domain both encourages and contains the women in their march towards freedom. Female sexuality was for him always a deeply problematic sphere. He situates women within the traditional parameters of the familial and domestic. His answer to the problem of prostitution is to "...quarantine them and warn the public of the danger of falling an easy prey to the temptation forced on it"(Sen 181). The prostitute representing promiscuity can only be a figure of ruin for him. In fact, Gandhi's critique of western civiliastion in his *Hind Swaraj* too is offered in "the connotations evoked by the prefix, 'Swa' against that evoked by the image of the veshya, who is always at (sic) someone's control and whose agency is perforce without". Gandhi who "reconceptualises resistance as the recovery of resistance" and "questions domination by insisting on a subaltern responsibility for subordination; not as a loss of power, but the loss of Swa"(*EPW, 2006, 49,* 5065) inhabits a deeply contentious space in the film and does not sit easy with the sweeping romance of Narayan for Kalyani. Indeed, in the lack of agency for the women characters of the film, who are either forcibly taken or given they are reduced to objects and are denied control of the Swa or self. Significantly, in the film, Kalyani who is forced into prostitution by the contingent demands of the ashram is never seen offering any resistance – except once timidly to be overpowered by Gulabi and her client.

What is more, Gandhi's views on the widows too fluctuate between "a voluntary widowhood" which he calls the "priceless boon in Hinduism" and the desirability of the "remarriage of virgin widows" (Sen 241). The liberation of the "widows of India" that Narayan refers to is really within very narrow parameters. Indeed, in the film the figure of Shakuntala inhabits a stoic if "voluntary widowhood" and the only widow to be finally rescued from the ashram is Chuyia, the child widow.

The struggle over the meaning of India thus is really the struggle over the site of the female body in whom the right wing invests the responsibility of tradition and "Indian civilisational" values. Especially, in the case of *Water,* where the construction of the widow, as a site of desire is not only fundamentally flawed – from the right wing logic – but also entirely unacceptable. For the diasporic filmmaker eager to recover this site the danger lies in not providing the female subject the space from which to speak.

If the nation indulges in myth-making to bind its people together then surely, the diasporic filmmaker works with mythical names to project an India frozen in a time-wrap. Is it any surprise then that the names of the various characters in the film are named after mythological and historical characters: Kalyani, was earlier to be called Janaki. Shakuntala, Kunti, Devaki are some of the other female characters. Narayan himself is modelled on Krishna, he is shown playing the flute, arranging meetings with Kalyani near the river. His best friend, the feckless poet, is none other than Rabindra happily colluding with the British, content to recite their poetry, drink their whisky and play their music. The parallels are too close to be overlooked, and not conclude that the Rabindra of the film must also be the Rabindra Nath Tagore of Bengal. Indeed, the use of his name is deeply ironical in that Tagore himself and his family were at the forefront of women's emancipation.

It is in keeping with the logic of the film that just as it begins with the epigraph from Manu's injunction on how widows may lead their lives the film ends with the unhappy declaration that "35 million widows exist in India and many still live in situations similar to those shown in the film." Bringing the film full circle in its attestation of the decree of Manu still reigning in a timeless India. In validating Manu over all other lawgivers, "like Narad and Parashar" who as Rajni Sogani, quoting Iswarchandra Vidyasagar's monumental essay *Marriage of Hindu Widow (1856),* in her book *The Hindu Widow in Indian Literature,* tells us "allowed for widow remarriage under certain circumstances" (31). Mehta passes over the entire discourse on widow remarriage that raged in nineteenth and first half of twentieth century India and the reformist movement that undertook to rehabilitate the widows and projects her film into 1938.

Even before the passing of the Widow Remarriage Act 1856 the debate over the issue of remarriage had gained tremendous notoriety. It is therefore a little difficult to understand that why even when the film is located in 1938 it takes almost a century for the above knowledge to reach Shakuntala who knows how to read and write. Novel after novel in late nineteenth and early twentieth century talks of the plight and dilemmas of widows left high and dry by their relatives and oppressive customs. To mention only briefly some of these novels: *Yamuna Paryatan* (Marathi 1857) by Padmanji Mulay, *Bhagyaati* (Hindi 1877) by Shraddharam Phullauri, *Sansar* (Bengali 1886) by R.C. Dutt, *Indirabai (Kannada 1899)* by Gulavadi Venketa Rao, *Choker Bali (Bengali 1902)* by Rabindranath Tagore, *Muthumeenakshi* (Tamil 1903) by A Madhavaiah, *Hum Khurma O Hum Sawab* (Urdu 1906) by Premchand, *Pathnirdesh* (Bengali 1914) by Saratchandra and many others. But the film does not mention even in the passing the anxiety of social reformers as Iswarchand Vidyasagar for the plight of widows and the work done by them to redress the issue.

In the final analysis, it may be said that Mehta's film even though it purports to represent the suffering of women at the hands of a deeply patriarchal society is compromised by an orientalist and neo-imperialist slant in its narrative. In its portrayal of the perpetual mourning that the widows are forced to undertake, the film does however evoke a deeply emotional response. But as denizens of a 'post-colonial third world' one is forced by the contingent demands of contemporary global politics to view with suspicion all representations emerging from 'first world' benevolence. Indeed all such films thrive on the dilemmas and sharp polarisations they create though their texts in 'third world' nations over issues of feminism and nationalism forcing one to side with one or the other but never with both.

References

Adorno, Theodore. *The Culture Industry*. London: Routledge. 1991.

Appadurai, Arjun. *Modernity at Large: Cultural Dimensions of Globalization*. New Delhi: OUP. 1997.

Baxi, Upendra, " 'The State's Emissary': The Place of Law in Subaltern Studies" *Subaltern Studies* VII. Eds. Partha Chatterjee and Gyanendra Pandey. New Delhi: OUP. 1992. 246-264.

Foucault, Michel. "Of Other Spaces" Trans. Jay Miskowiec. *Diacritics* 16 (1986) 22-27.

Mill, James. *The History of British India*. Vol. I. 1826. London: Routledge. 1997.

Parameswaran, Uma. "Contextualizing Diasporic Locations in Deepa Mehta's *Fire* and Sriniwas Krishna's *Masala" In Diaspora: Theories, Histories, Texts*. Ed. Makarand Paranjape. New Delhi: Indialog Publications. 2001. 290-300.

Said, Edward. *Orientalism. New York:* Vintage Books. 1979.

Saltzman, Devyani. *Shooting Water: A Mother-Daughter Journey and the Making of a Film*. New Delhi: Penguin Books. 2005.

Sen, N.B. *Wit and Wisdom of Mahatma Gandhi.* New Delhi: New Book Society of India. 1960.

Skaria, Ajay. "Only One Word Properly Altered: Gandhi and the Question of the Prostitute" *Economic and Political Weekly of India,* Dec 9-15 2006 Vol. XLI No 49. 5065-5072.

Sogani, Rajul. *The Hindu Widow in Indian Literature.* New Delhi: OUP. 2002.

Water Dir. Deepa Mehta. Cast. Lisa Ray, Seema Biswas, John Abraham, Sarala, Raghuveer Yadav, Kulbhushan Kharbanda, Vinay Pathak, Manorama, Waheeda Rahman. Mongrel Films. 2005.

16

The Diasporic Gaze

Deepa Mehta's and Bapsi Sidhwa's *Water*

Sudha Rai

The chequered history of the making of Deepa Mehta's *Water* is well known. Caught in the resistance ideology of Hindutva nationalism[1], the emphasis on the theme of widowhood was viewed as denigratory of Indian tradition, and the original sets of the 1930s period film on the ostracisation, marginalisation and exploitation of Brahmin widows in Varanasi, was sent up in flames, with a vandalisation of the sets and properties obtained for it. Subsequently, the film was secretively shot in Sri Lanka, with a changed cast, and released in Canada.

Within three months of the completion of *Water*, Canadian publisher Anna Porter commissioned Bapsi Sidhwa to produce a novel based on the film script, to time with its release in the US. The novel then, is a product specifically prepared for the market and audiences in the US and the kind of ethnographic and sociological 'data' that has been woven into the text, as one can see, is a reflection of such specific market needs. The creative recycling and adaptation from film to novel, a 'reverse adaptation,' (Wikipedia), (a first for the novelist Sidhwa), and the 'collaboration' between the two diasporic artists Mehta and Sidhwa, raise several issues pertaining to 'the diasporic gaze.'

Deepa Mehta's film on the condition of widows in Bengal in the 1930s and the commissioning of a novel based on the film, raises many questions pertaining to wellknown debates in diasporic art. Do diasporas project representations of India that encourage a narrow view of India's poverty, superstition, caste-bound abyss and static religious positions? Have these realities been authentically portrayed, or appropriated and misrepresented? For whom are diasporic writings or films made? Are they put together primarily for the western readers and viewers? Are there distortions[2], gaps in knowledge and over generalisations in these representations?

Other, more positive perspectives on diasporic representation, advance the argument that the diasporic eye can confer the strengths of a double-vision, imparting a necessary critical distance, and, as Rushdie claims in his essay "Imaginary Homelands" (1991), upholding the virtues of the fragmented perspective: "The broken mirror may actually be as valuable as the one which is supposedly unflawed" (11).

With the virtual canonisation of diasporic fiction and film, sophisticated products of research and technology, other questions have been raised pertaining to viewership and audiences for these diasporic artistic creations. To recapitulate a few – Do diasporic writings and films have greater visibility? If so, what gives them visibility? With the specific example before us of the re-production of *Water*, we need to examine carefully the factors operating in the construction of a canon and how that affects novels and films, on similar themes produced within India.

The present article, structured in three parts, reviews in the first part the concepts and theories of the 'gaze', relating it to the diasporic perspective. In the second part, I dwell on the common ground of the two *Waters*, a fairly strict one to one equation of history, plot, character, theme, symbol, incident and conclusion, and also of a common diasporic slant, despite the intertextuality of an inter-genre transcreation. In the final part I bring together the problematic of the diasporic gaze in its characteristic style of 'framed image', marked by stylization and textbook cultural interpretation, that fragments and freezes the subject in stereotypical scenes.

It is the projection of *Water* as the definitive text of widowhood, despite a wide range of positions occupied by widows in India, in the

30s, and most certainly in contemporary India that comes across as a stark subsuming of differences. Mehta's intent in the film is to cast shadows of epic dimensions by capturing an essentialised and homogenised India, as the film's conclusion highlights in its informative message about the 35 million widows of India, who continue, many of them to be victims of prescriptive traditions. Their plight (a common and uncomplex fate), is summed up as a grand finale, obliterating modern and contemporary realities and specificities of the condition and treatment of widows in different regions of India. Of course this may bring us to another countercharge of whether 'we' essentialise diasporic art?

In his comprehensive review of 'theories of the gaze' Jeremy Hawthorn (2006) characterises the gaze as an exploratory tool for conceptualising differences in perspectives and location and distinguishes between the literal meaning of looking or being looked at, and the metaphorical sense in which authors, readers and narrators 'see' the substance of reality, whatsoever it may be:

> The gaze does not define a well-defined theoretical or critical movement or school. In some ways the term is used like 'discourse': as a means to encourage a particular way of considering a text or an utterance, and relating it to broader socio-historical and ideological matters. Theories of the gaze cannot be traced back to a single place of origin or time of birth; they build on and incorporate a number of traditional literary-critical concerns, along with ideas and concepts from movements and bodies of theory such as psychoanalysis, discourse studies, and film studies. As a familiar umbrella term, the gaze is little more than a quarter of a century old movement or school.

For Hawthorn, the 'gaze' (relevant to a narrative and cinematic perspective), can be related to "a number of characteristics of interpersonal looking", namely (a) "exchange of looks between two individuals is an interactive two-way process, we reveal things about ourselves, including things that we may not wish to reveal, or of which we are unaware;" (b) "Looking is a cumulative process: each look we give is informed by – and displays – the fruits of previous looks;" and more importantly, (c) "looking is far from a neutral process of information gathering". Hawthorn points out that "our looking activities are saturated with the residues of our social and cultural existence – for example, those relating to class, sexuality, economics." Basing the interpretation of looking and seeing, imagining and representing, in Hawthorn's basic parameters of the gaze, I submit that the diasporic gaze is 'unidirectional' rather than 'interactive,' stilling and pacifying the agency of the subject.

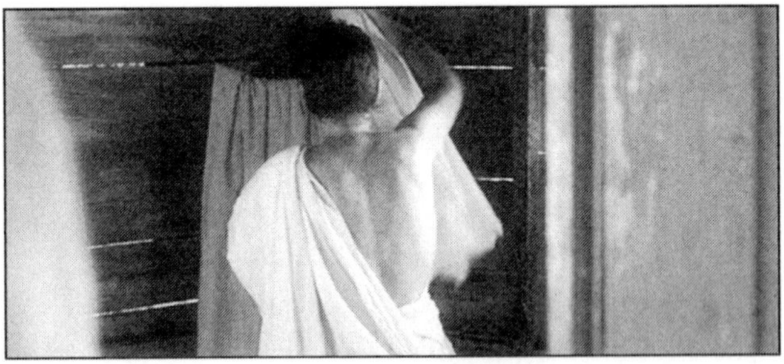

Kalyni: Undraping the female body

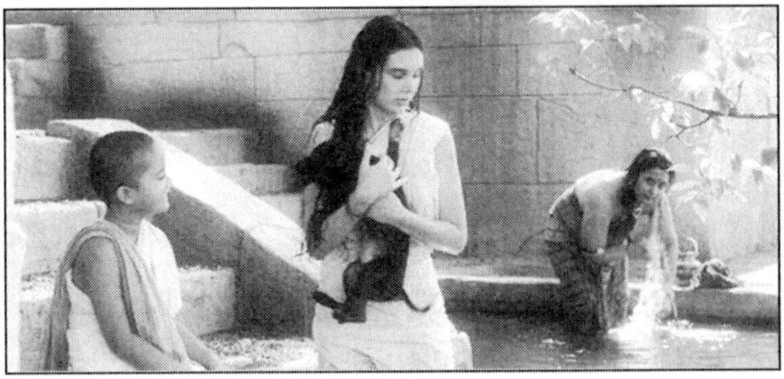

For the male gaze

Two studies Hawthorn puts forward, oft cited in considering the gaze within gender and psychoanalytical perspectives, are John Berger's *Ways of Seeing* (1972), and Laura Mulvey's "Visual Pleasure and Narrative Cinema" (1975). The first theorises the knowledge and belief systems that are behind the way we see the *codes* within visual representations and the ways we *decode* them as viewers or readers. The second text offers a feminist position on the male gaze that sets up a hierarchy of 'active male' vs 'passive female', so that women are represented to fulfil male needs of 'to-be-looked-at-ness'. Mulvey's central thesis is that, the forms of looking that are depicted *in* a work of art can not be separated from the forms of looking *at* that work of art conducted by reader or spectator, even though the latter forms of looking are literal in the case of the cinema and metaphorical in the case of the reading of literature." Another theory cited for its relevance to the gaze by Hawthorn comes from Foucault's *Discipline and Punish: The Birth of the Prison* (1977), where the structure of the panopticon (prison cells laid out in a ring permitting total surveillance of the imprisoned) makes the gaze "unambiguously a means of control" (Hawthorn 512). In discussions on the 'perspective' of the cine–camera, what emerges is the power of the camera as 'voyeur.'

With the attaining of freedom by the former colonies of Europe, and the proliferation of postcolonial theories and writings in the last quarter century or so, such as Edward Said's theory of colonial representation as distortion and stereotype, Hawthorn picks up Said's focus on 'exteriority' (*Orientalism*: 1978) and the imperial gaze.

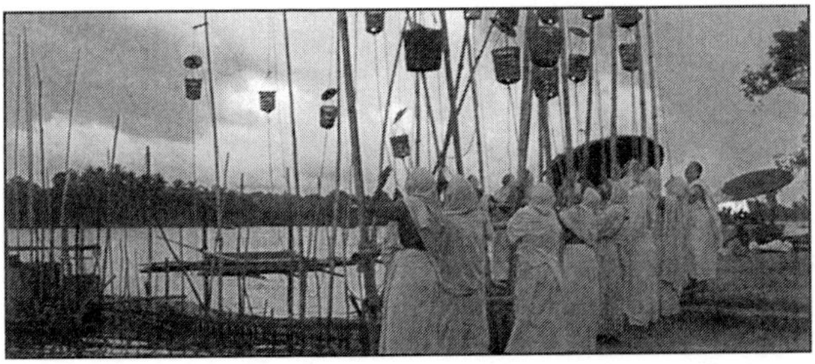

Exteriority: Widowhood as spectacle

Gandhi's intervention in countering the gaze, was in returning the imperial gaze, in claiming an interactive space for looking and interpreting. The writer Mulk Raj Anand was caned for staring at an official of the British Raj: "I salaamed the Adjutant Sahab of my father's regiment and stared at him out of curiosity. He hit me with a cane and I went crying to my father, who did not say anything but accepted the punishment I got for the crime of looking up to the sahib." (71)

Expounding the discovery of self as a postcolonial, V.S. Naipaul's fictions and travel narratives hinge on unravelling colonial epistemological conditioning, making a transition to a new way of looking and seeing[3] that re-engages with history and the present. Himani Bannerji (*The Dark Side of the Nation)* problematises the gaze as a form of control by the machinery of the Canadian nation, to contain 'visible minorities.'

In my construction of the diasporic gaze and its crucial components, I pinpoint five features: exteriority, silence, thickness of sociological detail, spectacle, and conventions of stylization. The features working together determine the duration of the gaze and foregrounding of selected imagery and symbolism that will be substantiated in the discussion that follows.

Gathered together in the shabby interiors of an ashram by the stigma on their social condition, the widows in *Water* become visible in the real world outside only as performers for the divine in temples, as objects of repugnance and pity. The widows' ashram located in Rawalpur is the home of its destitute inmates, each one of whom has been 'cast off.'

The film and novel *Water*, bring together a group of widows the youngest child widow eight year old Chuyia, the fair and comely Kalyani, the blighted fairy tale princess of the widows who tries to live a pious and humane life, untouched by her sordid exposure to prostitution; Shakuntala, caregiver and scholar of the scriptures, confronting experiential realities and trying to sort out the conflict in her own mind between the faith religious tradition demands, and the stirrings of her own skeptical mind; Madhumati, doyen of the ashram, hardened to the suffering of her fellow widows, tuned in only to the fulfillment of her cravings for opium and the delicacies in food prohibited to widows; Kunti growing more bitter by the day, venting her frustration on young Chuyia; and the aged widow Bua, who drools at the memory of the sweets served at her own marriage. The film and the novel *Water* work out the tragic fate and simple yearnings of each of these characters, for food or comfort, company and love.

The cultural prohibitions on looking and gazing within the inter-personal domains of a caste and tradition that bound North Indian social and Brahminical caste structure of the 1930s, can be decoded within the film *Water*. Sarala with her child's curiosity and spirited attitude, looks all around, contesting Madhumati's cruelty and power; she glances back in anger when her mother-in-law chastises

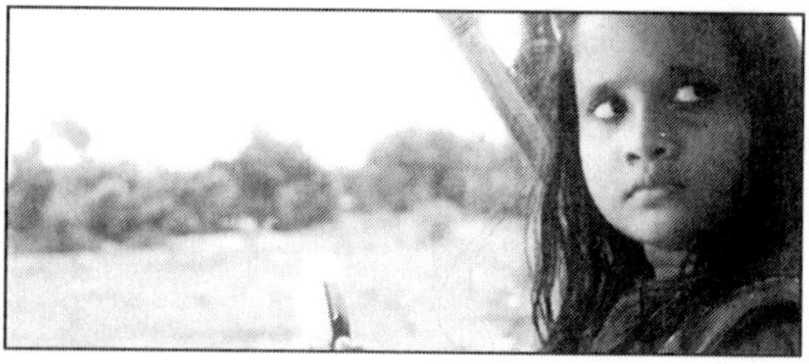

Chuyia: The centred self

her for her playfulness in the opening sequence of the bullock cart ride, where she accompanies her ill and virtually dying husband to the banks of the river. As Shakuntala understands the horror of Kalyani's and eventually Sarala's sexual exploitation, her decorous ways of looking change as her eyes confront the world and convey anger, extreme shock and alarm and a determination amidst despair. The 'gaze' takes us "to culture, history, politics and most of all unto power" (Hawthorn 509).

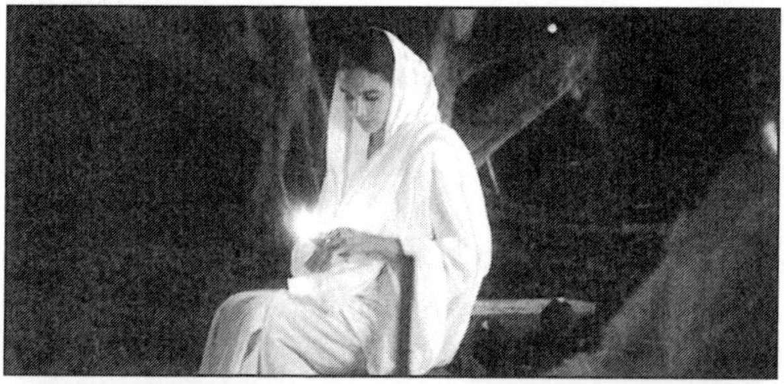

Stylisation and the Indian feminine

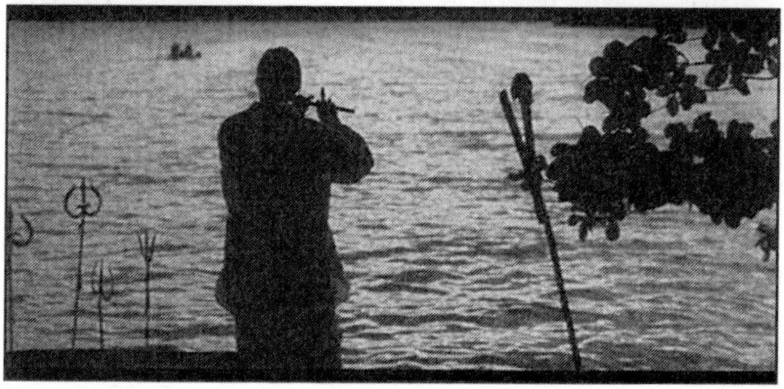

Framing Indianness: Krishna, the flute player

Within the stylised romantic frame of the Radha-Krishna narrative of ideal love, (reinforced through the background melodies) the relationship between Narayan and Kalyani gradually flowers. Kalyani begins to exchange looks expressing her confidence and her status as an equal with Narayan, an idealistic lover and Gandhian. Her relationship with him shows an opening of her self, whenever she is outside the boundaries of the social gaze that denies her this freedom. From this "literal interchange of looks" that are interpreted within a cultural semantics by reader or viewer as cultural insiders, to the theorisation of the diasporic 'gaze', entails an overall consideration of the poetic, picturesque, framed representation of an essence of the city of Benares too, whose teeming cultural life is virtually stilled, intended by Mehta perhaps to draw attention solely to the isolation and reclusive life of the stigmatised widows. The few scenes where the widows cross the path of the other people, while begging, or bathing, or performing rituals, are quite obviously 'staged' to incite melodrama.

Major portions of Mehta's gaze in *Water* are directed by the need to fulfil western needs for oriental fixities – the unchanging horror tale of a barbaric India. A contrastive Gandhian thread of the changing order of widowhood[4] within family structures in a representative South Indian village, was worked out by Raja Rao in *Kanthapura*, a novel that captures the cultural dynamics of pre-independence India, where we see that the widow Ratna is liberated from the fixities of the gaze.

Another textual example from the Brahminical social context for widowhood is the Kannada novel *Phaniyamma* (1976)[5] by M.K. Indira that looks at widowhood within the structure of the joint family. Phaniyamma too is widowed at the early age of eleven, accepts social structures of pollution and purity, and internalises the patriarchal norms of transgression for widows. She is given a *depth* and an *inner life* in her interrogation of the system of widowhood, that Mehta denies Kalyani.

The transformation of self for Phaniyamma in Indira's novel occurs when she boldly ventures out at night, transgressing caste codes and assists in the delivery of the child of an untouchable woman Sinki, in the small village. In the same novel, another widow Dakshayini transgresses sexual barriers, entering into a relationship with her brother-in-law, declaring her pregnancy through him, and flouting social conventions. The transitions and new choices Phaniyamma and Dakshayini make, revision the old social text of widowhood, a history that represents virtually the same time period as Mehta's *Water*. It is interesting to speculate whether it is *Water* that is likely foregrounded as a canonical text displacing *Kanthapura* and *Phaniyamma*, through the dissemination of film by diaspora, markets and the global media.

The creative recycling and adaptation from film to novel and the 'tuning' between the two diasporic artists, Mehta and Sidhwa, raises several questions about whether the novel can be loosely regarded as an intertextual[6] reworking or recycling in another medium – a transgenre transformation. The case of *Water* holds interest on aesthetic grounds and the visibility it provides for rendering and reading social texts.[7] The interpretation of the diasporic gaze must necessarily engage with issues such as the geographical location of the artist, allegiances to abroad and/or home, the intended audience, the cultural imagination called into existence by Mehta or Sidhwa and finally, the politics of the present be it Hindutva or neo-colonisation.

A review and comparison of the two texts – the film and the novel – carried out initially in terms of plot, structure and character reveal a close parallel. The plot repeats the tragic fate of the 6-year-old child bride Chuyia who becomes a widow within two years of her marriage and is confined to the widows' ashram on the banks of the Ganga. The plot of the film and the novel, focus on Chuyia's friendship with Kalyani, a widow who is exploited as a prostitute, a valuable source of income for the self-centred leader of the ashram, Madhumati, addicted to the pleasure of her body and impervious to the woes of the widows who surround her.

The novel and film also echo the narrative of Gandhi's impact on the young law student Narayan, committed to reformist ideas about widow remarriage and their emancipation from cultural taboos, confinement and a virtual death in the eyes of their society. Following closely, the trail of Mehta's cinematic narrative, Sidhwa pins her conclusion on the 'rescue' of Chuyia, (after Chuyia's rape by Seth Dwarkanath), when Shakuntala, running frantically to spot Narayan in a moving train, hands over Chuyia to him. With the suicide of Kalyani, the beautiful young widow, and the anti-climactic ending to the tender love story of Narayan and Kalyani, Shakuntala the emergent awakened, protesting consciousness of the ashram, is determined to release Chuyia from the shackles of a system that cannot be changed.

While the adaptation of novels into films for commercial reasons occurs on a regular basis, reverse adaptation, an artistic process where a novel is commissioned out a film to promote it commercially (Wikipedia, 'Film Adaptation') is somewhat less common. In cases of reverse adaptation, the form of the novel allows for a more sustained delineation of character, incident and socio-cultural milieu. Sidhwa's novel provides more space for scholarly, text-bookish commentary, and is evaluative and judgmental of patriarchy. However in common, the film and the novel's processes of expression are dominated by a quest for stereotypical forms of response and behaviour and the construction of the bleakest forms of deprivation

The novel allows for the detailed reworking of scenes, imagines a childhood for Chuyia, marked by spontaneity and play and develops her family background. Her father, a priest, has accepted the remarriage of a 44 year old widower to 6 year old Chuyia and her apprehensive mother, cherishes anger against the gender injustice of a Brahminical religious and social structure, but ameliorates her protest, rationalising her husband's decisions. While no new characters are introduced for the novel, each character expands in 'character time' and becomes a mouthpiece for explicit sociological commentary on Indian concepts, customs and rituals, allowing a certain 'growth' within another artistic medium, despite a structural equivalence of character, plot, history, image and symbol. The novel, with its relatively more concrete and expressive use of *language*, exhibits more fully the *exteriority* of the diasporic *gaze* and the distant location from the native milieu.

Let us first focus on the predilection of the male gaze that looks sexually at children and women. What does this gaze select, despite Mehta and Sidhwa being women artists? The following illustrations from the novel should make it clear:

1. Bhagya's body 'thickened with childbearing'.
2. Her daughter's chest was flat and her small nipples dimpled inwards. Bhagya had an urge to hold her. (12)
3. Her [Chuyia's] mouth was an inlaid bud in the moon of her face. Impulsively, she bent to lightly kiss the sweetness on her daughter's lips. The wash-worn rag that served as Chuyia's tiny sari had ridden up her limbs, she looked like one of Krishna's cherubic gopis. (9)
4. Sadananda's sexual desire for Shakuntala's woman's body is opened up fully in the novel, the male gaze feasting on explicit details of her anatomy, though the ostensible intent is to malign religion and priesthood. (156-7)

The binary of 'coloured' vs 'white' races inherent in the diasporic gaze is cast into relief in Sidhwa's narrative where "chocolate" and "ebony" and "brown skin the colour of creamed coffee" are used as descriptive adjectives for the Indian women characters. Predictably, Kalyani is 'fair' and the woman who gives Shakuntala a pot of water for Chuyia's revival, in the concluding part of the novel, is visibly dark (a Sri Lankan, who stands out in the film contrastively).

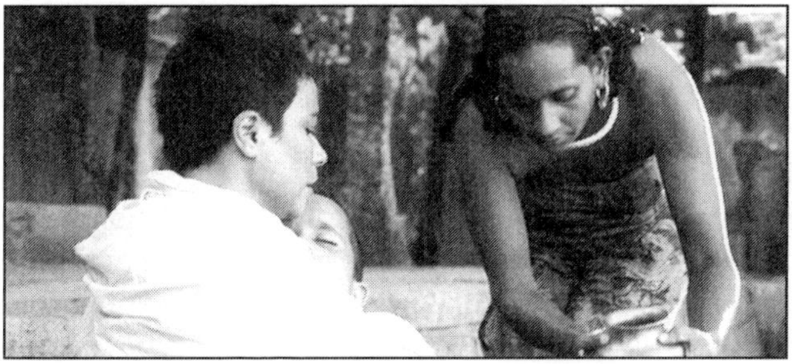

Foregrounding the 'dark' body

The denial of subjecthood and agency by the diasporic gaze is the limitation of these narratives of victimhood. It is important to problematise the historical and ideological distance of the treatment of widowhood, from the contemporary spaces of India. In terms of the debates on 'narrating the nation,' Mehta's most gross errors consist in advocating the specific histories of the widows of Bihar and Bengal as the reality of the 'nation,' both in 1930s India and the 21st century. Cultural specificity is recreated at the level of period locale, architecture, habits and customs, rituals and traditions, song and dance, while selectively obliterating the forms of protest emanating from the voices of educated widows.

The iconisation of Gandhi, is a conscious choice and Mehta's gaze excludes the more positive forms of women-centric protest on the issue of widowhood. Why, one asks, could Shakuntala, a courageous and caring woman, who had attempted to save Kalyani from a loveless life of prostitution, not have herself boarded the train with Chuyia rather than relegate her frantically to a male saviour Narayan? Is it because Mehta has decided to contain Shakuntala's strength and decisiveness. Any further upsurge in Shakuntala would perhaps have upset the colonial binary too strongly.

The point being advanced here is that the progressive and thinking Indian woman of the 1930s is sacrificed to put the submissive woman on a pedestal. The diasporic privilege to occupy a third space, to stir the nation's past from the 'inside' as Monica Flundernik (2006:13) theorises in her reading of internal difference, based on a confluence of heterogenous cultures and traditions: "Differencing therefore is carried into the inside from its former position on the outside to which it had been relegated by the colonial, racist or nationalist episteme"[8], is bypassed.

Water is a moving film but empty of real political redefinition and subversion at the level of gender, class and race. The symbolic fascination with the medium of water submerges the voices of the women's community. The case of *Water* (film and novel as diasporic texts) brings us to the question of the relative identity of diaspora, searching 'home' for subjects of ethnic interest and 'abroad' for captive markets: "Diasporas develop and maintain crucial networks of material and symbolic exchanges with their homelands as well as with various social groups in receiving countries," as Ali Behdad comments (Shwarz and Sangeeta Ray: 2000).

India is constructed through many routine devices and conventional symbols in the film *Water*. The opening epigraph from Manu, voices a normative text of widowhood. The journey of a dying man on the boat journey across the river suggests the crossover from life to death – to the other bank – lit up by the shimmering orange of the funeral pyres. The yellow ingredient of haldi paste smeared on Chuyia's head to ease the rawness of her tonsured head, applied by Shakuntala, apparently stands in need of explanation, even to a common village girl. 'This is Haldi...it will cool your mind,' Shakuntala explains. The gaudy pinks and yellow that the widowed inmates of the ashram fling around and smear on each other's faces, is again 'held' for the camera gaze, as spectacle, capturing an essence of India.

Lisa Ray (Kalyani) is particularly targeted as an ethereal beauty for the male gaze. With her dark long tresses, she is a Rapunzel leaning out from the balcony. 'She walks in beauty,' her expressions and demeanor, virtually a still pond, despite her exposure to prostitution. The draping and undraping of selected portions of Kalyani's fair body, revealing her nakedness in crucial scenes are clearly directed to the male gaze and her idealised virtues to the male fantasy. Kalyani is 'displayed' and 'held' in close-ups that offer her up to detailed scrutiny, objectifying her.

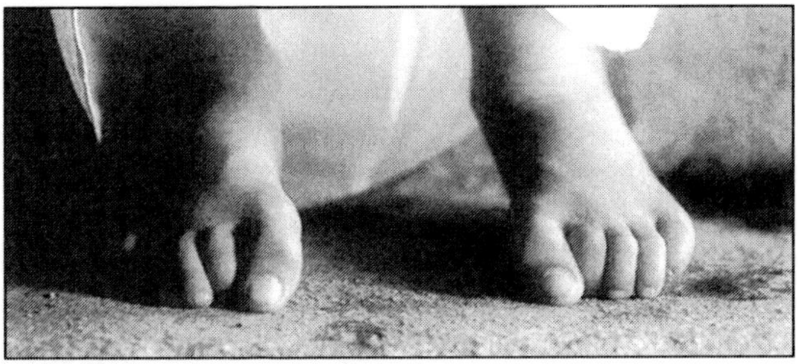

Imposing a culture of silence

The filmmaker imposes a culture of silence on her positive female characters. Chuyia does not wriggle or yell out during her slow and tortuous tonsuring. All the camera focuses on is her clenched toes. This seems to be designed for the foreign 'gaze.' The same Chuyia, is allowed to show her real mettle, when she protests her father and mother-in-law's decision to abandon her in the ashram, or bites Madhumati when the latter orders her around sternly. The point being made here is that the 'passivisation' of the female/racial subject concerned, is of crucial significance in interpreting the political slant of the diasporic gaze. The held image, and the spelt out cultural data seem to me to be as relevant to interpreting the start of this gaze as other technical aspects of a cinematic shots such as "distance, focus, movement, and point of view" (Monaco 195).

The critical distinction of the diasporic perspective that I have argued by juxtaposing the film and novel *Water*, suggests the historical and cultural fallacies of the gaze, by prioritising stylisation and spectacle, women as objects, homogenising the state of widowhood and thereby the nation.

Arun Prabha Mukherjee argues the problematic of Western cinema and its representation of the Third World, critiquing "the misrepresentation, manipulation and fantasisation of the people of the Third World" (Mukherjee 1994:39). Her points are well taken and applicable to the representations generated by the diasporic gaze that equally in *Water*, panders to 'the male gaze' and a dominant thrust on the barbaric practices sanctioned by Hindu religion. The spectacle of poverty and helplessness endorses colonial binaries, sanitising the colonial presence in Gandhian India or the life of Varanasi.

Thus though there is a certain leeway at the level of agency given to some of the widows like Shakuntala or Madhumati, the dominant governing mode for the diasporic eye continues to be the victim syndrome[9] of widows and women. The scenes are also designed for the male gaze, where women are looked at most of the time. The cinematic technique of spectacle and fragmentation of subjectivity works against the social concern the text declares as it overt intention.

The diasporic gaze has a predilection to engage with the construction of an unchanging India – mythical and exotic in reimagining and interpreting the past. The framed image uses a conscious technique of stylization to contain (for the male and Western and diasporic gaze) the dynamics of action or thought. The frame may be one of mythical story (Radha and Krishna), the eternal and the timeless quality of reality, disallowing protest and change. The widows, especially Kalyani, are muted, forming a framed composition, pretty in play, but allowed no real introspection and sharing on the tragedy of their lives. Rarely are the widows allowed the privilege of looking, even as indiscretions or transgressive acts.

The picture of a "pink-cheeked English girl, clasping a bouquet of flowers in her white hands," hanging on the walls of the ashram, that Chuyia gazes at (46), is unconsciously/or consciously (?) constructed as a symbol of the racial/hierarchical binaries of self and the other in a colonial era. Sidhwa gives a description of Chuyia's reverential gaze before the portrait, building in a poor village child's prayer to a 'white' child, seen as a "strange goddess" who may perhaps transport her home. A similar condescension invests the scene where Gandhi addresses the crowd gathered at the railway station, to listen to his discourse. Gandhi makes no clear eye contact

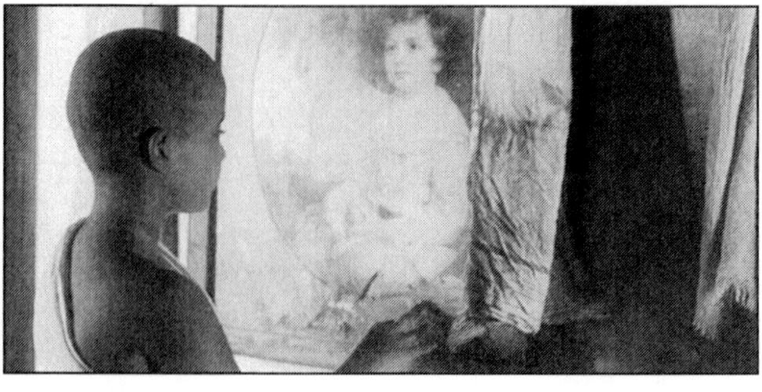

The colonial gaze: Self and the other

with the audience and neither do the viewers of Mehta's film. This comes through again as the intention of the filmmaker to control Gandhi's subversiveness.

As marker of status and power, 'looking' and 'gazing' are manifestations of a characters place within a social hierarchy (of religion, caste, patriarchy). The 'look' and the 'gaze' considered alongside other aspects of a character's body language contribute to an interpretation of both ease and equality in interpersonal relations. 'Looking' and 'gazing' within the cinematic frames of *Water* become expressive of a graph of attitudes from passivity, modesty, subjugation, fear, acceptance and resignation to the empowered traits of curiosity, interrogation, imagining, defiance and determination. The maximum growth in empowerment of attitudes is visible through Shakuntala's expressions. Mehta chooses, however, to fix Kalyani in a stereotype of silent suffering paving the way for her suicide, after the disclosure that the 'client' Seth Dwarkanath whom Gulabi takes her to, is none other than her prospective husband Narayan's father.

Deepa Mehta's *Water* remains imprisoned within the prescriptive codes of Manu shastra – that "a widow should be long suffering." The film does not create from the stance of the politics of the present, a counter discourse of strong currents of protest[10], within the deep waters of a hoary tradition. Chuyia's anger and rebellious spirit come to naught. The film (and its sibling novel) are monuments to the reinvocation and deification of the widow as victim, impaled within the negative fixities and sociological prison of the diasporic gaze.

Notes

1. When Deepa Mehta was asked in an interview about what was the central issue that she wanted people to take from the movie *Water,* she responded: "The kernel for me is the movie's exploration of the difference between conscience and faith. People must listen to and be honest with themselves rather than accept intolerant ideologies, which are at odds with their moral conscience and the realities of life." (Mehta and Phillips, 15 May 2006)
2. See Uma Parameswaran on the question of "disjunction of sensibility," in her article "Disjunction of Sensibility: Deepa Mehta's Film *Fire*" in *Writing the Diaspora* (Rawat: 2007).

3. See Naipaul's opening paras in *A Way in the World,* (London: Heinemann, 1994), for discriminations between looking and seeing.
4. Rajul Sogani in the introduction to her work *The Hindu Widow in Indian Literature* (OUP: 2002), focuses on canonical and non-canonised Indian texts to examine the theme of tradition and change in the context of widowhood.
5. See my article on the film *Phaniyamma* and the representation of widowhood: "Breaking the Silence: Gender, Caste and Transgression in *Phaniyamma* and *Bandh Jharokhe*" (179-93) in Jain and Rai, Eds. *Films and Feminism* (Rawat: 2002).
6. See Stam for the concept of 'intertextuality.' "All works of art inevitably get caught up in the ongoing whirl of dialogical transformation, of texts generating other texts in an interminable circuits of recycling and transformation" (65) in *Literature through Film* (Oxford: Blackwell Publishing, 2005).
7. See Robert Stam's Introduction to *Literature through Film* (Oxford: Blackwell Publishing, 2005), for the social and ideological questions that are raised in an adaptation and the chosen style of representation. Stam asks: "Does a novel or its adaptation push society towards a more egalitarian condition by critiquing social inequities based on axes of stratification such as race, gender, class, and sexuality, or does it simply assume (or even glorify) these inequities and hierarchies as natural and God-given...in what language and style is the representation framed, and what are the social connotations of those styles and languages?" (6)
8. The problematic of the politics of 'inside/outside' is sounded out by R. Radhakrishnan (196) in his essay " Nationalism, Gender and Identity" (*Postcolonial Discourses.* Ed. Gregory Castle. Oxford: Blackwell, 2001). What Mehta constructs as a seeming opposition to the religious conservatism of the inside, is also fraught with problems pertaining to homogenisation and selection of conventions of femininity.
9. See Priyamvada Gopal's essay, "Of Victims and Vigilantes" in *Signposts*. Ed. Rajeshwari Sunderrajan, (New Delhi: Kali for Women, 2000) on the film – Phoolan Devi, the Bandit Queen. Gopal asks: "Do depictions of victimisation/oppression with the putative goal of raising political awareness do further harm by showing women as victims rather than agents?" (294).
10. *Samaj Ki Bhool*, a film directed by Homi Master in 1934, was one of the early films to address the issue of widow remarriage. V. Shantaram's *Duniya na Mane* (1937) focuses on a young woman's protest at being married to a much older husband and her resistance becomes the basis of his realisation of the social malpractice.

References

Anand, Mulk Raj "The Source of Protest in my Novels," *Creating Theory: Writers on Writing*. Ed. Jasbir Jain. Delhi: Pencraft International, 2000.

Bannerji, Himani. *The Dark Side of the Nation*. Toronto: Canadian Scholars Press, 2000.

Fludernik, Monika. ed. *Hybridity and Postcolonialism*. Jaipur: Rawat Publications, 2006.

Hawthorn, Jeremy. "Theories of the Gaze", in *Literary Theory and Criticism*. Ed. Patricia Waugh, London:OUP, 2006.

Indira, M.K. *Phaniyamma*. (1976) trans, Tejaswani Niranjana. New Delhi: Kali for Women, 1989.

Jain, Jasbir and Sudha Rai, eds. *Films and Feminism*. Jaipur: Rawat Publications, 2002.

Monaco, James. *How to Read a Film* (2000). Indian Edition, OUP, 2007.

Mukherjee, Arun. *Oppositional Aesthetics*. Toronto: TSAR Publications, 1994.

Naipaul, V.S. *A Way in the World*. London: Heinemann, 1994.

Parameswaran, Uma. *Writing the Diaspora*. Jaipur: Rawat Publications, 2007.

Phillips, Richard. Speaks with Deepa Mehta. http://www.wsws.org/articles/2006/May 2006/deep-m15.shtml

Radhakrishnan, R. "Nationalism, Gender and Identity" in *Postcolonial Discourses*. Ed. Gregory Castle. Oxford: Blackwell, 2001.

Rao, Raja. *Kanthapura*. (1938) Delhi: OUP, 1989.

Rushdie, Salman. "Imaginary Homelands", *Imaginary Homelands*. New Delhi: Penguin Books, 1991.

Shwarz, Henry and Sangeeta Ray. *A Companion to Postcolonial Studies* (2000). Oxford: Blackwell Publishing, 2005.

Sidhwa, Bapsi. *Water*. New Delhi: Viking Books, 2006.

Sogani, Rajul. *The Hindu Widow in Indian Literature*. New Delhi: OUP, 2002.

Stam, Robert. *Literature through Film*. Oxford: Blackwell Publishing, 2005.

Sunderrajan, Rajeshwari. *Signposts*. New Delhi: Kali for Women, 2000.

Wikipedia. htpp://en.wikipedia.org/wiki/film_adaptation

Water (2005). Dir. Deepa Mehta, Prod. David Hamilton, Cinematography: Giles Nuttgems, Perf. Seema Biswas, Lisa Ray, John Abraham, Sarala.

17

Deepa Mehta's Film *Water*

Constructing the Dialectical Image

Tutun Mukherjee

Even if *Water* had not been nominated for the Oscars, which constitutes peer approbation of its cinematic distinction, it would have been marked as a singular achievement for the sheer grit and determination of the director to complete the film surmounting all odds. As is wellknown, even in ordinary filmmaking circumstances, it is a challenge for individual filmmakers to find encouraging producers, capable technicians and support staff who would help give ultimate shape to their vision. To be able to sustain interest and pursue the project after the serious setback of the kind 'Project Water' suffered, bears out Mehta's intrepid nature and tenacious love for her craft as well as the producer David Hamilton's faith in her ability.

Mehta's trilogy that binds the elemental with the feminine intrinsically and probes the way women are preyed upon and shackled by social institutions, pulverised and bartered by patriarchy, represents in its totality a powerful and significant cultural challenge to the dominating masculine values and practices of oppression, subjugation and exploitation of women. Since Mehta happens to be a woman director, her courage in the face of intimidation by the largely patriarchal forces must be acknowledged as the immensely relevant Preface to her film *Water* that documents, perhaps a little melodramatically, the marginalised life of forgotten Hindu widows battling to survive the harsh realities of neglect and poverty.

In a society where a woman's identity is governed by her male relative – whether father, husband, or son – and eventual patrilocality, it would appear that after the death of the husband, she 'ceases' as a person and passes into a state of 'social death'. Since a woman is regarded primarily as a vessel of reproduction, her 'social death' also signals her 'sexual death'. As a widow she is pushed to the margins of the functioning social unit of the family and is alienated from reproduction and sexuality.[1] She begins to be regarded as a disrupter of the social order and the society is not at ease about other categories because a woman is not regarded as an independent being. As a widow, she is reduced to a void, a zero. The question rises about where to place her? Unlike the elaborate marriage rituals that mark a woman's entry into legitimate sexual activity, the rituals marking the renunciation of the widow's sexuality are simple but deeply humiliating and traumatic, the most visible being the breaking of bangles and tonsure or the shaving of the head. These enforced signs of widowhood – signifying symbolic restraint or castration – along with the effacement of colour from her garments and taste from her food (a widow must wear white – or black in certain communities – borderless sari and eat bland vegetarian diet and on some days be denied food altogether) are the ways by which the society/community (such practices were especially prevalent and severe among the brahmins) reiterates its power to control a widow's sexuality. Two other signs of marriage that are removed are the *sindhoor* or the vermilion mark in the parting of the hair and the *bindi* or the red dot on the forehead (a widow may wear a bindi of ash if she wishes as a reminder of the ash from her husband's pyre or the heap of ash her life has become). In addition to removing the symbols of marriage, a widow is expected to renounce all adornments, cosmetics and is forbidden from looking in a mirror. The fear of female sexuality and the need to control it have figured in all patriarchal societies and this desire has assumed various forms in different societies at different times. Through these ritual processes, symbolic ideas are acted out to suggest the real human interaction which would subsequently follow. The customs and rituals represent an attempt to find a social and ideological resolution of the tensions inherent in the conceptualisation of widowhood where a widow continues to exist but is sexually a non-being. The worst of all is the lifelong shame a widow must bear of being considered inauspicious and hence banned from attending celebrations. A widow is feared and imagined as a bad omen. Of the eight incarnations of the Devi in Hindu mythology, the most feared is 'Dhumavati' in the form of a widow accompanied by the raven as her vehicle.

That there is an economic angle to the way widows are treated must not be overlooked. Often social norms restrict a widow's rights to residence, property, and employment, and impose a gendered division of labour as well as seclusion. Without any source of income, she is reduced to helpless dependency and penury. There is hardly a family in India that does not have a widow – a grandmother, mother or an aunt – as an omnipresent figure. When supported and cared for she is the matriarch who rules the household with love and wisdom. But increasingly with the dismantling of the joint family system, she is left to fend for herself and as Martha Alter Chen puts it, "symbolizes the imminent collapse of the social order" (2001:1). According to the Government of India 1991 Census, there are more than 33 million widows in India of whom some thirty thousand are below fifteen years of age. According to Chen, the reasons for the high proportion of widows is because "marriage in India is near universal; husbands are five years older on average than wives; male mortality rates are still very high; women begin to outlive men after their reproductive years; and, most importantly, widow remarriage is infrequent" (2001:3). Till recently, two linked social practices: *gauri daan* or child marriage to avoid social ostracism if a daughter remains unmarried after attaining puberty and *kulin pratha* that allows polygamy among the brahmins, were the major causes for widowhood in that community since very young girls were wed to much older and much married men. To avoid the problems of both economic and familial nurture of the widows, the convenient way devised by the communities was, and still is, to send them away to pilgrimage centres like Mathura-Vrindavan and Kashi/Varanasi ostensibly to let them pass the remainder of their life in devotion and worship. These pilgrimage centres, as well as others, teem with widows sent away by their families invariably without financial support living in pitiful condition and trying to combat grim poverty, caught between life and death. Their status is of being "lifted from the pyre but left in the cremation ground" (Kitchlu viii).

Though the plight of the Hindu widows has captured the attention of the people in India and abroad, and the Indian National Commission for Women presented its Report on widows living in Mathura, Vrindavan and Varanasi in 1996, their lot remains unchanged. Three images in particular – the child widow, the ascetic widow, and the widow who burns on her husband's pyre – have never failed to evoke pity and consternation. The current work of social reformers and women's rights activists focus on the financial well being and the customary rights of widows to property as both daughters and daughters-in-law (e.g. Kitchlu; Chen). The urgent need is to highlight the widows' rights in principle and the reality of their denial. However, these matters are yet to be satisfactorily resolved, given the patrilineal laws and customs in India as well as the existing social norms in patrilineal communities.

The nineteenth century is considered the most eventful period in the history of women's struggle for the rights of equality and freedom. Effective campaigns were launched in India by social reformers like Rammohan Roy, Iswarchandra Vidyasagar, Dayanand Saraswati, Pandita Ramabai, Narmadashankar Dave, Tarabai Shinde and so on, against 'sati', 'polygamy', 'child marriage' and 'widow remarriage' to mention a few relevant issues. The reformist rhetoric and the success of these movements translated into various legislative enactments and amendments making 'sati' and child marriage – those who perform and also those who incite – punishable offences and legalising widow remarriage. The latter (by The Hindu Widow's Remarriage Act of 1856), however, was not a totally new concept because certain communities of Punjab and Rajasthan permit the levirate custom of the widow marrying the younger brother of the deceased husband. This is in keeping with certain allowances made in the *Dharma shastras*. For instance, Sage Parashar (*Parashar Samhita* Ch IV) suggested three ways of life for widows: to lead celibate lives, to die with their husbands or to re-marry. Indian myths offer examples of all three: Kunti (*Mahabharata*) lived a celibate life; Madri (*Mahabharata*) died with her husband; and on Rama's advice,

Mandodari (*Ramayana*) remarried Vibhisan. Despite all this, remarriage of widows is not a socially accepted practice; for instance, Vidyasagar's efforts to conduct remarriage of widows met with stiff resistance and antagonism and even attracted physical attack; the remarriage of Anandi Bai Joshi to D.K. Karve in 1893 created a furore[2]. Such was the unease and tension regarding the issue that many literary leaders of the century like Bankim Chandra Chattopadhyay, Saratchandra Chatterjee, Rabindranath Tagore dealt with the image of the widow in their fiction but did not (dare to?) permit her the happy resolution of a marriage. Though such fictional characters are treated with initial sympathy by their creators, they are slowly developed as transgressive and disruptive agents who threaten the moral and social order of the family and the community. Young and beautiful widows free of male control circulate as objects of desire and illicit passion. Therefore they must be and eventually are removed by some narrative connivance. According to Meenakshi Mukherjee, since marriages were arranged and the brides were sometimes very young, the only possibility of romance of an adult male could be with a courtesan, prostitute or a widow (70). Thus, novels like *Vishabriksha, Krishnakanter Will, Charitraheen, Palli Samaj, Chokher Bali, Yamuna Paryatan, Saraswatichandra* to mention a few memorable representations of widows, address widowhood and its difficulties by pivoting the plot on it but do not break social conventions nor introduce liberal thinking to radically change the social attitude towards widows. In fact, their treatment confirms society's subliminal fear of young widows as sexually disruptive agents.

The development of analytical awareness of social-cultural evils takes time. Effecting radical changes takes even longer. The emancipation movement of women began gradually to take bigger and more successful strides in the twentieth century and reflected the positive change and aggressive stance vis-à-vis regressive customs in various kinds of writing.[3] Stories were written with widows as protagonists who were admired and respected for their conduct and ethics. With films becoming widely popular by mid-century, another medium became available as an expressive mode to explore and represent various social issues. While the usual social and family dramas had widows as ubiquitous characters, a few memorable films inspired by equally remarkable novels confronted the subject more directly and courageously. These films have received both audience appreciation and critical acclaim for their sensitive treatment of the conditions of widowhood. While the several film versions of *Vishabriksha, Krishnakanter Will, Charitraheen, Palli Samaj, Chokher Bali, Saraswatichandra* present the cautious attitude of the earlier generation, films like *Ek Chadar Maili Si, Vamshavriksha, Ghattashraddha, Rudali, Adajya* explore the various aspects of widowhood and their social implications with realistic, nuanced and sensitive maturity.

Deepa Mehta's film *Water* contributes to this discourse on widowhood and makes commendable attempts to embed the cinematic images in the dialectical force-field. In all the three films of the trilogy – *Earth, Fire* and *Water* – Mehta's treatment is informed by a strong feminist stance. This means that she is sensitive to the gendered way of seeing the world and therefore consciously creates a frame of reference or a standpoint in each film to critically examine the issues that particular film intends to bring into discussion. Since it is the woman's eye directing the camera, her understanding and sensitive presentation of both subject and subjectivity are intended as interventions in the received ideas that have been allowed to perpetuate conventional attitudes unquestioningly. There can be no fixed characteristics that identify a typically 'feminist text' because, as Annette Kuhn explains, "no set of meanings already inhabits the text, but rather a text is, in some measures at least, created in its reading or reception" (14). Hence, no intervention in culture can work at the level of the text alone but becomes effective by the way of its reception. In her films, Mehta tries to invest each frame and each image with such properties and detailing as to provoke interrogation/intellection. Since a text is based on its relationship with the receptor/spectator, it becomes a feminine text in the moment of its reading/viewing that makes one aware of the film's questioning and problematising of the taken-for-granted stereotypical representation of women and/or issues that concern them.

Water opens with a beautiful visual of an expanse of blue water covered with lotuses beyond which a bullock cart crosses a bridge and trundles along a narrow path overhung with green deciduous trees. A dark skinned man passes swinging clay pots in a bamboo carrier slung across his shoulders. The exotic oriental setting is immediately registered but not in idealised timelessness since the specific time is quickly announced as "India 1938". The stylised panorama is interrupted by closer shots of the passengers of the bullock cart comprising a montage of small anklet-adorned feet dangling from the back of the cart; a small cheerful girl with curly hair chewing sugar cane with relish; a very sick man being attended to by an older man and a woman. The innocent playfulness of the small girl indifferent to the seriously ill patient, the boat ride across a river, the death of the sick man and the girl being awakened by the old man her father with the information that her husband is dead, follow in a quick economical succession of frames. Remarkable is the expert play of colours and tonalities to contrast the changing contexts and of the intermittent vista shots with closer montage. As would become evident, this cinematographic technique, matched with subdued and sometimes evocative mood music of *ragas*, controls the pace and mood of the entire film and weaves the fine poetic texture of the narrative. The view of the cremation ground by the river with burning pyres cuts to the close shots of the breaking of the bangles adorning small wrists, a small head being shorn and then shaved by a barber. The girl's exasperated face devoid of any understanding of what is being done to her changes to bewilderment when dressed in a white sari she is taken to a dilapidated house and left there by her father. She asks repeatedly about her mother and starts to cry. She is carried screaming and struggling by a widow into the courtyard of the house where sit several other widows of different ages, all emaciated and sad looking. She is summoned by Madhumati whom she bites in a helpless animal-like rage, and after futile running around, backs into a corner. Thus the eight year old Chuyia (Sarala Kariyawasam) enters the *bidhva-ashram*, the widow home where she must spend the rest of her life.

The inmates of the widow home are women of different ages and temperament. Though the characterisation reveals a basic formula that feeds the plot, the director's efforts towards individualising and fine-tuning of some of the characters becomes evident through the progressing narrative. While the fat Madhumati (the well remembered Manorama of countless villainous roles) is like a madam of a brothel – immoral, greedy and exploitative – earning their expenses by prostituting the beautiful Kalyani (Lisa Ray) in collusion with the transvestite pimp Gulabi (Raghuveer Yadav); Shakuntala (Seema Biswas) is literate, reserved and disciplined, kind-hearted, respected by others and the only one calling Madhumati by her name when the others call her 'didi' or elder sister; Kunti and Snehalata are the serving menial types as are several others; and the oldest inmate 'auntie' shows an ironic sense of humour and spends her time in nostalgia. None of them can recall exactly how long they have lived there but that they were very small when they came after their husbands, the old men they were married to, died. The semiotics of the dark and dismal interiors emphasised by crumbling and peeling walls baring the bricks underneath as though exposing the skeletons of the society, the bars on the windows, the closed doors (interestingly, the panel of Kalyani's door has an aperture!), a caged parrot – convey the poverty-stricken, cloistered and circumscribed life of the inmates struggling to survive. Their religiosity consists of *bhajan* and the mechanical chanting of the names of gods, listening to sacred texts or *pravachan* and observing fast. The only instance of real fervour and joy is Holi the festival of colours, and especially that year when Shakuntala dresses Chuyia up as frolicking child Krishna among the *gopikas*. So effective in the film has been the representation of the dreary colourless life of the bidhva-ashram that the sudden splash of the hues of Holi and unrestrained laughter make a startling impact. The drab bidhva-ashram hemmed in from all sides is to be contrasted with Narayan's home: airy, opulent and comfortable. The juxtaposition uplifts the meaningful use of colour, tone and atmosphere by the director.

The widows tacitly accept Kalyani's exploitation since she brings the money for their food and Kalyani appears to stoically accept her own functionality. Most of the inmates sleep in ground floor halls, Madhumati has a separate room, Shakuntala has created separate space for herself – physically and metaphorically, and Kalyani enjoys the privilege of a small room on the first floor where she has a niche for her deities, a balcony, and a puppy Kallu. She is also the only one who has long hair. Into their midst comes irrepressible and lovable Chuyia – literally, a small mouse – who becomes Kalyani's playmate and the reluctant Shakuntala's ward.

The sense that conveys itself most powerfully in the film is that of appetite of different sorts. Madhumati does not deny her palate and gets *ganja,* savouries and men through Gulabi. Snehalata eats greedily in the kitchen before serving food to Madhumati and old 'auntie' longs for the kind of *laddoo* she ate when she got married. A fascinating scene ensues when Chuyia places a *laddoo* that she has inveigled from the sweet shop in auntie's hand as she sleeps. The aroma awakens auntie and she swallows the laddoo greedily, letting the taste revive the scene of her being fed a laddu during her marriage, a vivid spot in her memory surrounded by the darkness of forgetfulness. Another appetite is the lust of the rich men that feeds on the widows who are not even referred to by name but by their bodies as the fat one, the thin one, the young one etc. and which does not even spare a vulnerable and innocent child like Chuyia. Contrasted with the sensual excesses is the denial of the senses and asceticism – of Shakuntala, of the ideal celibate widows, and of Gandhi. Narayan (John Abraham) is a true Gandhian and refuses to indulge in the epicurean lifestyle that his friend Rabindra (Vinay Pathak) seems to accept as his patrimony. Kalyani and Chuyia both hunger for and like Narayan are ready to share warmth and affection.

The metaphorical and metonymical use and the multilayered connotations of the river are integral to the plot. Besides reflecting the shifting moods of the characters and the twists in the narrative in tandem with the changes in Nature, the river operates at once as a regenerative element as well as a purifying agent; it is the resting place for tired bodies, the last sip for the departing soul and a site of rituals for both marriage and death; it is a source of hope where Chuyia floats a boat to carry her home and of hopelessness when it bears both Kalyani and her as objects of lust. It is by the river that the young and handsome Narayan sees Kalyani and is immediately captivated by her natural and winsome beauty in the stark widow's weeds. We know that the film was shot near a lake in Sri Lanka with a new cast after the Varanasi fiasco. Mehta is able to create a fair semblance of the Varanasi river-front with its varied and crowded activities. Obviously she can not help that the lake and the river in the film appear too calm and tranquil to be Ganga. The turgid currents of the Ganga at Varanasi hinting at its powerful undertow would have enhanced both the metaphorical depth of the plot and the painterly splendour of Giles Nuttgens's cinematography.

The bank of Ganga in the film narrative recalls the bank of Jamuna where, under a massy tree, the flute playing Narayan awaits Kalyani in a strong reminder of the Krishna-Radha rendezvous. The romance of Radha and Krishna is deliberately invoked as Kalyani leaves for her clandestine meeting with Narayan after bowing to the figure of Krishna in the niche and lining her eyes with kohl from the burning lamp. Under the tree, by the side of many Shiva Lingas and symbols of Navagraha as silent witnesses, Narayan tells her of the fragrant flowerets of the *kadamba tree* and recites lines from Kalidas's *Meghadutam.* Their attraction for each other is spontaneous and natural. Narayan, a liberal Gandhian, is honest and warm hearted. Kalyani is too simple to be coy. Their blossoming love is both charming and touching because, as with the romance of Radha and Krishna, there is a prescience of their separation.

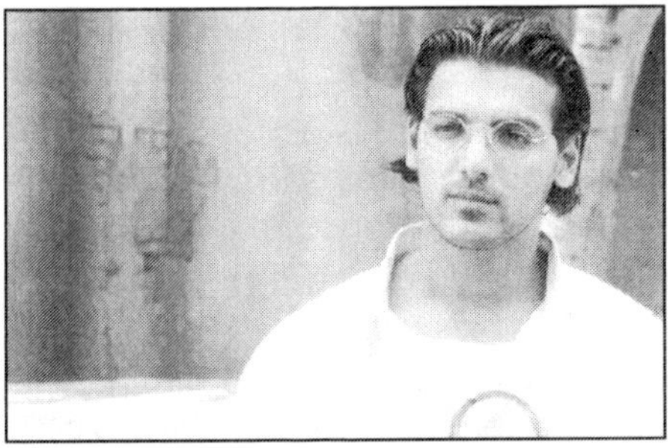

Narayan : Discovering his self

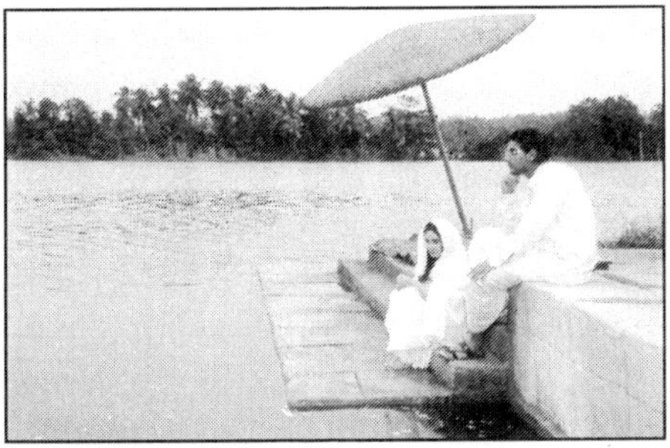

The lovers at the riverside

There are other forms of water shown in the film. Walking below Kalyani's balcony, Narayan is showered with water from her rinsed clothes. Kalyani and Chuyia play in the room to match the vigour of the rains outside. Recalling Narayan's recitation from *Meghadutam,* Kalyani watches the gathering dark clouds from her balcony and murmurs secret messages to the 'cloud messenger'. The rains come and drench them as they rejoice in their new-found love for each other. A vibrant oral tradition is recalled too, as the following verses explain:

titar pakhi badli bidhva kajal rekh
woh barse yo ghar kare ya main nahin bisekh
[a dark grey cloud is bound to burst
a widow using kohl is bound to remarry]

and,

kachchi imli gadrai savan mein
rand lugai mustai phagun mein
[a young girl matures in the month of rains
a widow frolics in early spring][4]

Narayan wants to marry Kalyani and does not hesitate to tell his mother (Waheeda Rahman) that she is a widow. As expected his mother is shocked and cries 'What will the people say!' But he is convinced that his father is broadminded enough to accept his decision and persuade his mother's consent. Shakuntala believes that Sadananda who reads the sacred texts to them by the river side is a wise and sympathetic person. She learns from him that dharma allows widows to remarry and in fact a Government Act permits them to do so. She wonders why such socially relevant information is suppressed and decides to help Kalyani find a new future. That she is trusted is demonstrated by Kalyani asking her unhesitatingly to read Narayan's missive for her. Shakuntala is neither judgmental nor punitive. But when Madhumati learns of Kalyani's decision from Chuyia, she cuts off Kalyani's hair and locks her in the room. The gesture is a symbolical one recalling the controlling of sexuality. Shakuntala opens Kalyani's door and importunes her to fearlessly follow her destiny. Kalyani's trauma is expressed in her sobs as she rushes into Narayan's arms. Narayan takes Kalyani across the river but as they near their house, Kalyani asks the name of his father and then demands that the boat be turned back. She tells him that he should ask his father the reason for her action. Back at the bidhva-ashram, Madhumati tells her to get ready to go with Gulabi. But like a bird that has once stepped outside the cage, Kalyani is no longer willing to pawn herself. Despairing of ever finding happiness or a life of respectability, she very deliberately chooses the river as her haven. Shakuntala, Chuyia and Narayan sit by the river and grieve over Kalyani's death. Narayan is shocked when his father tells him that he need not marry a widow but could keep her as a mistress as he himself has been doing. The father that he has idolised exposes his feet of clay. Disgusted by the debauchery, Narayan leaves home and boards the crowded train that Gandhi is travelling in, thus exchanging one father-figure for another (Gandhi was fondly called 'Bapu' or 'father' by his followers which translated easily into 'Father of the Nation' after Independence).

Water does not allow the happy closure of a widow's marriage but like the early novels on the subject, probes the reasons for Kalyani's action. It succeeds in making apparent the helplessness of a woman trapped within the social grid when she has neither the means nor the opportunities of standing by herself in defiance of the community/society. Without the protection of a male, she is merely an object for exploitation, whether inside or outside a home or a bidhva-ashram, by men or by colluding women. Women's utter helplessness becomes emphasised when Shakuntala, after cradling the traumatised Chuyia through the night, runs to the station where a huge crowd has gathered to listen to Gandhi (Mohan Jhangiani), looking desperately for some means to save the child from the quagmire of oppression and exploitation. She sees Narayan on the train and hands Chuyia over to him. Her poignant and loving cry, "Girna mat...girna mat!" – may translate as 'don't fall, don't fall' but seems to convey a far-reaching admonition of 'watch out, take care'. Though they are a man's hands that take Chuyia, but as Narayan is not the typical patriarchal man, there is the sense of hope for the child.

The date and place announced in the film as "India 1938" serve as significant pointers that in India's fight against colonialism, the colonised subjecthood of women has been forgotten. Since the fight for freedom should mean the freeing of shackles for every individual, the train bearing Gandhi, the messenger of freedom, bears Chuyia away too towards emancipation. Shakuntala, who had earlier accepted the strictures of widowhood as the norms given in the *Dharma sastras*, learns from Sadananda and Gandhi the need to seek inner truth. Her decision to defy norms and be the agent of change is based on her realisation of the dignity of life and her acts of freeing Kalyani and Chuyia indicate the growing awareness of a woman's subjectivity. The film's message is that of arousing women's social awareness and building resistance – of not succumbing to the implacable forces, and of finding plausible routes of escape – as conveyed

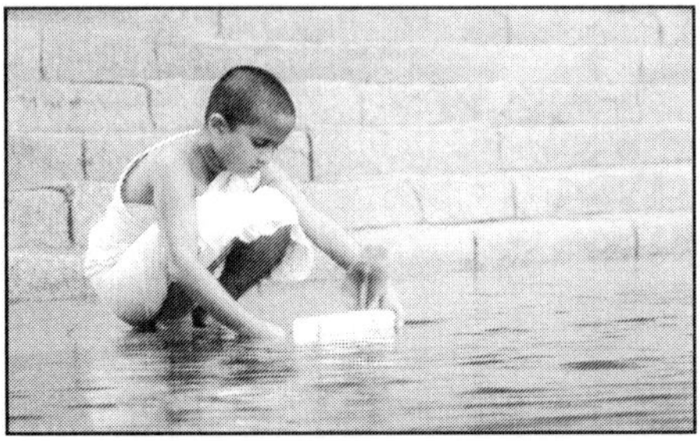

Sailing a boat

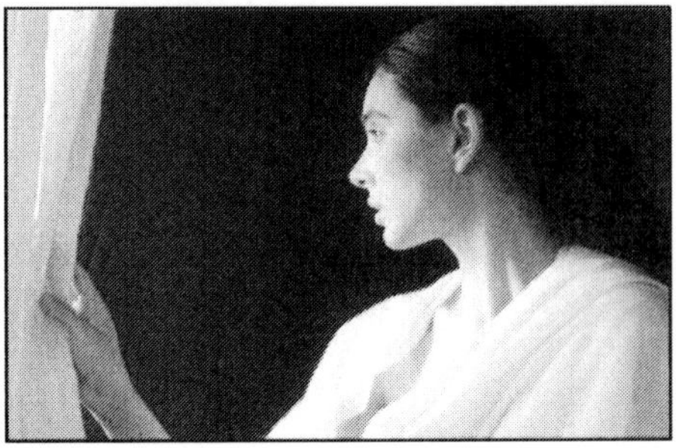

Gazing at the world outside

by Shakuntala's looking back at the audience with a burning glance as the film ends.

Water is a treat to watch. There are unforgettable images crafted with sensitivity and subtlety to convey beauty and pathos: like that of auntie eating the laddoo or Chuyia sailing a boat made with banana stem and banyan leaf; Narayan's upturned umbrella with a twig of neem leaves dancing away in the currents; Kalyani gazing out of the window or her face lit up by the light of the lamp; and Chuyia taken like a lamb to slaughter, standing at the threshold of a semi-darkened bedroom under slanting rays of light that enhance her innocence and vulnerability, saying trustingly 'I have come to play' to a sinister shadow waiting within the nets of the fourposter. Mehta's cinematic aesthetics is pleasing but the film is intended to disturb the mind and shake the complacency of the postmodern world. It speaks of issues long neglected by the Indian society so that the widows of Mathura, Vrindavan and Varanasi seem to be the forgotten inhabitants of an oppressive and archaic world. The success of the Mehta's cinema lies in juxtaposing the beauty of nature with the sordidness of the man-made world.

The productivity of textual analysis is premised on the notion of the film as a dynamic process of meaning construction. As Kuhn

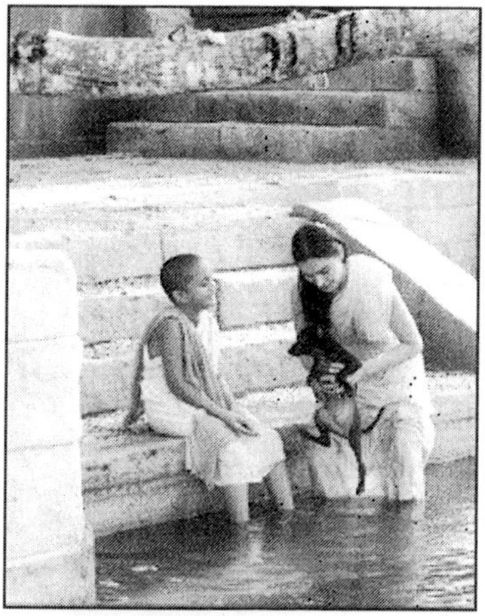

Looking for a cause to live

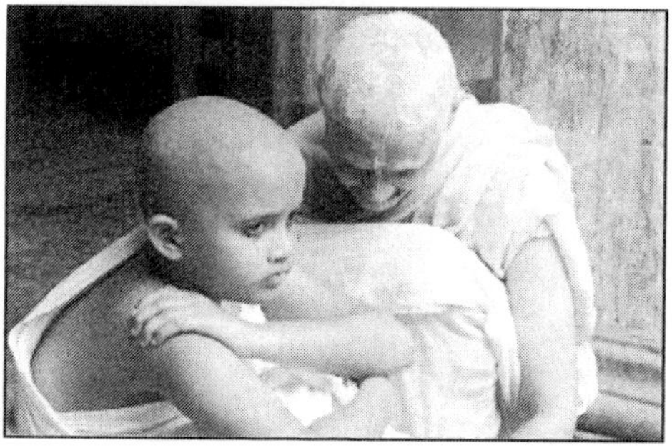

Chuyia with Bua

points out that "social meanings centring one way or the other on women can be constituted as the focus of textual analysis whose objective then becomes to expose the processes by which such meanings are constructed" (81). Deepa Mehta succeeds in engaging the spectator in a dialectical exchange by constructing powerful images that lay bare the working of patriarchal ideology. The film addresses a global audience in an attempt to nudge the conscience of the world to the continued neglect of a section of women even after the successes of feminism and the political reforms initiated by feminist ideology into many areas of women's life to secure for them their rights and equality. By enabling the silent pain of the Hindu widows reach out to a wider audience, Mehta creates meaningful cinema and gifts the world an extremely significant and provocative social text.

Notes

1. Various injunctions illustrate this. For more details see Chakravarti and Gill.
2. See Chakravarti and Gill for documents and personal narratives on widow remarriage.
3. See Chakravarti and Gill. 251-284
4. Prem Chauduri in *Widows in India: Social Neglect and Public Action* (New Delhi: Sage Publication, 1998) p. 95.

References

Altekar, A.S. *Position of Women in Hindu Civilization.* Delhi: Motilal Banarsidass, 1959 rpt.

Chakravarti, Uma and Preeti Gill. eds. *Shadow Lives: Writings on Widowhood.* New Delhi: Kali for Women, 2001.

Chen, Martha Alter. ed. *Widows in India: Social Neglect and Public Action.* New Delhi: Sage Publications, 1998.

— *Perpetual Mourning: Widowhood in Rural India.* New Delhi: Oxford UP, 2000. 2001 rpt.

Kitchlu, T.N. *Widows in India.* New Delhi: Ashish Publishing House, 1993.

Kuhn, Annette. *Women's Pictures: Feminism and Cinema.* London & New York: Routledge and Kegan Paul, 1982; Verso, 1993 rpt.

Mukherjee, Meenakshi. *Realism and Reality: The Novel and Society in India.* Delhi: Oxford UP, 1985.

Water; Director, Story and Screenplay Writer: Deepa Mehta; Producer: David Hamilton; Cinematography: Giles Nuttgens; Music: Mychael Danna and A.R. Rahman, 2005.

18

Meaning Through Contrast

Colour and Image in *Water*

Rama Rani Lall

When the film *Water* was released in Canada, the high acclaim it won for itself aroused our curiosity and we had a private viewing session at a friend's house. The earlier controversy, which had surrounded its plans of production in India, no doubt was another reason for our keenness. Needless to say, our first response was of appreciation, a sympathising with the young girl-child and a sense of nostalgia as the 30s were recreated with all the political and personal struggles, impending socio-political changes, and the music of the period. The simplicity was touching. The camera caught the changing moods of nature and human life in an effective manner. The contrasted images of light and darkness, gaiety and despair, made a deep impression on my mind.

A second viewing brought forth other dimensions. As I was watching it at home, it caught the eye of my Bengali maid. She quickly summoned her friends from the neighbouring houses and they all joined me in this viewing where the dynamics of film-viewing were somewhat different as they moved across class and region. As they watched attentively, they broke out into an excited exchange every now and then. I realised that it had moved them a lot. The experiences of the unfortunate widows in the film were very close to what they had often seen in their own villages and towns. They could not believe that some compassionate filmmaker had taken the trouble of making a film on the psycho-dynamics of isolation and single sex community formation in a society apparently hostile to widows.

Recently, when it was released in India, it eluded the masses completely. Commenting on the hits and flops in the first half of the year, Ziya Us Salam remarked, "*Water*, completing Deepa Mehta's trilogy of elements, got critical acclaim but little else".[1] There was no storm of approval or protest. I was disappointed.

Water is an exceptional film. It was never meant to please the masses with the usual components of song and dance. Mehta has catered to this in a very modest and oblique manner by introducing the Holi celebrations and the romantic episode. The celebrations, when Chuyia is dressed as Krishna, bring music, colour and cheer to the women even as the festivity remains within the confines of religion and, at the same time, acts as a relieving factor in the overall heaviness of the theme. But perhaps an additional factor was its low publicity in the media and the carefully orchestrated projection of the theme, almost a self-censorship by both the filmmaker and the media, thereby limiting it to academic discussions and a largely upper class modern and urban viewing public.

Deepa Mehta, born in India and settled in Canada, has finally completed her trilogy and framed an aspect of Indian culture and social life, which continues to inhabit several sections of life both in economic and regional areas. She has brought to our conscious recognition some of the glaring injustices perpetuated in the name of tradition and religion. The excellence of its aesthetic dimensions has been recognised by the fact of its being selected for nomination as one of the five films competing for the prestigious Oscar award in the Best Foreign Language Film category of the year 2006, as a Canadian film. Perhaps Mehta's Indian half should also wake up to its merits.

All films are time specific and space specific. The historical time frame and the location help the filmmaker in focusing her attention on a community of women living in a particular geographical area and faced with a kind of social ostracism with their brahminhood forbidding them normal employment and widowhood depriving them of normal environment. The young Chuyia is forcibly removed from a family background and dismissed into oblivion just as the nearly middle-aged, educated Shakuntala is placed in the widow's home. The film chooses its time and placement carefully. Why? Is it that this is no longer happening or is it that the Gandhi factor is important? Or, more than all this, it is an analysis of the factor of change at a particular time in the nation's history when idealism had a role in public life? All these are important questions that need to be addressed and thought about. The specific time frame of the film *Water* is the year 1938 and the location is the holy city of Rawalpur, on the banks of the river Ganga.

Since, Hindi is the language of the film and Indian religious and social environment is examined in it, those of us who are located in India, have a large area of socially shared experiences to fall back upon. The mythical references and hidden nuances of the film are crystal clear to us. We have no need to rush to dictionaries and encyclopedias to unravel its deeper connotations. Thus the cultural density that is either passed over or elicited artificially does not exist for us. Here I should add that this may not always be the case. On one hand modernity has charted out new distances and alienations with the young seduced by western music and literatures and on the other an overdose of academic documentation often fails to respond to the gap between factual data and social reality, between representation and reality.

Film studies are a part of the modern discipline of cultural studies. According to Glenn Jordan and Chris Weedon, such studies exist everywhere and provide a focal point for the development of critical theory, "It has sought to theorize the role of literature in society in new ways, and to look at literary texts in relation to cultural institutions, cultural history, and other cultural texts, forms and practices".[2] By asking new questions and finding new ways of theorising modern critics try to understand cultural phenomena and their social implications.

Indian culture and its social imperatives are diverse and heterogeneous. Especially the gender equations in the social setup are governed by age-old traditions and religious codes. Though it is difficult to have an all-encompassing theory of cognitive aesthetics to explain all its complexity we can make a sincere attempt to do so. According to Jasbir Jain, "It needs constantly to be stressed that feminism is not entirely of the west. It has its indigenous roots."[3] Both postcolonial theory and the post feminist critique of the west will have to widen their scope and terminology to fully explain some of the unique Indian experiences.

Deepa Mehta does not write back from the privileged position of a diasporic writer but writes home to the country of her origin to nurture her roots. She points out some of the glaring weaknesses of our social setup. Surely an active awareness of what ails us can lead to a happier and healthier outlook on life. In many Indian holy texts women are often glorified in public speeches and functions. The most quoted of Sanskrit verses is the one that says that gods reside where women are respected. Years of foreign subjugation combined with political and economic constraints downgraded the position of women and reduced them to the status of second-class citizens who are condemned to be always on the margin of all social discourse. They were conveniently denied their basic rights of leading a life of self-respect and dignity. After the Independence of the country their condition has gradually started improving.

The film, *Water,* seems to identify three major power structures responsible for the victimisation of widows. First of all, it is the ideological aspect, in which the priests interpret selected holy texts to subjugate women and widows. Secondly, the patriarchal hegemony of rich landlords and gentry, who with their overt and hypocritical concern for institutionalised widows, never fails to exploit them for their own physical needs, in a callous manner. Lastly, it is the socially empowered women themselves who have no qualms of conscience in tyrannising over their own less fortunate sisters. This threefold oppression and the denial of normal food, normal clothing, and normal living conditions to the widows placed in such institutions have reduced them to the position of the poorest of the poor and the weakest of the weak. In the movie, the contrasts (and disruptions) together allow the meaning to emerge.

Our Vedic hymns often enjoin us to pray to the Almighty to lead us away from darkness to light. In the movie *Water* the camera moves artistically from the brightness of morning to the everlasting gloom of the evening and night. Thus, one of the most striking contrasts in the movie is between darkness and light. It acts as an all-encompassing metaphor. The film begins with the freshness of dawn, where we watch the cheerful lotus leaves and buds dancing in the breeze. The next scene is of a brightly clad girl child of eight years, Chuyia, happily chewing on her piece of sweet sugar cane on her bullock-cart journey, by the side of the lotus pond. This proximity of a bright child and the rising sun lead us to expect a full and happy life for this child who may soon bloom out in all her natural beauty, with the help of love and protection.

In contrast to our hopes we soon have a glimpse of a sick man in the front part of the same cart with his stern mother taking care of him. As evening comes they sail on a boat in gloomy silence. Soon the burning funeral pyre inform us that the sick man is no more. Unaware of the disaster, Chuyia sleeps. Her father wakes her and tells her with infinite pity that she is now a widow. To the viewer's shock and horror the traditional rituals are performed mercilessly. Her bangles are broken and her hair shorn off. Soon she is made to don the dull, white attire of a widow and is pushed into the everlasting gloom of a widow's home. The innocence and liveliness of childhood are condemned to the everlasting horrors of inhuman deprivation and confinement.

The most powerful visual image in the film and the most valourised practice in the Indian society is of the white homespun sari, made mandatory for the widows, as a badge of their being inauspicious. In contrast to them the women devotees who frequent the temples wear rich multicoloured dresses. Even the eunuch Gulabi, who pimps for the richer classes, dons on the brightest of colours and jewellery. This contrast between the dull monotonous white and the rich red and green of other normal women, distinguishes the widows as social outcasts.

Coming to another of the basic human needs – the need for food, the film highlights the amount of injustice meted out to the widows. Food has been widely accepted as one of the most significant signifiers of any culture. The widows in the institutionalised homes are only given a little bit of boiled rice and watery lentils by the priests in return for their singing holy songs in the temple for long hours, they are also strictly forbidden to eat any fried or delicious food. All indulgence of the senses is taboo.

This cruel denial has again and again been emphasised in the film by one of the old wrinkled widows Pitirajji, who was called 'Bua' by the other inmates of the ashram. When Chuyia meets her for the first time, she asks her to give her some laddoos. Bua soon recalls her marriage feast where there was an abundance of the choicest sweets. She admits that whether she is awake or asleep, even in her dreams she only sees sweets. Her constant verbal refrain of laddoos, gulabjamun, rasgullas, kaju ki barfi, sone ki asharfi, hurts the sensibility of all sensitive viewers. As for the third basic human need of a suitable place to stay, we find that the widows are condemned to stay in old dilapidated houses, while their clients lead a life of luxury and comfort in well-furnished palatial mansions. The widows' houses are the cheapest of the cheap places and yet, in order to pay the rent, some of them have to sell their bodies.

Water has a number of contrasted scenes, in addition to a number of contrasted characters. The very opening scene of the film is well contrasted to some of the last scenes. The vibrant, vivacious Chuyia of the opening scene is reduced in the end to an unconscious little bundle lying like a heap in the boat, She has become a victim of the greed of the matron, Madhumati, who sends her to the same rich clients, under the pretext of sending her back to her parents. When her friend and guardian, Shakuntala, finds her in this state, all the viewers share her horror and shock. This episode leaves an indelible impression on the mind and encompasses the whole tragedy of a child widow's exploitation and suffering. Finally to everyone's relief Chuyia is handed over to Narayan, to be placed under Gandhi's custody.

Images of light and darkness, daybreak and evening, alternate artistically throughout the various scenes. While morning and light symbolise hope and vitality, darkness and shadows symbolise despair and destitution. The widows lead a life of penance and prayer under compulsion. Their mornings are spent in bathing in the holy waters and listening to the sacred texts and singing prayers in the temples. The evenings bring some cheer when small earthen lamps are lit in the temples. The melodious tunes of the flute, played by Narayan, the young Gandhian hero, sometimes create an ambience of peace and tranquility by the waters of the river. But very soon Narayan watches the shadowy figures moving about in darkness. He learns that the white sari glimmering in the darkness is that of some unwilling widow being forcibly transported by the pimp to the house of some rich client. The contrast between the edifying rituals of the morning and the sinister activities of the evening reveal the double life the widows are condemned to live. The everlasting funeral fires on the banks of the river add to the gloom of their lives.

To dispel the darkness and sorrow in the life of the widows, Deepa Mehta has interspersed some scenes of hope and rejoicing. When the young and vibrant Kalyani meets Narayan, they fall in love. Kalyani's heart blooms out in joy and in harmony and with her excitement come the rejuvenating showers of rain. Kalyani and Chuyia dance happily with the rhythmic, cheerful songs in the background. Soon all this gaiety vanishes when Madhumati cruelly punishes her for her unforgivable sin of having even thought of remarriage. Her beautiful flowing hair is roughly chopped off and she is locked in her attic. Kalyani can do nothing but by herself bewail her misfortune. Soft lilting songs like "*naina neer bahaye*" heighten the impact of her plight. The misfortune of Kalyani touches the heart of Shakuntala and, defying Madhumati, she opens the lock and asks Kalyani to go to her lover, assuring her that she would take care to inform him. As this harbingers a shift in the widows' self-perception and introduces the possibility of happiness, we as viewers, begin to register the meaning of such a step not merely for Kalyani but also for Shakuntala, Madhumati and the other inhabitants of the home. The shift of power from one to the other, from Madumati to Shakuntala, is silently achieved and has a remarkable resonance in the outside world. It would imply change in the Narayan household and the real process of a nation's self-discovery through self-analysis and social critiquing would be initiated. This is directly contrasted with the passivity of Chuyia's parents and the acceptance of an old-age code by women like Madhumati.

In happy anticipation of the coming wedding we have scenes of 'Holi' celebration in the ashram. The next scene reveals the lovers sailing in a boat with the sun shining benignly over them and the waves dancing all around. As the lovers talk happily of their future, Kalyani learns that her future father-in-law is no other than the Seth

Dwarkanath, who had been one of her clients. Her despair and disappointment are clearly palpable and finally lead to suicide as all other options are taken away from her.

In the film not only are the scenes of rejoicing contrasted with those of utter despair, but also the characters are sharply differentiated. We have a scholar and a broadminded Gandhian gentleman in Narayan, who acts as a complete foil to his selfish and mean father. And then we have an innocent child like Chuyia, who has to deal with the cunning, hypocritical Madhumati. The presence of four generations in the home goes to show the slow pace of change and is additionally presented in the shape of a future where Chuyia is concerned. Shakuntala's being of a middle generation is enough reason for her to be the initiater the change.

Deepa Mehta has used various contrasting images artistically to heighten the emotional impact of her film. They not only throw light on each other, they also act as counterpoints. Visual representations of serious social issues force the viewers to question their age-old beliefs and assumptions. An objective assessment of the film reveals that the director has skillfully used all the devices of plastic theatre to drive home her message. Suitable and symbolic songs add to the charm of the film, while appropriate light effects foreground its emotional centre. In addition to all this Deepa Mehta has successfully used all the resources of dramatic presentation as dramatic irony, verbal repartee, and colour contrasts to make her film a masterpiece.

Notes

1. Ziya Us Salam. "Business, as usual", *The Hindu, Friday Review,* July 6, 2007.
2. Glenn Jordan and Weedon Chris. "Literature into Culture: Cultural Studies after Leavis" in *Literary Theory and Criticism,* Ed. Patricia Waugh (Oxford: OUP) 2006 p.245.
3. Jasbir Jain. "Preface" *Indian Feminisms* Eds. Jasbir Jain and Avadhesh Kumar Singh (New Delhi: Creative Books) 2001.

19

Variations on a Theme

Water and *Banaras*

Santosh Gupta

The year 2006 saw the release of two remarkable films: *Water*[1] and *Banaras*. Some striking similarities in the two – of location and theme – make for a comparative juxtaposition, for both are highly impressive films. While *Water* is directed by the diasporic filmmaker Deepa Mehta, an Indian based in Canada, *Banaras* is the work of the stay-at-home director, L.C. Singh, an engineer by profession whose deep love for the city Banaras and interest in its long traditions of philosophical and religious learning moved him to equip himself for the art of filmmaking. This is so far his only film and he has now created a blog where several viewers discuss with him different aspects of the film and the ideas around which the film evolves.

Both *Water* and *Banaras* are the outcome of the keen involvement of their directors with the themes they have taken up. These themes approximate each other in ways that raise interesting comparisons. In both the films it is the rigid social values and practices relating to the status of women, class and caste divisions which function as agents of oppression. The victims in these films are weak, helpless persons from the marginalised classes of Hindu society such as women, widows and lower castes. In *Water* Hindu widows of all age groups are portrayed living in extremely oppressive conditions, enduring physical and emotional deprivations. In *Banaras* the young lovers, Shwetambari and Soham, are prevented from finding happiness in their love for each other by the rigid social class and caste divisions. Soham is killed before their marriage can take place; Shwetambari is left with a life time of bereavement with the loss of love and all hope of happiness.

The portrayal of these social rigidities and their destructive impact on human life is realistically presented in the two films, avoiding melodrama and any kind of exaggeration. Yet as one film, *Water,* becomes depressing at the end, the other, *Banaras* opens up hopes of redemption and faith in the future. Their treatment of the subject, of the city and river, which are the central spaces within the two films are indicative of the perspectives that the two filmmakers have worked with. In presenting the conflict between tradition and modernity, between harsh social structures and practices and the search for freedom and love of people at all times become framed by the positionality/the location of these two filmmakers. Deepa Mehta's perception of Indian social life and its evils contrasts with that of L.C. Singh for while one film suggests social change the other looks beyond social structures, to the spiritual and mystical dimensions of human life.

The two tropes inhabiting the two films are water in the film by that title, and seed in *Banaras*. The river Ganges is seen frequently in both the films, but it is in *Water* that its role as a purifying and redemptive river – the traditional religious view of this river in Hindu society and culture – is questioned and subverted. It becomes an important location – the space in which widows, like many others regularly bathe, pray, and perform different rituals; lovers meet at night, and again, at night, the widow-whore is taken across the river by boat to meet her 'clients', the rich elderly men. This trope plays an important function in the film's ironical questioning of religion, mythology and the social situations of that period.

In *Banaras* the seed becomes a symbol linking together the past, present and the future. It also connects the different subtexts in the film, interlinking the social dimension with the philosophical and the spiritual. A seed is gifted by Babaji, a mystical and mysterious religious figure, to the child Soham, as part of his training and initiation into knowledge of philosophy and the universe. The seed grows into a small plant, which Soham gives to Shwetambari, as Soham intuitively learns about his impending death.

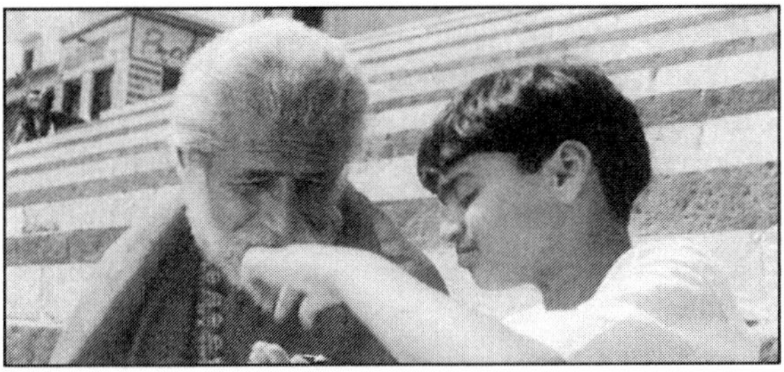

Handing over the seed to the chosen one – *Banaras*

The location of both the films in Banaras, the ancient and holy city of pilgrimage for Hindus, becomes an important aspect of the films. The city has been associated with orthodox Hindu beliefs, religious and scriptural learning since ages. It has attracted enlightened persons and is the place where Buddha in the 3rd century BCE delivered his first Sermon; where scholars come to engage in learned dialogue with the Pundits of ancient Hindu scriptures to give their discourses through poetry on social issues; it is a city connected with Adi Sankaracharya in the 8th century, poets like Tulsidas and Kabir during the Bhakti movement in the 14th and 15th centuries CE. The city has witnessed constant intellectual questioning, debates and formations of new sects. It has been a strong centre of Hindu religion and also a big centre of trade and commerce. Mehta and Singh both use the city as the location of their stories of the human struggle for freedom to love and live with dignity. But their perceptions of the city vary radically, perhaps, due to their very different relationship with the city itself. As they present different historical moments, they also visually construct the city differently. While Mehta's narrative of widows is placed in the 1930s, the time of the emergence of Gandhian social-political national movements, Singh's film is located in contemporary Banaras.

In *Banaras* the river Ganges is shown in the first few opening shots, as men and women are seen in the early morning, against a backdrop of bright sunshine, and then at the time of sunset against golden, orange hues, offering prayers at the temples of Lord Siva. Throughout the film, diverse kinds of people living in Banaras are shown – at the ghats, college rooms, houses of well-to-do people, the quarters of the poor, the gardens, Sarnath, and the temple where Tulsidas wrote *Ramcaritmanas*. For Singh the film, is his homage to the city he loves deeply. One views the natural beauty of the wide banks of the river flowing in its wide expanse. These locations are shown in vibrant and bright shades and at different times of the day. As Shwetambari and Soham go together in a boat across the river, the harmony between the human and natural worlds is beautifully created. Its crowded streets, with roaming bulls, sadhus, and biers being taken for cremation, (usual sights in Banaras) come up at different points in the film.

Deepa Mehta's failure to shoot *Water* in Banaras in 2001 is quite wellknown. She met with live demonstrations from the representatives rigid, destructive traditional orthodoxy which is the subject of her film. Strategically locating the story in recent history she then quietly shot the film in Sri Lanka, changing also some of the lead performers. The use of the substitute Banaras perhaps restricts Mehta's use of the ghats and open spaces, as it also further distances her from a city which perhaps she knows only through library material. She perhaps thought of Banaras only as a city associated with orthodox Hindu faith, its rituals and the refuge of widows, who spend their lives in lonely seclusion. For though she has shot some scenes on the ghats any one familiar with Banaras can notice the difference.

The portrayal of the river in *Water* uses it as a heterotopic space associated with tradition where the prevalent myths about the river are to be subverted. Mehta raises serious doubts about its regenerative and redemptive powers. In one scene, one sees a boat carrying a female passenger across the river at night. Rabindra and Narayan, two young men belonging to the aristocracy, are shown sitting by the ghats. As they see the boat, Rabindra informs Narayan that the passenger is a 'whore', a widow engaged in prostitution. The boat and the river become part of the exploitative situation, witnessing and facilitating the exploitation of the poor women. The boat also is a space that becomes implicated in the use made of it. Foucault, discussing spaces of different kinds, says with regard to the 'boat' that it has provided man's imagination avenues for adventure, journey towards freedom and has been constantly present in formation and expansion of civiliastions(27). Here, Mehta uses the boat as a part of the system of exploitation as she presents scenes where the widow-whore is taken to the other side of the river to the houses of the rich aristocrats. It may be noted that the houses of rich aristocrats in Banaras are not always on the other side of the river, away from the rest of the town. They usually have their houses within the streets inside the main town along with the rest of the city. The other side of the Ganges is, for the most part, open spaces, or has houses close to one another. The director uses both the river and the boat for creating scenes where the mobility of the widows, especially of Kalyani, does not bring her any freedom. The film invites subversive reflections upon the impact of the river. It is in a boat that Kalyani goes with Narayan, the young idealist Gandhian who wants to marry her, to the house of his parents. When she recognises Narayan's house to be that of one of her 'clients' (whom she has visited as a prostitute), she asks for the boat to turn back. Kalyani's journey ends in the loss of hope, of freedom, dignity and love, and, taunted by Madhumati, she quitely drowns herself in the river the very water that had taken her out of her confines in more ways than one.

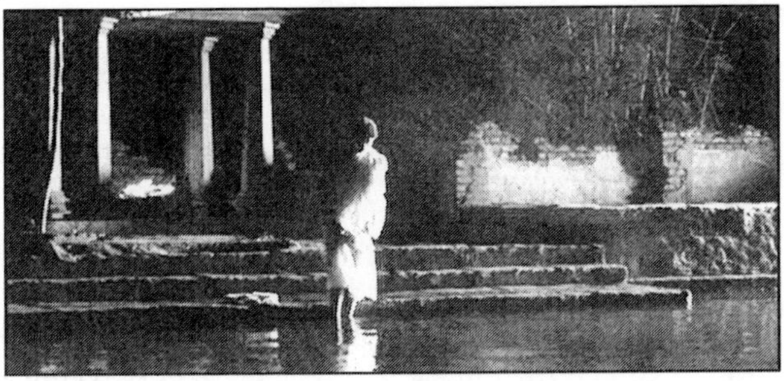

Stepping into the river of death – *Water*

Mehta's visualisation of the river and the city to depict the lives of widows is very functional and also subversive. She looks at the river as still water which fails to provide relief and redemption to the suffering that is going on around it. Though constantly evoked to provide salvation, no feeling of a faith in a future world emerges in the film where these hapless women could hope for a better life. A world beyond death is also not suggested anywhere. Mehta's focus is on the material reality, on human suffering and the exploitation of their weak social status. Very early in the film, Chuyia's journey with her dying husband is also across these river waters.

Mehta's narrow and detailed focus on her main subject – the degradation of women as widows – makes her treatment of all the devices very effective. It however becomes a slice of the reality that leaves out several other related strands in the social fabric. Uma Parameswaran, the Canadian critic, feels that as a diasporic filmmaker Mehta's perception becomes distanced from the subject, which also allows for a greater objectivity.[2] The lens of the diasporic eye leaves out, as in this case, all the social discussions and actions that were being taken for improving women's and widows' condition, since the middle of the 19th century. In Bengal, UP, Punjab and Maharashtra leading reformists were engaged sincerely in opening schools and providing education and employment, and, a new kind of dignity to women. Mehta's perspective is made clear at the opening of the film, where certain edicts from Manu serve as a prologue. These foundational ideas of the Hindu social system are then placed in 1930s. The patriarchal hegemony of the orthodox views on women clearly frame the of the small community of widows in that social milieu. The widows living in the home have suffered deprivation and exclusion from normal human life. The entry of the eight year Chuyia into this small house helps to show how the entire life's experience of these widows will now be repeated in the life of Chuyia, establishing an unchanging continuity in social practices.

The film begins with the little girl Chuyia chewing sugar cane in a carefree manner travelling in a bullock cart. Her transformation into a widow, and entry into the widows' home leave her confused, unhappy and unsettled. While she tries to befriend some of the more likeable widows, she resists degradation as well as the finality of her dislocation from home. She tells Narayan that she is here visiting someone. Her desire for freedom is used to dupe her into a final acceptance when, a few months' later, she is shown going in a boat across the river accompanied by Gulabi, the transvestite, who also functions as a pimp. Madhumati although herself a victim of the deprivations imposed on the whole community becomes an oppressor pushing the pretty young widows into prostitution. Chuyia's journey towards freedom turns into one of trauma, leaving her numb and shocked.

In the next few scenes a clear move is made from the depressing dark scenes and the seclusion of the river. Now we see Shakuntala, one of the middle aged widows, take yet another step towards change. She had, in earlier scenes, been instrumental in setting Kalyani free from Madhumati's hold. When Shakuntala discovers the plight of Chuyia, she takes her, carrying her in her arms, towards the railway station where Mahatma Gandhi's train will halt. Shakuntala runs through the streets where hundreds of men and women are also shown going in that direction. At the station Shakuntala pushes through the crowds to reach Gandhi. Narayan who is also moving out of the confines of his home, extends his arms to hold Chuyia as Shakuntala lifts her up.

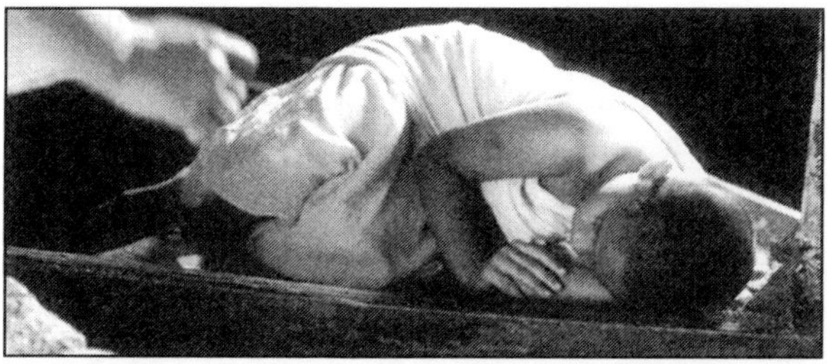

Trauma and its aftermath – *Water*

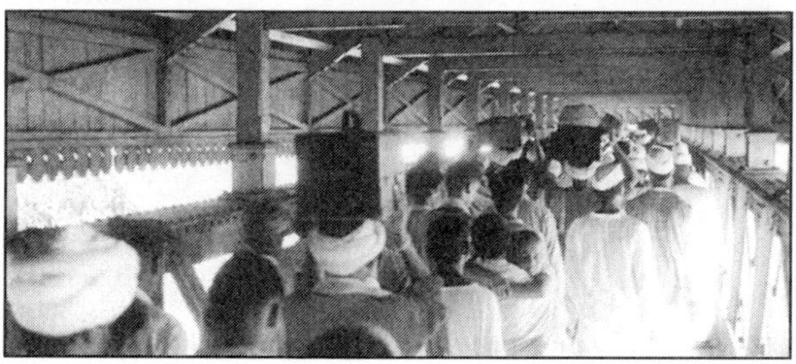

In search of freedom

The train in the last scene becomes an effective symbol of the arrival of modern era, thought and spirit in the old, slow moving world. So far characterised by the trope of the 'water' of the river, Ganges, which has become a stagnant cesspool of decadence and corruption, the train then suggests the coming of changes under Gandhi's leadership. Gandhi's appearance in the film is backed up by the singing of his favourite bhajan '*Vaishav Jan to Tene Kahiye*' in the background. But no interaction between the public and the Mahatma is shown. Perhaps the appearance of Gandhi is sufficient to indicate the changing social conditions. The abruptness of the end, and the vague message regarding the condition of Chuyia, of Shakuntala herself are disturbing. What would be Chuyia's future and would the other inmates of the widow home also live more freely, some such questions nag the viewer although a positive development has been shown. Once again, the end shows data about widows in contemporary India, relating the past with the present day problems of widows, commenting upon the slow pace of change.

What one wants to examine here is Mehta's use of historical archival material in the film. A narrow perspective determines the picture of the Hindu social thought and discourse that is presented here. Kumkum Sangari's view of a 'hybrid' writer, placed in the local and international location provides useful insight. Looking at the diasporic writers she thinks such writers are open to two worlds and are "constructed within the national and the international, political and cultural systems of colonialism and neocolonialism". She feels that "to be hybrid is to understand and question as well to represent the pressures of such historical placement" (144). As a filmmaker who targets the international film markets the desire to present historical situations for the eyes of the western world can become an important deciding factor. Mehta reconstructs Banaras and Hindu society from an angle which underlines the backwardness of the society, and the misery of the widows. By not showing the changes that were already taking place among the Hindus, the flexibility in tradition and the impact of reform in that period is ignored. Vasudha Dalmia's study of Bhartendu Harish Chandra relates the rebel poet and thinker to the context of new intellectual spirit of questioning (of tradition) and changing attitude towards the suffering of widows in the middle of the nineteenth century. In her work, *The Nationalization of Hindu Traditions* (1997), Dalmia provides extensive support for the view of Banaras as a centre of enlightenment and new learning in the Hindu world.

I would also like to raise a question about Mehta's silence about the abuse of the girlchild in contemporary India. The physical abuse of the girlchild is increasing in proportion to the rise of as affluence and urbanisation. Social values, cultural norms are also caught up in change under the impact of high capitalism, consumerism and the rise of new norms sexuality.

Besides the narrow perspective, the complete failure of male figures to ameliorate or liberate these suffering women also becomes too heavy-handed. The ineffectual angel, Narayan, is accompanied by the cynical Rabindra who quotes verses from English romantic poets, plays the piano and comments upon the foremost evils of Banaras

"Rand, sand, seedhee aur sadhu,
Inse bache to pahunche Kashi"

These young men are unable to make an effective protest against the exploitative behaviour of their fathers. Narayan tries to help Kalyani, but her own sense of guilt stops her from marrying him. The Pandit at the ghats gives Shakuntala sympathetic advice. But when he insists that she should not give up "faith", one wonders, faith in whom or what? Gandhi's brief appearance fails to make an impact strong enough to wipe off the horror one experiences at Kalyani's death and Chuyia's devastation.

Mehta's perception of tradition as fixed and fossilised seems to be reflected in the idea of still stagnant water. Her view leaves out other aspects of social life, of traditions that are also present all the time. In Singh's portrayal of the city's day to day life, its crowded spaces the flowing glistening river, all create an ambience of living within a natural world that changes and regenerates. The film explores the different facets of tradition, philosophies and religious ideologies that were located in Banaras. He weaves the strands from the past into the story of contemporary society, showing the social evils as well.

In this city traditional Hindu scriptural knowledge is imparted to the child Soham by a mysterious 'Babaji'. In the modern college Quantum Physics is being taught, to young students, to explain the

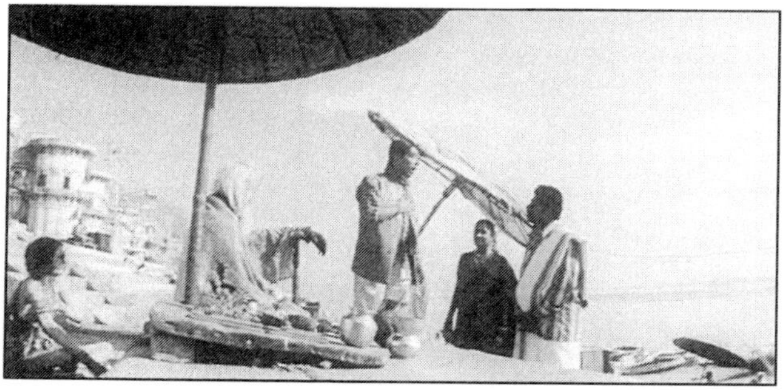

Religion on sale – *Banaras*

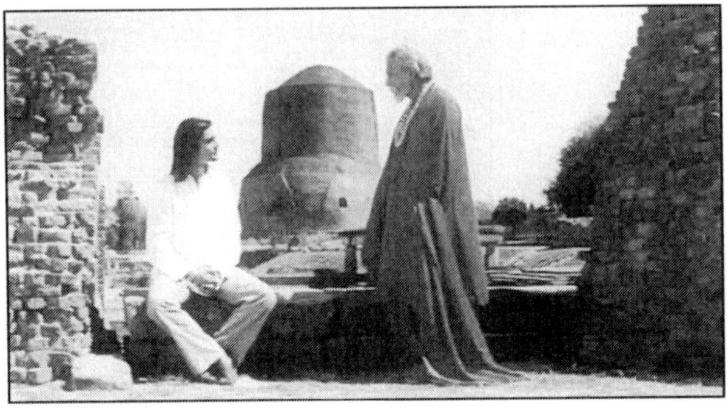

Spaces of knowledge: From Sarnath to the future

higher abstractions of space and time. Tradition co-exists with modern new ideas. One of the ideas, social equality for all, irrespective of caste divide, is suggested through the relationships between Soham and Shweta. Soham is a foundling child, brought up by a woman of low caste, who teaches him Kabir's ideas of looking at *the human being*, not at his caste. Shwetambari belongs to a well-to-do Brahmin family. Her mother's more aristocratic family links are teasingly hinted at by her father who is the principal of the college.

The friendship between Soham and Shweta attracts social disapproval although the parents are willing to be more liberal and are

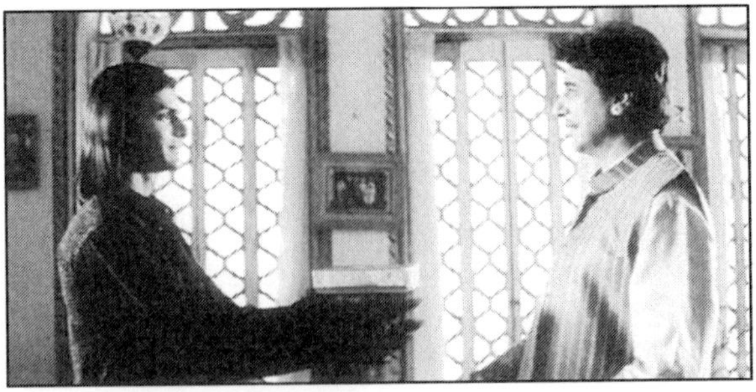

Reaching out across caste

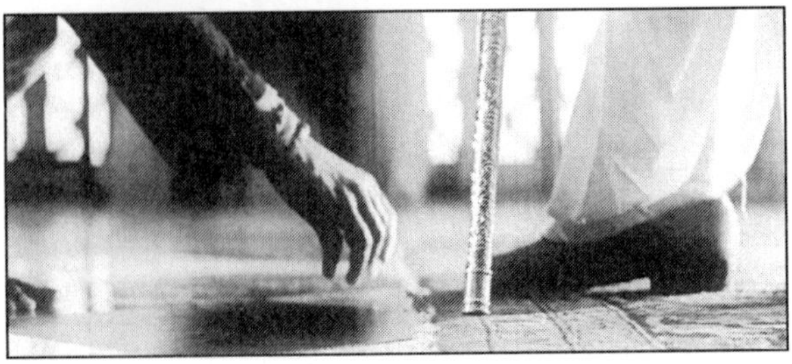

Caste as the dividing shadow – *Banaras*

prepared to accept Soham as a son-in-law. As other members of the community object, Soham's murder is organised, with the connivance of her mother, highlighting the pull of caste, social status and traditional biases prevalent in Hindu society that tends to ignore individual differences.

Other aspects of tension between tradition and modern views and different forms of knowledge emerge after Soham's death. Soham's enlightenment in Sarnath is an important turning point for the young man, and his views begin to influence the science educated Shwetambari, whose response to Soham's thinking is indicated through her revival of interest in music. Dr. Bhattacharya, a psychiatrist, who is suffering from lung cancer has returned from the US in order to die on his own soil. His wife, an American, leaves him when she learns of his illness (however it is not necessarily meant to be representative of the behaviour of a culture, for it is an individual's response). He tries to 'treat' Shweta by telling her that she must accept Soham's death as the final truth of life. She insists on her sense of truth by saying that for her Soham is still alive and she feels his presence all the time.

Shweta's response to Soham's death is the most significant aspect of her intellectual development. Through the influence of Babaji, whom she had met a few times, and Soham, she insists on thinking of the soul as indestructible and immortal even after the body's destruction. One day, she takes Dr. Bhattacharya to meet Babaji and is shocked to learn that Babaji does not exist physically in her contemporary world; he had died about a hundred years ago.

At this point Shweta turns to the plant Soham had given her for her care and protection. Sensing his impending doom, Soham had handed over the plant that has grown out of the seed given to him by Babaji had given him. Now Shweta realises the true significance of the plant: it connects the past to which Babaji belonged, to the present when Soham nurtured it grow, and to the future as it is now under her custody, for her to save and pass on to a worthy receiver. Both Soham and Babaji belong to the past but for Shweta their presence is a felt experience, the plant being a living symbol of that truth.

The seed and the plant become the governing trope of *Banaras*, as it links Shweta with Soham. The past, present and the future are connected in it. As a growing plant it symbolises birth, rebirth and successive births in continuation. The life span of an individual merges with that of another, and others after it, just as a tree lives for several decades and centuries in new forms through its seeds.

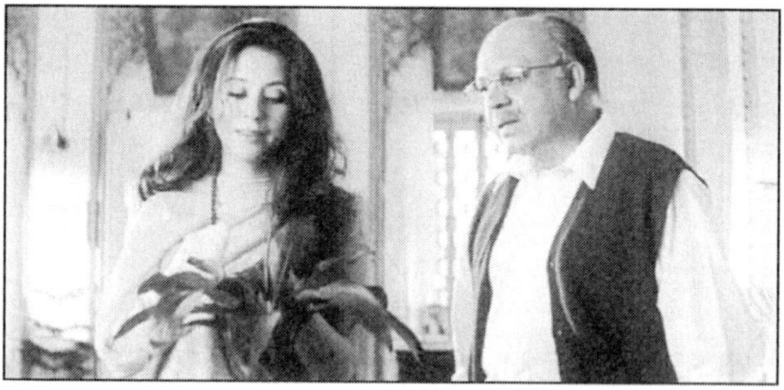

The believer and the non-believer

The scenes depicting Babaji's teachings to Soham about the nature of Truth and Knowledge about reality of space, universe and matter and the scenes of the professor in the classroom teaching modern theories of the universe in western science follow in quick succession. The juxtaposition relates the opposing forms of knowledge, till one begins to see the limits of modern science, and the extensive reach of ancient knowledge. As Shweta tells Dr. Bhattacharya that it is *he*, rather than she who needs to be treated for depression, loneliness and his limited perceptions of the world around him, the old man discards his former discipline and sets out in search of Babaji. He finally has a vision and dies happily on the steps he is ascending in pursuit of his goal.

Death is not the final truth of human life, of this world. The film tries to present this supra-natural view of life and death. Shweta claims that can feel his spirit around her. The presence of Babaji uses a mystical suggestion that can become a stumbling block for modern rationalistic viewers. The overwhelming surge of emotional identification with a dead person can be a 'rational' explanation of such a feeling. *Banaras* presents the idea of the soul's presence on a level that is beyond material ground, yet felt deeply and intuitively, a truth expounded clearly in the Gita and other holy books of the Hindus.

Singh has emphasised the idea of evolution of persons in his discussions about the film, on the blog on *Banaras,* to be one of the central themes of his film. Many characters in the film grow in intellectual, moral and spiritual terms. Shweta, Soham, the parents of Shweta evolve through different experiences. Shweta learns to forgive her parents who had been involved in Soham's death. She expresses her deep love for them. She becomes a world renowned spiritual teacher, expanding like a tree, but she returns to the ground where her roots are located. When her mother tries to commit suicide, Shweta stops her, and asks her to seek peace through love and penance.

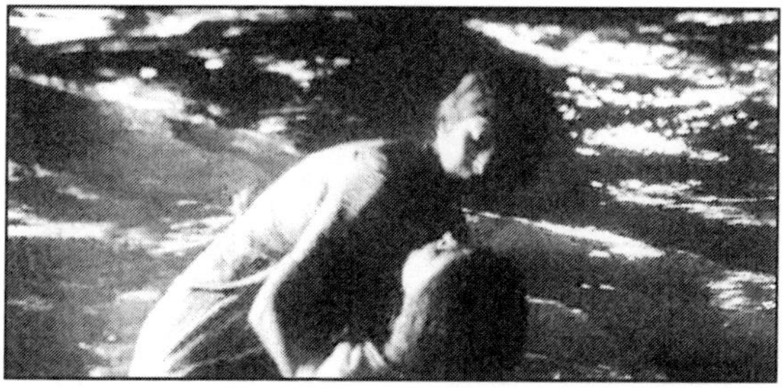

The final forgiveness – *Banaras*

The death of Soham in *Banaras* fills Shweta with immense grief, but it leads her also to further involvement with philosophy and religious learning creating a stronger selfhood. Shweta and Kalyani, the central figures in the two films, suffer due to repressive and rigid social beliefs and practices. But as Shweta is able to attain an intellectual depth, maturity and strength from her 'faith', Kalyani is destroyed by the pressure of social injustice. The suicide of Kalyani, in *Water*, creates a feeling of tragic despair. Kalyani seeks freedom and fulfillment but the whole social world is so confining and repressing that it is difficult for her to see beyond the dark visible horizon.

Banaras presents several aspects of tradition while the social structures can be destructive, the intellectual and spiritual traditions associated with Hindu religion, and with Banaras can be enlightening and uplifting. The commingling of these strands is attained through the love story of Soham and Shwetambari. The forward looking faith of Shweta builds links between people and helps them come to terms with their grief. In the scene where she is shown in Mauritius, she helps a young girl cope with her bereavement and continually advocates a search for higher truth. The film presents the multi-layered and multidimensional nature of tradition. The river and the city have many possibilities, many different moods and colours, just as human life goes through different stages of happiness and grief. Social divisions remain, but individuals learn to reach out to people across such barriers. *Water* in contrast, presents a more negative view of tradition, the city and the river. Its insistence on the destructive aspects of social system prevents a recognition of other more liberating forces of life.

Notes

1. *Water* was made in 2005. By 2006 the DVD had reached India and preceded the official release, which took place in March, 2007.
2. Uma Parameswaran spoke on Mehta's films in a talk she delivered at the Conference 'The Diasporic Eye: Theory and Cultural Interpretation" held in Jaipur in February, 2007.

References

Banaras. Director and Script Writer, L.C. Singh; Producer, Pankaj Parashar; Performers: Urmila Matondkar, Amish Patel, Dimple Kapadia, Raj Babbar, Naseeruddin Shah. 2006.

Banaras: http:/www.blog on *Banaras*

Dalmia, Vasudha. *The Nationalization of Hindu Traditions: Bharténdu Harischandra and Nineteenth Century Banaras*. New Delhi: OUP. (1997), 1999.

Foucault, Michel. "Of Other Spaces" (1984), translated by Jay Miskowiec, *Diacritics* Spring 1986. 22-27.

Sangari, Kumkum. "The Politics of the Possible". *The Post-Colonial Studies Reader*. Eds. Bill Ashcroft, Gareth Griffith and Helen Tiffin. New York: Routledge, 1997.

Water. Director, Deepa Mehta; Producer David Hamilton; Perf. Lisa Ray, John Abraham, Sarala, Manorama, Seema Biswas, Kulbhushan Kharbanda. 2005.

Contributors

Avinash Jodha teaches English at Dungar College, Bikaner. He worked on the *Poetics of Exile: A Study of Michael Ondaatje's Fiction* for his doctoral degree. Interested in creative writing, currently he is researching on South Asian Diaspora.

Bandana Chakrabarty is in Rajasthan Education Service. Co-editor of *Contemporary Indian Drama*, Chakrabarty's dominant interest lies in music and narratology. Her doctoral work was on Alice Munro.

Jasbir Jain is an independent critic currently working on Indian language literatures, subcontinental writing and gender studies with a focus on the interrelation between history and narratology.

Jayita Sengupta teaches English literature in South Calcutta Girls College affiliated to Calcutta University. A translator from Bengali to English and vice versa, her research interests include gender, postcolonialism, and psycho-analysis.

Jennifer Heath is the author/editor of ten books of fiction and non-fiction, including *The Scimitar and the Veil: Extraordinary Women of Islam* (Paulist Press, 2004) and *The Veil: Women Writers on History, Lore and Politics* from the University of California.

Madhuri Chatterjee teaches English at Subodh PG College, Jaipur. Her current interest areas are in gender studies and travelogues. Chatterjee's doctoral work was on John Updike.

Neelam Raisinghani teaches English at Dungar College, Bikaner. Raisinghani did her doctoral work on Fanny Burney and is the editor of *Realism, Reality and Fiction*. Her interest areas lie in feminist and postcolonial studies.

R.R. Lall worked on Satiric Fables for her doctoral work. Since then she has extended her areas onto other concerns including feminist, postcolonial writing and American drama.

Santosh Gupta has worked extensively in 20th century fiction and literary movements. Currently on a UGC Fellowship for research on prison narratives, her recent publication is *Contemporary British Fiction* (Ed) and her major interests are in critical theory.

Shamini Shankar-Jain is a practising architect. She did her dissertation on *The City Square* with special reference to Chotti Chaupar. Currently she is exploring the relationship between gender and space.

Simran Chadha teaches English at Dyal Singh College, Delhi University and is pursuing her doctoral research on *Writing Militancy: Literature, Identity and the Politics of Location*. She has published articles on Bollywood and Sri Lankan Writing.

Somdatta Mandal teaches at the Department of English & Other European Languages at Visva Bharati. She has recently published *Film and Fiction: Word Into Image* and is currently engaged in working on South Asian Diasporic Cinema on a Rockefeller Foundation Award.

Sudha Rai is Professor of English at the University of Rajasthan, Jaipur. She has worked on Expatriate Sensibility and her major interest areas are literature of marginalised categories. She has published *V.S. Naipaul* and *Homeless by Choice* and is the co-editor of *Films and Feminism*.

Sudha Shastri is Associate Professor at the Department of Humanities and Social Sciences, IIT, Mumbai. Her research interests lie in Narratology and Indian Writing in English. She worked for her doctorate on intertextuality.

Tutun Mukherjee is Professor and Head, Centre for Comparative Literature, University of Hyderabad. Her specialisation in Literary Criticism and Theory urged her interests in Translation, Women's Writing, Theatre and Film Studies which have very often become contiguous subjects for her to teach and discuss.

Uma Mahadevan Dasgupta, an IAS officer, and a regular book reviewer for leading newspapers, is engaged in doctoral research at IIT Mumbai.

Uma Parameswaran is a creative writer, living and teaching in Winnipeg, Canada. She has authored fiction, plays, poetry and numerous critical essays on postcolonial literatures. Her recent publications are *Riding High with Krishna* and a *Baseball Bat & Other Stories.*

Vijaya Singh, a poet and short story writer, has worked for her doctoral work on film adaptations of E.M. Forster's novels. A Fulbright Fellow, her major interests are in cinema and cultural studies.